A SHORT BUT FULL BOOK ON

DARWIN'S
RACISM

A SHORT BUT FULL BOOK ON

DARWIN'S RACISM

LEON ZITZER

A SHORT BUT FULL BOOK ON DARWIN'S RACISM

iUniverse books may be ordered through booksellers or by contacting:

iUniverse
1663 Liberty Drive
Bloomington, IN 47403
www.iuniverse.com
1-800-Authors (1-800-288-4677)

ISBN: 978-1-5320-2129-9 (sc)
ISBN: 978-1-5320-2130-5 (e)

Print information available on the last page.

iUniverse rev. date: 04/20/2017

To all the children,
throughout history, throughout the world,
who never had a chance

Contents

Preface and Acknowledgments

This book is based on my previous one, *Darwin's Racism*. That last book was an 800 page tome. Not for nothing did I subtitle it the definitive case. It did not take long to realize that a short book was needed. Six months after *Darwin's Racism* was published, I tackled this one and wrote it in about four or five weeks. The big one had to come first so I could see the whole landscape. I have made what I hope is a judicious selection of the evidence from the longer book. More importantly, I have completely reorganized the order the evidence is presented in. This may help certain items to stand out more.

Since nothing has changed for me personally in so short a time and since I said it all in the previous preface, there is no need for a new preface. I will just repeat the old one below. To attempt anything new would just be to mess up what I got right the first time.

I only want to add two comments here. First, without the help of my friend Susan Rowley and my sister Ruth Mann, I would not have been able to publish this book. If this book means anything to anyone and awakens or reinspires a love of science and humanity, you can thank them.

Second, I am indebted to Ilya Kaminsky (see Bibliography) for two quotes from poets. The one from Austrian poet Ingeborg Bachmann is referred to in a later chapter. As for W.H. Auden, he said of Yeats, "Mad Ireland hurt him into poetry." For my part, I can say bad scholarship hurt me into clarity. I don't know why (though I have a strong hunch) but bad scholarship—the kind that suppresses evidence—hurts me personally. It feels like a kick in the gut. The only relief I get is to seek clarity with a vengeance. That is the only reason I ever pick up my pen.

That said, here is the previous preface (with only a few minor changes):

I came into this world unwanted and it looks like I'm going out the same way. In between, I had to do something. Maybe a few somethings. This book has been one of them.

My talents could have taken me in a lot of directions. I could have been a dancer, a boxer, an actor. The gifts were there, but health and other circumstances were not. So I had to pour whatever love and talent I had in me into research and writing. It was the only thing I could do with my limited energy. I hope this book has turned out to be the kind of book that a good actor or director would love to have written. A long time ago, I had an acting teacher, Jane Dentinger, who told me that a good actor is a good detective. I hope I have remained true to that.

As with any acting role, some parts of myself have found their way into the final performance. When people meet actors whom they have seen in roles they admire, they tend to assume they know this actor, they know all about him or her, they have seen their most intimate soul. People do this with singers too and all sorts of performers. But any artist will tell you that there is only a piece of me in this performance, and if I have done my job well, you won't know which piece or where in the performance it can be found. The same goes for authoring a book. Undoubtedly, I am in this book, but equally undoubted, there is no telling where I can be found inside these pages. Also, there is whole lot more to me that never found its way into this product I worked on for so long. You cannot read this book and know me. I, the whole of me, am not here, but some things that are important to me are definitely here. Just don't assume too much. We're all destined to disappear, leaving only bits and pieces behind.

The whole of Charles Darwin is not in this book either. I only wish to restore to common knowledge an important part of him that is too often suppressed. I see all the work I have ever done on any subject as a major *corrective* to what has gone before, but not as the complete story of what I am dealing with. Completeness won't be possible until we make the needed corrections to the standard story. It will be several generations before that happens.

This particular book has to be painful for anyone who adores Darwin as a champion of scientific truth. In his anthropology, he was not as objective as we would like a scientist to be. The pain that comes in realizing this is the main difficulty in confronting this history. The facts are otherwise very clear. Darwin was not shy about expressing his prejudices. He didn't believe they were prejudices. They were objective facts to him. Scholars have avoided or misrepresented the evidence from his writings which clearly tell us what he believed about other races. Each person will have to answer one question for him- or herself: Which is more important, telling the truth about this evidence or letting emotions cover it up?

I used to have a lot of respect for people who think so highly of Darwin as a scientist. But this study has disabused me of that. If great science is the goal, then why haven't we remembered those who achieved an even better, more objective anthropology than Darwin did? There were others in his time who were purer scientists of the human species than he was and yet academic tradition has seen fit to erase their accomplishments from history. If people really loved Darwin because they love science, then they would remember these others also. Robert Chambers followed pure scientific method and cared not whom he might offend. He stood up for objective examination of nature, when all the established scientists vilified him. When you meet Georg Gerland, you will see that he was a far more accurate anthropologist than Darwin. These are just two examples of great scientists who have been dumped on the side of the road, while a questionable science has been celebrated to no end.

There were many things about writing this book that have been frightening to me (but then, I suppose, it is helpful to know that I'm frightened of my own shadow). Not least is the length of it. Honestly, I want to throw up when I think of how long this book has become. There was no one to advise me. I write alone, in the dark almost. I kept discovering facts that have been removed from history by the powers that be. The details are so fascinating, they glitter before me like golden nuggets. I can't help myself. I kept collecting and reporting them, not quite every piece I came upon, but a lot of them. This book is a compendium of wonderful nuggets. When I started this, I had no idea of all that I would find. Looking back on it now, I think it is possible that all along I was unconsciously aiming for a magnificent panorama of evidence. Was I wrong to do this? I may never live to find out.

I have been lucky to have some people in my life who have helped me survive and lucky to have stumbled on resources that were incredibly useful in doing the research for this book. In the past, I found that people can sometimes be embarrassed by what I have said about them in the Acknowledgments, so bearing that in mind, I will be succinct this time. As usual, I owe my sister Ruth Mann and my friend Susan Rowley all the thanks in the world for keeping me on my feet and in my apartment. Or have I said too much already? Never mind, they deserve to be thanked for their generosity. My friends Mark Felber, Sean Moran, and Susan have kept up conversation with me, and many thanks to Mark for help in translating Georg Gerland and to Ruth for purchasing two books for me, especially that very rare one by J. Langfield Ward. My neighbor across the hall for many years, Bruce Rutherford, read a previous version of the first chapter. Thank you for your feedback. I changed a couple of sentences because of your comments.

I would never have started this book were it not for one author and two letter writers to *The New York Times Book Review* (for all three, see the Bibliography). It was Sven Lindqvist who planted the first seeds of doubt in me about Charles Darwin. Lindqvist is also one of those writers who make it their business to spot overlooked people in history. If not for him, I don't think I ever would have discovered Georg Gerland, J. Langfield Ward, and Helen Hunt. Then there were Peter Quinn and Daniel Newsome whose letters to the *Times* put my doubts about Darwin into action. I read *The Descent of Man* because of their remarks and was blown away by the obvious racism. What I got from all three was the best gift you can get from a writer: The stimulus to take a more careful look at the evidence.

I am grateful to all the websites which have pdf files for so many old books (see Abbreviations for some of these sites). Most of the research for this book would have been impossible without the existence of these sources. In addition, the Columbia University libraries and their staff have been of great assistance. Everyone was willing to help with whatever questions I had. The facilities of the NYPL with all its branches are a godsend and, in particular, without their wifi at my local branch, I would have been up a creek.

It's been a glorious ride discovering all the humanitarians presented herein. They sacrificed more comfortable lives so that they could tell the truth to their society. If anyone paid attention (a very big if), it earned them only ostracism. They were not prophets. They could feel more than they could see that the western world was tottering, not inevitably advancing, towards extraordinary organized violence and a more intense racism. Very few in their time were willing to listen. How many of us can hear them now?

In a previous manuscript for a book I have never published, called *Disappearing Jews from History*, I recorded my memory of a favorite line from a movie I saw. At the end of the film *A Thousand Acres*, one of the sisters is dying in the hospital. She complains to her sibling that she accomplished nothing in her life, she created nothing and has nothing to leave behind. There is only one thing she says she achieved: "I saw and I did not flinch from telling." Surely that is one of the best epitaphs any scientist or artist could wish for.

The film of course is based on Jane Smiley's novel of the same title. It is about these three sisters who try to establish some independence for themselves as they confront the fact that their father abused them, sexually and with beatings, when they were growing up. They make their family history public in a community that regards their father as a model citizen, even a saint. I recently looked up this scene in the book (355-56). The sister is Rose. She says, "I have no accomplishments." She didn't teach long enough, or work the farm successfully, or have a good marriage, or shepherd her daughters into adulthood, and a lot of other failures. "I was as much of a nothing as Mommy or Grandma Edith." I know the feeling. How that nothing stings in my ears. She winds up with this statement, much longer than the brief comment I remember from the movie: "So all I have is the knowledge that I saw! That I saw without being afraid and without turning away, and that I didn't forgive the unforgiveable. Forgiveness is a reflex when you can't stand what you know. I resisted that reflex. That's my sole, solitary, lonely accomplishment." She saw and did not flinch from telling, as the movie has it (if I remember that correctly).

Probably a majority of academics would like to forgive Darwin and all the mainstream scientists in the 19th century who went down a wrong path. And their way of forgiving is simply not to tell what went wrong. Let us turn away and forget. That is not a true forgiveness. Among other things that are wrong with this is that if we are going to forget all the bias in their work, and Darwin's in particular, we also have to erase all those humanitarians who fought against such bias and stood for something better. We have to erase them because allowing them to speak will be a reminder that Darwin cannot be counted among them. So forgetting the bad also means forgetting many of the good people who valiantly struggled for a voice in their culture and who put to shame everyone, like Darwin, who did not join them. I am not against forgiving and even occasional forgetting. But to forgive and to tell the whole truth without flinching—now that would be an accomplishment.

My job in this book has been to tell the story, fairly, accurately, and clearly. If I did that, then I did what I set out to do, and the story lives.

And with that, I am done.

Abbreviations and Explanations

Abbreviations:

ARW – *Alfred Russel Wallace: Letters and Reminiscences*, ed. by James Marchant

BAAS – British Association for the Advancement of Science

BHL – Biodiversity Heritage Library

http://www.biodiversitylibrary.org

CCD – *The Correspondence of Charles Darwin* edited by Frederick Burkhardt *et al*

D-O – Darwin-Online

http://www.darwin-online.org.uk

(As of this writing, their pdf files were not searchable.)

DR – *Darwin's Racism* by Leon Zitzer

Essay – Malthus's *An Essay on the Principle of Population*

Founders – Founders Online

http://founders.archives.gov/about/Washington

(For other founders, type in last name of founder, in place of Washington; such as Jefferson, Adams, Madison; each page also has links to the other founders.)

H – Hathitrust Digital Library

http://www.hathitrust.org

LL – *The Life and Letters of Charles Darwin*, ed. by Francis Darwin

ML – *More Letters of Charles Darwin*, ed. by Francis Darwin

NYPL – The New York Public Library

http://www.nypl.org

pdf – Portable Document Format (for presenting and viewing documents)

Report – 1837 *Report* of the House of Commons Select Committee on Aborigines

Explanations:

Italics and all caps – Most of the time, I indicate whether an italicized portion of a quote, or anything printed in all caps, was original to the source or whether it is my added emphasis. Whenever I fail to do so, you can assume it was in the original quote.

multi-volume works – In referencing multi-volume works, I use volume and page number. Thus, 2.245 means volume 2, page 245.

savages – This term was common in the literature of the day in 19th century Europe and America. My writing reflects that. But I mix it up quite a bit with Indigenes, Indigenous peoples, Natives, and Aborigines, all of which were also used back then. I don't judge any of the older writers by whether they used 'savage' more often than 'Native' or 'Aborigine', though admittedly 'savage' always had pejorative connotations. Even the expression 'noble savage' was meant to sound contradictory. The nastiness inherent in the word 'savages' colored their thinking, but in general, it is *what specifically* was being said about savages or Natives that concerns me, not the terminology itself. And we should not forget that some humanitarians were capable of seeing savagery in Europeans and Americans. Also, I am following one new practice which I did not use in the previous book—using initial caps for terms like Native, Indigenous, etc. It seems many Native writers in America, Australia, and elsewhere are doing this, so I have adopted it too. It makes sense. However, since it is a new practice for me, I may have slipped up in some instances and failed to use an initial cap. I apologize for any such errors.

sic – I very rarely use this to note incorrect spellings in quotations from old books. It would be presumptuous because spellings in an earlier time varied so much. This applies as well to grammar and punctuation. What looks incorrect today may well have been acceptable then. I have proofread all quotations more than once and can only offer this as reassurance that each one corresponds word for word and punctuation for punctuation to the original. I apologize for any errors that may have crept in.

spellings modernized – I am not entirely consistent in this. In my transcriptions from older texts (generally prior to 1800), I do retain some older spellings in order to preserve the sense of a different time period. My main, almost exclusive, effort is to replace the old, elongated *s* (which resembled an *f*) with our usual *s* (they used both types of *s*).

EXPLANATIONS CONCERNING VARIOUS AUTHORS:

Bonwick, James – References to Bonwick are always to *The Last of the Tasmanians*, except for the one time I referred to his other book.

Chambers, Robert – References to *Vestiges* are to the first edition (1844) unless otherwise noted. For *Explanations*, I am using only the second edition.

Darwin, Charles – *The Origin of Species* – The first edition of this book has been reprinted many times with varying pagination. For *DR*, I used a modern reprint. For this book, all page citations are to the first edition as originally published in London in 1859. One reason for doing this is that I have found the occasional typo in the reprint I previously used, but fortunately nothing that affected the meaning of a sentence. A second reason is that the original British edition is now available to everyone online at BHL, so it makes more sense to use it for citations. For editions two through five, citations are always to the first British printing. For the sixth, I am using the Modern Library edition. All are listed in the Bibliography. The original title was of course *On the Origin of Species*, but it is usually referred to without the first word or just as *Origin*, a practice Darwin himself followed in his *Autobiography*. I too follow this.

Diary, Narrative, Journal, Voyage – These are the editions of the journal or diary Darwin kept while on board the *Beagle* in his five year round-the-world trip from December 1831 to October 1836. The full titles are listed in the Bibliography under his name. I believe that the original *Diary* was not published until after his death. When I refer to the published editions of the journal, I mean *Narrative, Journal*, and *Voyage*. *Narrative* (1839) was actually a three volume work to which Darwin's contribution was Volume 3. (Volume 2 was Captain Robert FitzRoy's account of the same voyage and Volume 1 was Captain P. Parker King's account of a previous *Beagle* voyage.) References to *Narrative* are always to Darwin's Volume 3, unless otherwise noted. The publisher put out Darwin's volume as a separate book, with no changes, at the end of that same year under the new title of *Journal*, which was republished in a second edition with changes in 1845. References to *Journal* are always to this 1845 edition. The last published edition was under the title *Voyage*. I am using the 1909 text, reprinted in 2004 by Barnes & Noble, Inc. with an introduction by Catherine A. Henze.

The Descent of Man – There were two editions, 1871 and 1874. I am using the second edition, but not the one originally published in 1874, rather the one edited by Adrian Desmond and James Moore, mainly because, as a Penguin Classics, it is readily available to the public. When I refer to *Descent*, I almost always mean Part I and/or the last chapter, summarizing Darwin's views on racial descent. Parts II and III are on sexual selection and have very little in them that is relevant to the topic at hand.

1842 and *1844* essays – These are Darwin's early essays on the origin of species, unpublished in his lifetime. Both are in the same volume, *The Foundation of the Origin of Species*, edited by his son, Francis Darwin. Pagination is continuous from one essay to the next.

Darwin, Erasmus – References to his poems are by Canto and line number; e.g., I, 295 means Canto I, line 295.

Gerland, George – Both the original German edition of his book and the French translation are listed in the Bibliography. All page references are to the German edition. As far as I know, Gerland's book has never been translated into English, so I had to make my own. Since I have never studied German, I had to rely first of all on the French. When I came across any interesting passage I wished to quote, I then checked the corresponding German and looked up every German word in a dictionary, and finally consulted my friend Mark Felber who has spoken German since he was a child. I take all responsibility for any errors. My verb tenses in particular may be off. I use square brackets to provide alternative translations of a word. For those who do know German and in order to facilitate spotting anything I got wrong, I have provided the original German following each of my translations. If I made any mistakes, I would like to know.

A pdf version of Darwin's copy of Gerland's book is available at BHL as well as Darwin's Supplemental Notes on the book (this is on separate sheets of paper, about six in all). The information provided on Darwin's markings in Gerland at BHL indicates that the annotations (the translations and close paraphrases written in the margins) were not made by Darwin. German was difficult for him. Is it possible that someone in Darwin's family (possibly his daughter Henrietta) worked with him on reading this book? Did this person translate out loud and then Darwin picked out the particular bits he wanted translated in the margins? Or did this person make their own decisions about what to put in the margins? I don't know the answers to these questions. Whether Darwin made these translations on his own or someone else made them for him, these were the parts of Gerland's book he would have paid most attention to. He was very aware of what Gerland was saying and this stands regardless of who made the translations in the margins. His Supplemental Notes (a few pages of which are in his handwriting, I believe) also indicate that he or his helper was reading the book very carefully.

Malthus – All references to his *An Essay on the Principle of Population* (abbreviated as *Essay*) are to the first edition (1798), unless the sixth (1826) edition is indicated. Since the sixth is in two volumes, whenever I refer to a volume and page number for Malthus, this is obviously the sixth edition that is being referred to (the original 1826 publication can be found online at **H**); this is the one Darwin read. For the first edition, I am using the Penguin Classics, edited by Antony Flew, for the reason that anyone can easily purchase it. In addition to modernizing the spelling, Flew incorporated Malthus's footnoted material into the main body of the text.

Rafinesque, Constantine – His poem *The World, or Instability* is divided into twenty parts, but the line numbers run continuously; there are over 5,000. It is possible that the line numbers I cite may sometimes be off by one or two. Line numbers are given in the text of the poem every 20 lines and sometimes every 40, but when I count the lines, they do not always come out to 20 or 40. I don't know whether I am doing something wrong or there are mistakes in the original text. My line counts are close enough that it should not be difficult to find the relevant quotation.

It is well known that those who suppress history have to relive it.

—Hubert Butler (469)

~ 1 ~

Brother Ant, Sister Worm

Here is a good example of how popular writing about Darwin constantly mythologizes him, giving us a Darwin who never existed. In a *New York Times* review of a book on the causes of World War I, Margaret MacMillan, a professor at Oxford, writes, "Struggle, so Darwin could be twisted to say, was a natural part of human existence." I suppose she meant to imply that Darwin was more humane than that. She wants to distinguish Darwin from "social Darwinism and the racialist theories it spawned." But you don't have to twist Darwin to make him elevate struggle to a primary feature of life or to make him espouse racist ideas of inferiority and superiority. He says these things himself.

Chapter III of *The Origin of Species* is entitled "Struggle for Existence". The last words of Chapter VII are "let the strongest live and the weakest die." Those words remained in place through all six editions (in the sixth edition, this was at the end of Chapter VIII). For the first ten pages or so of "Struggle for Existence", Darwin is reminding the reader of the great destruction of life in nature, and, using plants as an example, states that "the more vigorous … gradually kill the less vigorous." No one has to make Darwin say any of this. He is quite clear about it and never tries to pretend that he sees life as anything less than a struggle to the death—"fatal competition" as he says at the end of Chapter IV on natural selection. Extinction, which is the subject of one of the sections of Chapter IV, is what the losers get; it plays a large role in Darwin's thinking. And lest we forget (how careless of me to leave this as the last example), the struggle for life was so important to Darwin that he put it in the subtitle of his book: *The Preservation of Favoured Races in the Struggle for Life*.

In case anyone is wondering, struggle and competition also feature prominently in Darwin's book on humans, *The Descent of Man*. Here is just one illustrative quote: "Man has multiplied so rapidly, that he has necessarily been exposed to struggle for existence, and consequently to natural selection" (*Descent*, 172). As he continues his exposition, he will argue that the struggle has produced many different races of man, or as he would prefer to call them, sub-species (204, 210). The inferiority of some of these sub-species is a principle theme of Part I of *Descent*.

I think the reason writers have felt enabled to so shamefully misrepresent Darwin's views is that Darwin (the fictional Darwin) has been encapsulated in one sentence. This is the last sentence of *Origin*, which in truncated form reads as follows: "There is grandeur in this view of life ... from so simple a beginning endless forms most beautiful and most wonderful have been, and are being, evolved." This is the romantic Darwin and it is the chief source of the idealistic vision of him. But the real Darwin also wrote a sentence immediately before that, in which he explained how this evolution comes about. It results "from the war of nature, from famine and death." This gives us, says Darwin, "the production of the higher animals." And in the sentence immediately before that, he references "a Struggle for Life" and "the Extinction of less-improved forms." These sentences, the second and third from the end of *Origin*, express and capture what most of *The Origin of Species* is about. The very last sentence is a romantic departure from the main thrust of *Origin*.

That final sentence of *Origin*, quoted probably more often than any other from Darwin, has been used to create the fictional Darwin. No one ever bothers to tell you how atypical it is for the historical Darwin. The real Darwin can be found in the sentences leading up to the uncharacteristic last one. Darwin would go on to make clear twelve years later in *The Descent of Man* that he believed Indigenous peoples all over the world were among the forms of life that would soon be exterminated by civilized Europeans (in at least one letter, he made it the Anglo-Saxons). He regarded this extermination of human beings as a natural process of extinction of the less improved forms of life. This historically real Darwin has been done away with by the majority of writers and scholars who continue to present to the public their romanticized, dream-like image of him. That image may be attractive to many people, but he never existed.

Darwin was a very clear writer and thinker. Most of the time. He rarely dissembled. We should be equally clear and precise about what he said and believed. Picking out that one sentence from the end of *Origin* is a way of obscuring his real beliefs. And so, in order to get rid of other distractions which get in the way of accurate historical study, here are several things to keep in mind about Darwin and evolution, as we endeavor to understand in future chapters how he could have allowed racism to infiltrate a legitimate scientific field.

First: Whatever amount of racism Darwin infused into his study of evolution, this does not mean that the theory of evolution is racist. Quite the opposite. Just remember that Darwin and evolution are not the same thing. They are not interchangeable terms. It is possible to criticize Darwin without criticizing the theory of evolution. It is true that many right-wing religious people try to promote confusion by treating Darwin and evolution as if they were identical or deeply interdependent, but for the sake of clarity and honesty, the two should always be kept apart. The theory itself does not have to lean in a racist direction. Darwin may have twisted things that way, but we must not follow suit and we must not tell lies about history as if everyone in Darwin's time thought about evolution or even nature the same way he did.

Second: The theory of evolution and the theory of natural selection are not the same thing. We must never confuse these two different theories. Darwin's theory properly speaking is natural selection. That is a particular version of the way evolution might be happening. It is often summed up as the survival of the fittest. This term was coined by Herbert Spencer and he based it on the subtitle of Darwin's book, *The Preservation of Favoured Races in the Struggle for Life*. Darwin himself approved it. In the fifth edition of *Origin* (1869), he retitled Chapter IV "Natural Selection; or The Survival of the Fittest", but he had first drawn an equivalency between the two a year earlier in *The Variation of Animals and Plants under Domestication* (1868).

Darwin was not very clear about making a distinction between his theory of survival and the general theory of evolution in *Origin*. He seems to meld the two into one and never points out which evidence goes toward the general theory and which helps to establish natural selection. It is not until *The Descent of Man* (1871, 1874) that he distinguishes between the two: "... I had two distinct objects in view [in *Origin*]; firstly, to shew that species had not been separately created, and secondly, that natural selection had been the chief agent of change, though largely aided by the inherited effects of habit, and slightly by the direct action of the surrounding conditions" (*Descent*, 81). He adds that some people forget this (82), but then he had helped them forget it by being unclear about it in *Origin*.

The general theory of evolution (which is not Darwin's private property) simply says that life evolves, without specifying a cause, and that plenty of evidence supports this even if the cause is unknown. More specifically, it says that species are descended from previous species (species change into new species gradually over immense lengths of time) and that if you trace things back far enough, all life on this planet came from a single source or progenitor. We are all biologically or genetically related. When it is put that way, you can see why evolutionary theory might be inherently antiracist. Darwin would thus have had to do a lot of spinning to inject racism into it. The opposite theory of special or independent creation claims that every species was created separate and apart from all the others and that it has been this way since the dawn of creation. Evolutionists believe in an ongoing creation and creationists believe that the creative energy of the universe expended itself in one burst a long time ago.

Third: Darwin does not own the general theory of evolution. He was not the first to discover it or invent it or propose it. He was not the first to promote and defend it. He was not even the first to prove that it is more probable than not (that is, more probable than independent creation). That credit should go to Robert Chambers, as we will see in a later chapter. Some might want the credit to go to Jean-Baptiste Lamarck, French naturalist. In 1809, the year Darwin was born, Lamarck published *Philosophie Zoologique* in which, as one small part of his work, he speculated in detail on how man may have evolved into an upright, two-footed creature from ape-like ancestors. In *Vestiges of the Natural History of Creation* (1844), published anonymously, Chambers assembled much of the same evidence for the general theory that Darwin would fifteen years later in *The Origin of Species* (1859). Darwin did some of his work independently of the others (his two unpublished essays of *1842* and *1844* were completed before Chambers's book appeared), but Darwin came into a world where work on the theory of evolution had been going on for several decades. He was not working from a blank slate.

It goes as far back as (and maybe further than) Erasmus Darwin, Charles Darwin's grandfather, who was writing about this at the end of the 18th century. Erasmus proved that evolution was a reasonable hypothesis worthy of further investigation, an accomplishment his grandson never acknowledged. In Erasmus's time, the theory was called generation—in part because it was seen to be similar to the birth of individuals. Life on an individual basis or in the larger case of species is always birthing or generating. Later on, when Chambers was championing it, it was known as the theory of development or the development hypothesis. The name kept changing but the idea was the same. All the early naturalists who believed in it would occasionally use the word 'evolve'.

Fourth: These other naturalists were far more humane in their pursuit of evolutionary theory than Charles Darwin was. They demonstrate that the theory of evolution is not intrinsically racist. They may be important for other reasons as well, but for the purposes of this book, this is their chief importance. They were more than precursors to Charles Darwin. They did good work in their own right at a time when the state of knowledge was much less advanced than it was for Darwin the younger. To call them precursors is to belittle their achievements. I believe that this belittling is done with an ulterior motive in mind. Scholars who dismiss Erasmus Darwin, Lamarck, Chambers, and Constantine Rafinesque, another early figure, want us to forget that the theory of evolution was headed in a more humane direction before Charles Darwin came along and that Darwin took a reactionary road, making the theory fit the racist and imperialist prejudices of his age.

Fifth: In a sense, evolution has two directions to it, both of which were important to Charles Darwin. It points back to a common ancestor and it points ahead to incredible diversity among the descendants. In those last sentences of *The Origin of Species*, along with a Struggle for Life, Inheritance, Variability, Natural Selection, and Extinction of less improved forms of life, Darwin listed Divergence of Character as another component of evolution. As we will see, Darwin was incredibly clear about this and he was just as clear about the implication of this as he saw it. He was not using divergence to celebrate diversity and tolerance. He did not believe that descent from a common ancestor meant that the descendants were all equal or spiritual brothers. Inequality was a feature of life and evolution for Darwin. It was one of the results of evolution. For him, divergence in evolution created unequal relationships, not brotherhood.

While the earlier evolutionists might have felt compelled to agree that there was some truth to this, they did not care to emphasize it. They looked back to the common ancestor, or the genetic commonalities of life, and chose to see life as a brotherhood or sisterhood. As Erasmus Darwin put it in his epic poem *The Temple of Nature* (IV, 426-28):

> ... man should ever be the friend of man;
> Should eye with tenderness all the living forms,
> His brother-emmets, and his sister-worms.

(Emmet was an older word for ant.) For Erasmus Darwin and all these early holistic evolutionists, not only was all life netted into one great whole in which every part plays a useful role, but scientific truth and justice should also be united in common cause.

To sum up these points: Charles Darwin does not own the theory of evolution; it was discovered long before Darwin came along and was given to him as a possible explanation for the varied life we see on this planet; a critique of Darwin's approach to both the general theory and his specific theory of natural selection, or survival of the fittest, is not a critique of evolution itself; any racism he put into either theory is his contribution and is not inherent in the theory; the earlier proponents of evolution did not incorporate racism into it and chose rather to see a deep brotherhood of life in its unwinding. With these necessary clarifications in mind, it will be so much easier to explore this history with a degree of honesty that scholars have done their best to avoid.

~ 2 ~

Never, Never Trust an Indian

It is not hard to prove that racism deeply infected the work of Charles Darwin. Turn the pages of his writings—his letters, his *Beagle Diary*, Notebooks, and published works—and it's there. There is hardly a source that does not contain it. It seems like every time he picked up his pen, he had something to say about the inferiority of certain races. As he saw it, it was an outcome of evolution and should be stated in no uncertain terms.

Getting rid of inferior savages was on Darwin's mind when he was writing *On The Origin of Species*. We know this because of a letter he wrote just a few weeks before publication to his friend and mentor, the geologist Charles Lyell. Lyell was never enthusiastic about Darwin taking up the idea of the transmutation of species, but encouraged him to get his work on this published. He would be the last of Darwin's friends to get on board and never quite wholeheartedly. He had argued vehemently against Lamarck and was capable of excoriating Chambers's *Vestiges*. Darwin knew that the main sticking point for Lyell was the implication that man was descended from the lower animals (a point Chambers had emphasized and was thrilled about). Lyell had read an advance copy of *Origin*. Darwin in his letter tried to convince him once again what a sensible idea it is that natural selection should act on mental abilities as well as on the physical features of an organism:

> I suppose that you do not doubt that the intellectual powers are as important for the welfare of each being, as corporeal structure: if so, I can see no difficulty [one of his favorite expressions in *Origin*, comparable to 'we can imagine'] in the most intellectual individuals of a species being continually selected; & the intellect of the new species thus improved, aided probably by effects of inherited mental exercise. *I look at this process as now going on with the races of man; the less intellectual races being exterminated.* [CCD 7.345; Oct. 11, 1859; emphasis added]

This is biological racism (though as we will see, Darwin is often both a biological and a cultural racist). Darwin is using a biological theory (natural selection) to explain that some groups are so inferior in their intellectual development that they will be exterminated by the intellectually superior. He casts no moral judgment on this. He rather presents it as if it were only natural that the intellectually inferior should perish at the hands of the intellectually superior. He is making a lot of assumptions about intellect and grades of perfection, but then that too is typical of racism.

Be it noted that he is not merely saying that this process took place eons ago. This is happening *now*, he says. Nature today is selecting the more highly endowed in intelligence for survival. Even though he uses the active word 'exterminated' rather than the more passive idea of 'extinction', it is clear that he does not intend to impute any immorality to the exterminators. This is nature's doing in his view.

In a letter (January 1873) to his cousin Francis Galton, who is often credited with inventing the concept of eugenics, Darwin responds to a point his cousin made in an article that nature does not care much for individuals and uses them to create improved races. Darwin is not sure that nature cares much more for races as one can see from the long line of "races and species which have become extinct." There is a better notion, thinks Darwin, which he puts in the form of a rhetorical question: "Would it not be truer to say that Nature cares only for the superior individuals and then makes her new and better races?" (ML 2.44).

Darwin often expresses his interest in better races. It is part of his theory. His book is *The Origin of Species*, not the origin of individuals. He wants to understand how the world became populated by a hierarchy of species and races; "groups subordinate to groups" is a phrase that occurs frequently in *Origin*. Mutations explain individuals, natural selection explains groups. I am making this point now because there are notable writers (such as Richard Dawkins, Stephen Gould, and Adam Gopnik) who deny that Darwin's theory is about groups or races or species. They claim that his interest was in explaining better fitted individuals and that it was not his intent to elevate groups to an important status. They are so obviously wrong about this. We will see plenty of evidence (in the next chapter) for how wrong they are. It is a fictional Darwin who is mainly concerned with the struggle between individuals. The real Darwin was interested in ranking groups and saw them in constant combat. The letter to Galton is just the tip of the iceberg.

What Darwin said in the letter to Lyell he would repeat publicly in *The Descent of Man*.

> At some future period, not very distant as measured by centuries, the civilised races of man will almost certainly exterminate, and replace, the savage races throughout the world. At the same time the anthropomorphous apes, as Professor Schaaffhausen has remarked, will no doubt be exterminated. The break between man and his nearest allies [i.e., the apes] will be wider, for it will intervene between man in a more civilised state, as we may hope, even than the Caucasian, and some ape as low as a baboon, instead of as now between the negro or Australian and the gorilla. [*Descent*, 183-84; cf. 153, 689]

This is a very famous passage from Darwin's writings. It is often quoted, in whole or in part, sometimes just the first sentence. Very few, however, pay attention to what he has said here.

I still find it shocking that Stephen Gould could quote this (*Mismeasure*, 417) and see only paternalism in it (416-20). Unlike some who would deny there is any racism in Darwin (e.g., Dawkins, Gopnik), Gould knows full well that Darwin had his prejudices: "The common (and false) impression of Darwin's egalitarianism arises largely from selective quotation" (*Mismeasure*, 417). Apparently (because he does not fully explain himself) what Gould gets out of the above quoted passage is that Darwin has ranked these groups from lowest to highest—that is, baboons, gorillas, savages (Negroes and Australian Aborigines), Caucasians. For Gould, these prejudices or "contempt" (417), "with white Europeans on top and natives of different colors on the bottom" (416), amount to no more than paternalism. I fail to see what is paternalistic about dooming savages to elimination from the earth. How kind of Darwin. Gould simply pays no attention to the first sentence, even though he quotes it. He does his own selective reading. Nor does he pay attention to the fact that Darwin argues that it is their own inferiority that dooms savages and that biology, or natural selection, has produced this inferiority.

Darwin never gave up thinking this way. In a letter near the end of his life (to William Graham, July 3, 1881; LL 1.316) where he is discussing the benefit of "natural selection having done and doing more for the progress of civilization," he brags, "The more civilized so-called Caucasian races have beaten the Turkish hollow in the struggle for existence." He continues with this general observation: "Looking to the world at no very distant date, what an endless number of the lower races will have been eliminated by the higher civilized races throughout the world."

One of his most egregious remarks came almost twenty years earlier, on February 6, 1862, in a letter to Charles Kingsley (CCD 10.72):

It is very true what you say about the higher races of men, when high enough, replacing & clearing off the lower races. In 500 years how the Anglo-saxon race will have spread & exterminated whole nations; & in consequence how much the Human race, viewed as a unit, will have risen in rank.

What makes this comment a little worse than the others is that he is practically declaring his hope for a purification of the human race—humanity as a whole will rise in rank when all the lower races are gone. I would not object if someone said this is perhaps the most awful thing he ever said. But I am usually knocked over by more subtle comments which almost accidentally reveal an author's prejudices.

There are two more letters to Lyell where Darwin makes very soft, but striking remarks. One is from May 4, 1860 (CCD 8.189): "I am content that man will probably advance & care not much whether we are looked at as mere savages in a remotely distant future." He is cavalierly dismissing all future criticisms that Europeans of his time once behaved like savages (I would have to guess that Darwin is referring primarily to the attempted exterminations carried out by Europeans). It is such a hardhearted thing to say. It comes from a sense of power that we can get away with our savage behavior towards other cultures. No one can stop us and all we will have to suffer is a bad opinion from future generations, which is easily shrugged off. What makes this especially disturbing is that he knew very well that the criticism that Europeans were savages was made in his own lifetime. He had read some of these authors. I will get to some of them in later chapters. I find Darwin's claim to be indifferent to such condemnation not convincing, and deeply cruel.

In another letter to Lyell (Sept. 23, 1860; CCD 8.379), Darwin writes, "White man is 'improving off the face of the earth' even races nearly his equals" (his use of quotation marks indicates this was a well-known expression), and approves of Lyell's insight that "man now keeping down any new man which might be developed." Darwin knows that other groups of human beings are still developing, and here he seems to celebrate the fact that one race is now able to prevent these groups from moving ahead. The white man is bringing his improvements to the rest of the world and is using them to clobber and erase other cultures, even those nearly equal to his own. In the wider context of his thoughts, one has to know that Darwin is attributing all this to natural selection. We are using our improvements to destroy and since this is just nature's way, no one can morally blame us.

This goes way back to the earlier part of his life. It is important to remember, as I said at the end of Chapter 1, that racism is not inherent in evolutionary theory or even specifically in natural selection. Darwin did not extrapolate racism from his ideas about evolution. He brought racism to evolution and natural selection, not the other way around. *Before Darwin thought of natural selection, he was already observing the world through a racist and genocidal lens.* We can see this in his *Beagle* journal and in the Notebooks he started keeping when he returned from his trip (which lasted from December 1831 to October 1836; he did not come up with natural selection until September 1838; the Notebooks cover a period from late 1836 or possibly January 1837 to around April 1840).

On August 16, 1833, Darwin entered the following in his journal:

> This war of extermination [by the Spanish against the Indians in Argentina], although carried on with the most shocking barbarity, will certainly produce great benefits; it will at once throw open four or 500 miles in length of fine country for the produce of cattle. [*Diary*, 172]

The following month, September 4-7, he made the following entry:

> If this warfare is successful, that is if all the Indians are butchered, a grand extent of country will be gained for the production of cattle: & the vallies of the R. Negro, Colorado, Sauce [rivers] will be most productive in corn." [*Diary*, 181]

Both these comments were deleted for the published version of the journal. It is possible that Darwin was shocked by the barbarity of his sentiment. But there is another possibility, or indeed both might be the case. Immediately after the above remark, he makes a comment on the Spanish Gauchos' savage behavior, one of a just couple of comments in his journal about Europeans as savages. He might have been embarrassed by his classifying Europeans this way and decided to eliminate the entire discussion. About the Gauchos, he wrote (after the above butchering quote), "The country will be in the hands of white Gaucho savages instead of copper-coloured Indians. The former being a little superior in civilization, as they are inferior in every moral virtue." (Cf. *Diary*, 99, 105, where he also referred to Gauchos as savages.)

Though these blatantly genocidal sentiments were not included in the published versions of the journal, he did say the same thing in the published account in a more polite, sophisticated way. When the remaining Indigenous people of Van Diemen's Land (or Tasmania) were removed so that the island could belong completely to white settlers (or better, invaders), Darwin noted, "All the aborigines have been removed … so that Van Diemen's Land enjoys the great advantage of being free from a native population" (*Narrative*, 533).

Darwin of course means it is advantageous to Europeans, an assumption he shared with most of his readers. In Notebook E 65 (Dec. 1838), he sums up his commitment to colonialism with "man is not an *intruder*" (his emphasis) and compares this to animals being transported on floating ice. Not being an intruder means for Darwin that man has a natural right to trample anywhere he pleases and to expel anyone he wants.

He could occasionally express sympathy for the Natives. In Argentina, he would observe, "It is melancholy to trace how the Indians have given way before the Spanish invaders" (*Narrative*, 122; *Voyage*, 86). Following this, he admires how an Indian and his son escaped their captors: "What a fine picture one can form in one's mind, the naked, bronze-like figure of the old man with his little boy, riding like a Mazeppa on the white horse, thus leaving far behind him the host of his pursuers!" In New Zealand, he gives us, "It was melancholy at New Zealand to hear the fine energetic natives saying, that they knew the land was doomed to pass from their children" (*Voyage*, 375). Neither of these comments were in the original *Diary*. As I suggested in *Darwin's Racism* (Ch.2, §2) and went to great lengths to establish, it is possible that Darwin added these for public consumption because it had become quite common for Europeans to express melancholy or compassion over the plight of Natives. Not all were sincere in this, but it had become an accepted convention. One had to express melancholy to prove you were civilized.

After that last melancholy remark, Darwin adds something that offsets his own seeming compassion. He emphasizes in his own unique way that colonial dispossession is natural: "The varieties of man seem to act on each other in the same way as different species of animals—the stronger always extirpating the weaker" (*Voyage*, 375). His belief in the naturalness of humans extirpating humans negates his professed melancholy. Did he make those melancholy remarks merely for public consumption? Did he express melancholy over this or over anything in the original *Diary*?

In the *Diary*, he had a chance to express melancholy for Aborigines who were losing their land in New South Wales, but he failed to do so. "The thoughtless Aboriginal, blinded by these trifling advantages [gifts from white people, like borrowing dogs or getting cow's milk], is delighted at the approach of the White Man, who seems predestined to inherit the country of his children" (*Diary*, 401-02; also in *Narrative*, 525; *Voyage*, 380). That is all he has to say. It is destiny. The Indigenous will lose their land, end of story. No melancholy here for the fate of the Aborigine. The only place he used the word 'melancholy' in the *Diary* (141, 143; 142 is taken up by an illustration; cf. *Voyage*, 191) was when he expressed chagrin that some Natives whom they had returned to Tierra del Fuego would likely revert back to their savage ways after having been half-way civilized in England. "It was quite melancholy leaving our Fuegians amongst their barbarous countrymen," he said and implied at the end of the paragraph that civilization will lose out to a barbarous culture.

While Darwin can sometimes express sympathy for Natives (he was after all a sensitive man), it is clear that his main sympathies lie with the colonists. There is the odd remark here and there in favor of Indigenes, but they do not add up to a consistent pattern or view of the world—whereas his comments in favor of colonial invaders do constitute a consistent pattern of thinking.

In Argentina, he knows full well that one General Rosas was exterminating the Indians, but Darwin never condemns genocide the way he would slavery and its cruelties. He is occasionally shocked by what Spanish soldiers are doing (such as killing all the Indian women over twenty, so that the Natives won't breed; *Diary*, 180), but then he also gives us the Spanish point of view without criticizing it: "Every one here is fully convinced that this is the justest war, because it is against Barbarians" (*Diary*, 180; *Voyage*, 85). Later on that same month (September 1833), he notes the colonists' "enthusiasm for Rosas & for the success of this 'most just of all wars, because against Barbarians'" (he makes no critical comments) and adds, "It is however natural enough, for even here neither man, woman, horse or cow was safe from the attacks of the Indians" (*Diary*, 190-91). Was Indian violence a response to white violence? Is genocide an appropriate response to sporadic Native attacks? Darwin never raises these questions.

This is a theme throughout Darwin's career: Genocide, if it is the result of colonization, is natural; nothing immoral about it because these Native peoples are inferior and troublesome and are doomed anyway. On January 4, 1835, Darwin found himself wondering about the absence of Indians from some of the islands on the Pacific side of South America. "The entire absence of all Indians amongst these islands is a complete puzzle … I should suppose the tribe has become extinct; one step to the final extermination of the Indian race in S. America" (*Diary*, 278). This is as callous a remark as the one he made to Lyell about not caring if in some remote future we are all regarded as savages (see above). He takes final extermination (final solution?) to be inevitable and, for all we can tell, not unwelcome. He can live with it—just as he found the ethnic cleansing in Van Diemen's Land to be advantageous. He is capable of occasionally noting European atrocities committed against Indigenous peoples, but right alongside that he will note that colonists feel justified, without making any criticism of this. One gets the general feeling that Darwin favors the colonial cause.

What troubles me about two of Darwin's sentences—"one step to the final extermination" and the one about being judged savages in a remote future—is that there is no trembling in those sentences. They are written so matter-of-factly, with no hint of emotion, or, as Darwin might have said if he had been inclined to criticize himself, so placidly. When Charles Lyell expressed no special concern for the way slave families were broken up, in his 1845 book *Travels in North America* (1.184), though he felt sympathy for the way poor whites were treated, Darwin told him how terrible this was to him: "How could you relate so placidly that atrocious sentiment about separating children from their parents; & in the next page, speak of being distressed at the Whites not having prospered; I assure you the contrast made me exclaim out" (CCD 3.242; Aug. 25, 1845), and then he promised Lyell "no more on this odious deadly subject."

Darwin well knew that much the same was being done to Aboriginal families, but never raised any humanitarian complaints. He was just as placid about their dilemma as Lyell was about slaves and their families. Darwin knew about the kidnapping of Native women and children from his reading James Bonwick's *The Last of the Tasmanians* (1870) and he knew about it even earlier, around 1832, from reading the government letters in James Bischoff's *Sketch of the History of Van Diemen's Land*. "The correspondence to show the necessity of this step [removing the Natives from Tasmania], which took place between the government at home and that of Van Diemen's Land, is very interesting; it is published in an appendix to Bischoff's History of Van Diemen's Land" (*Narrative*, 533). In the very first letter in that Appendix, Darwin would have read of random killings of Natives and Native women being kidnapped. Governor George Arthur reiterates "seizing their women" in a later letter (Bischoff, 200). The Appendix also contains the first Committee Report which keeps returning to the outrage of the kidnapping of children (205-07) and points out how justified the Natives are in their desire for revenge. Darwin admits that it all began with "the misconduct of the Whites" (*Diary*, 408; Feb. 5, 1836; also in the published journal; see *Narrative*, 533; *Voyage*, 385), which he probably got from these letters, but he has nothing to say about the particulars of this misconduct.

Darwin knew about these things from other sources as well, a particularly horrid example of a South American Indian woman being separated from her children presented by Alexander von Humboldt, one of Darwin's favorite authors, in his *Personal Narrative* (Vol. 5, Part 1, 5.234-38). Darwin could even match Lyell's placidity when he wrote in Argentina, "The children of the Indians are saved, to be sold or given away as a kind of slave, for as long a time as the owner can deceive them.—But I believe in this respect there is little to complain of" (*Diary*, 180; this is also in the published versions; see *Voyage*, 85, where the last line reads, "I believe in their treatment there is little to complain of"). Humboldt thought there was much to complain of, even recommending that legislation be passed to curb the excesses of missionaries using Native children as slaves (5.238). Darwin was unaffected. Several weeks later, Darwin writes as placidly as Lyell, "The children are sold for between 3 & 4 pound sterling" (*Diary*, 194).

These words about Indian slave children may surprise people who are familiar with Darwin's antislavery reputation, which I will take up in the next chapter, but they illustrate that when Darwin was in his colonialist mindset, he could tolerate a good deal of evil. It seems that for Darwin all this was just "the stronger always extirpating the weaker" (*Voyage*, 375), which I quoted above.

By the time he was recording his thoughts in his Notebooks, adapt or die had become a principle with him. Thus, "… certain physical changes at last become unfit, the animal cannot change quick enough & perishes" (Notebook C 153; probably around three to four months before he thinks of natural selection). His approach to evolution was already emphasizing inequality: "We see gradation to mans mind in Vertebrate Kindgdom in more instincts in rodents than in other animals & again in *Mans mind, in different races, being unequally developed*" (Notebook C 196; my emphasis). "With respect to future destinies of mankind, some of species or varieties are becoming extinct" (D 38; though he makes an exception for African Negroes who are "not loosing ground"; it is near the end of this Notebook that natural selection will occur to him).

Shortly after realizing natural selection, Darwin puts down these thoughts:

> When two races of men meet, they act precisely like two species of animals.—they fight, eat each other, bring diseases to each other & c, but then comes the more deadly struggle, namely which have the best fitted organization, or instincts (ie intellect in man) to gain the day.—In man chiefly intellect, in animals chiefly organization … intellect in Australia to the white.—The peculiar skulls of the men on the plains of Bolivia—strictly fossil <<& in Van Diemen's land>>—they have been exterminated on *principles*. strictly applicable to the universe.—The range of man is not unlike that of animals transported by floating ice.—I agree with M[r] Lyell., man is not an *intruder*. [E 63-65; his emphases; the Notebook editors' double angled brackets indicate Darwin's insertion.]

Extermination is a principle of nature, for human races as for other species of animals, and for humans it is intellect which will make the difference. This is exactly what he would tell Lyell over twenty years later in the October 1859 letter I quoted from at the beginning of this chapter. Early on, Darwin had made human genocide a principle of nature, a position he would never abandon.

The mention of "bring diseases" is a clear reference to one of the features of colonialism as is the claim that man is not an intruder. Whatever havoc man brings to other countries (like bringing disease or his own cultural practices), he is not intruding or invading. There is absolutely no sense here, as there never will be anywhere in Darwin's writings, that when any group of men arrives anywhere, they are intruding and therefore must learn to negotiate. Man is a negotiator precisely because he is an intruder. Darwin has completely erased this side of human life. He was a dedicated colonialist who believed in conquest because the superior in intellect had that natural right, and he would hold onto these ideas for his entire career.

For me, despite Gould's attempts to trivialize Darwin's racism into paternalism—or maybe precisely because Gould could trivialize this and other writers just want to erase it entirely—all these remarks on inferiority and extermination are the most serious part of Darwin's racism because they show the tight link between his racist ideas of ranking human groups from inferior to superior and his belief in the legitimacy of genocide. But many people might wonder if Darwin was racist in a simpler way.

Most of us think of a racist as someone who picks out certain physical attributes, which are disdained, and who then interprets these features as signs of mental and moral inferiority. Often, it is skin color and hair texture which are stigmatized. Darwin indulged in this kind of thinking too, though he made different choices about what traits to single out. He did not regard skin color and hair as significant. What he did find appealing was to look for any physical features which appeared to put savages closer to the world of animals than white Europeans were. He never quite classified savages as a missing link, but he comes close.

Scattered throughout *The Descent of Man* are Darwin's presentations of "facts" which seem to show that savages, generally darker-skinned, are more animal-like than whites. He does not think all of this is solidly established. He will occasionally grant that more research needs to be done, but he is clearly intrigued by any indications of the beastly nature of the Indigenous human beings of other lands, whom he usually calls savages but sometimes natives. This culminates in how much importance he ascribes to brain size.

Darwin informs his readers that "the dark-coloured races [have] a finer sense of smell than the white races," even though they don't need it for survival (*Descent*, 35, text and n36). The third eyelid, which is pronounced in certain reptiles, birds, and fish, is found in humans in rudimentary form, but is "apparently somewhat larger in Negroes and Australians than in Europeans" (35 n35). Darwin does not blare out the implication. He leaves it to the reader to draw his own conclusion about what this means for inferiority in human races.

We all know how closely male and female resemble each other among certain animals. Most of us cannot spot whether a dog or cat is male or female unless we examine it more carefully. For Darwin, it seems to be a distinguishing feature of human life that male and female are more sharply differentiated, so that if there are any human races where male and female are closer together, as among some animals, then those races are more animal-like. Darwin favorably quotes Karl Vogt (one of the scientists with problematic racist views whom Gould brings up in *Mismeasure*) on "a remarkable circumstance" that the difference in cranial capacity between the sexes increases with the development of race "so that the male European excels much more the female, than the negro the negress" (631 n26). Darwin notes Vogt's admission that more observations on this are needed, but relating such evidence, putting males and females closer together among savages than among Europeans and thus putting savages closer to the animal world, seems to please Darwin. He is not trumpeting his conclusion from the rooftops, but his point is unmistakable.

This particular evidence about male and female also pleases Darwin because he held a firm opinion that women are inferior to men. Citing his cousin Francis Galton's work, he states that "with woman the powers of intuition, of rapid perception, and perhaps of imitation, are more strongly marked than in man; but some, at least, of these faculties are characteristic of the lower races, and therefore of a past and lower state of civilisation" and concludes that "… the average of mental power in man must be above that of woman" (629). Take note that he sees women and lower races as sharing a bond in inferiority.

The most seriously racist distinctions Darwin makes in *Descent* in the physical features of human beings occur when he discusses brain size. He notes that there may be "extraordinary mental activity" in animals with small brains, like the ant, and he issues a warning that the intellect in any two men cannot "be accurately gauged by the cubic contents of their skulls," but then goes on to assert, "The belief that there exists in man some close relation between the size of the brain and the development of the intellectual faculties is supported by the comparison of the skulls of savage and civilised races …" (*Descent*, 74). His overall point seems to be that we cannot judge the intellect of individual men by brain size, but we can judge races this way.

He cites skull measurements taken by one scientist, which gave the highest number to Europeans and the lowest to Australian Aborigines (ibid.; "in Australians only 81.9 cubic inches"). He says this has been "proved, by many careful measurements" (ibid.). He clearly wants to convince us that this is sound science. That human skulls vary in shape from more elongated to rounder he regards as significant (76), but he does not spell it out. He leaves his readers with the distinct impression that savages are closer to animals. In the concluding chapter, he avers that reasoning power is more advanced in the civilized, while "with the less civilised nations reason often errs ..." (681).

Although Darwin does not believe characteristics like skin color and hair texture tell us anything, he sees all physical traits on a graded scale and can move smoothly from hair to brain convolutions: "There is, however, no doubt that the various races, when carefully compared and measured, differ much from each other, — as in the texture of the hair, the relative proportions of all parts of the body, the capacity of the lungs, the form and capacity of the skull, and even in the convolutions of the brain ... *Their mental characteristics are likewise very distinct*; chiefly as it would appear in their emotional, but *partly in their intellectual capacities*" (*Descent*, 195-96; emphases added).

It is true that Darwin sometimes stresses the commonalities among human beings. But two things have to be kept in mind about this. One is that even when he sees shared traits, affirming a racist view is never far from his mind. "Even the most distinct races of man are much more like each other in [physical] form than would at first be supposed; *certain negro tribes must be excepted* ..." (195; emphasis added). The second is that whatever the commonalities or differences between human races, Darwin always sees that intellectually, emotionally, and morally, they are very different: "... none of the differences between the races of man are of any direct or special service to him. *The intellectual and moral or social faculties must of course be excepted from this remark*" (229; emphasis added).

Darwin at his best understands how much human beings share: we "can hardly fail to be deeply impressed with the close similarity between the men of all races in tastes, dispositions and habits. This is shewn by the pleasure which they all take in dancing, rude music, acting, painting, tattooing, and otherwise decorating themselves; in their mutual comprehension of gesture language, by the same expression in their features, and by the same inarticulate cries, when excited by the same emotions" (207-08). But to pull this out of context is to completely miss what Darwin was doing with this information and it is to miss the tenor of the whole of his writings.

Darwin emphasizes common attributes to reach a limited objective. He wants to prove that all human races have a common ancestor. "Now when naturalists observe a close agreement in numerous small details ... they use this fact as an argument that they [various races or species of animals] are descended from a common progenitor who was thus endowed ... The same argument may be applied with much force to the races of man" (208). He was not the first to do this. Among others, Robert Chambers had made the same point in 1844: "The probability may now be assumed that the human race sprung from one stock ..." (*Vestiges*, 305; cf. 278, 283, 294). But being all cousins, so to speak, did not imply for Darwin equality or brotherhood or sisterhood among the descendants of that long ago progenitor. Drastic differences among the descendants were a hard fact for Darwin, despite their ancient link. It was inescapable. As noted above, the "intellectual and moral or social faculties" (*Descent*, 229) are racial differences which must be attended to.

Throughout *Descent*, Darwin expresses his low opinion of savages. Their immorality (which he assumed more than proved) was abhorrent to him. "Many instances could be given of the noble fidelity of savages towards each other, but not to strangers; common experience justifies the maxim of the Spaniard, 'Never, never trust an Indian'" (142). He gives it to the Irish too by way of favorably quoting a long passage from W.R. Greg which begins with "The careless, squalid, unaspiring Irishman multiplies like rabbits" (*Descent*, 164). The purpose of the entire passage is to evoke the fear that inferior races will cause a society to degenerate. An Irishman complained to Darwin and asked him to remove the offensive remark. Darwin refused or ignored the request (see Desmond and Moore, *Sacred Cause*, 368).

Darwin was convinced, "Most savages are utterly indifferent to the sufferings of strangers, or even delight in witnessing them ... humanity is an unknown virtue" (*Descent*, 142). One of the highest moral acts Darwin could conceive of was to risk one's own life to save a stranger who is drowning. A civilized man, "even boy," he says, will do this, but not savages (134; in his Notebooks, saving a drowning stranger comes up a few times). He seems offended by anyone who would disagree with his assessment of savages, but expresses himself politely about this: "I have entered into the above details on the immorality of savages, because some authors have recently taken a high view of their moral nature ... These authors appear to rest their conclusion on savages possessing those virtues which are serviceable, or even necessary, for the existence of the family and of the tribe [which Darwin agrees they do possess]" (144). His comment ends there. His disagreement with these authors is evident.

It was not only recent authors who had ventured a higher opinion of savages. He had to have known that older authors could have a more nuanced view of savages and could present them in a more positive light. In 1844, he would have read the following in Chambers's *Vestiges*: "when a people are oppressed ... they invariably contract habits of lying, for the purpose of deceiving and outwitting their superiors, falsehood being a refuge of the weak under difficulties" (*Vestiges*, 357). Chambers could see that what was deception from our point of view was a survival tactic to an oppressed people. Darwin, the supposed expert on survival of species, sometimes could not see the various stratagems a people employ to survive. He had no sympathy for their dilemma. He simply refused to take in any opinions or observations of Indigenous peoples that shook his faith in their immorality.

We can see how fixed his ideas were from a later letter to his friend, the botanist Joseph Hooker, who was about to embark on a trip to Morocco in 1871 (about one month after *Descent* was published). Darwin wrote, "Now don't be a fool, & do take care of yourself.—I know nothing about the natives, but I am convinced that they are blood-thirsty savages" (CCD 19.203). As a friend writing to a friend, this is certainly understandable. He is concerned for his welfare (further on in the letter, he reminds Hooker again not to be a fool and not to take risks). But as a scientist writing to another scientist, this is appalling. It shows how fixed was his mindset when he was writing *Descent*. These prejudices go back to his youth. In New Zealand, in his *Diary* (384), he opines that the "twinkling in the eye [which he sees in the natives] ... cannot indicate anything but cunning & ferocity." It was his general tendency to see violence or something nasty in savages.

Nothing could change his views about savages. Before publishing the second edition of *Descent* (1874), Darwin read Bonwick's *The Last of the Tasmanians* (1870) in which we find Natives helping a white farmer put out a fire threatening his crops (67), a young white girl lost in the bush and helped by Natives (39), and other reports of the friendliness of Natives to strangers (e.g., 36, 49). These were not just strangers but *invading* strangers, and still the Natives offered their help. Would Europeans have done the same when faced with invaders? Nothing positive which Darwin read about Natives ever had an impact on him. He shrugged it all off. Darwin saw only what he wanted to see when it came to savages.

The objection that this is only anecdotal evidence does not apply to Darwin. He loved anecdotes about nature and people. In *Descent*, he is delighted to relate observations about animals that give a favorable impression of them (e.g., 126, the heroic monkey who saved the life of a zookeeper attacked by a baboon, which Darwin liked so much he referred to it at least two more times,134, 689). But there is not one comparable example in *Descent* of savages doing something noble or marvelous for strangers. Darwin provided no relief from his relentless negative depiction of their character. He never sees a heroic savage (except when helping his own kind), whereas, for example, Charles Napier, a well-known British military hero who wrote a book on colonization in 1835, loved anecdotes of their "nobleness and courage" (Napier, 94; cf. 180 where he complains of the double standard whereby we record only the worst aspects of savage life and ignore their good actions). Napier also commented, "Every traveller's account of them, that I have seen, proves them to be by nature, equal to all other men" (94). Darwin saw what he wanted to see and did not see what he did not want to see.

We do not even have to go to other authors, whether read by Darwin or not, for examples of Natives helping strangers. Darwin seems to have forgotten that in his *Beagle Diary*, he himself had given some instances of savages helping strangers. He chose to forget these examples when he wrote *Descent*. Instead, he chose to write from the viewpoint of his society's prejudices about savages and neglected evidence, even his own, to the contrary.

In the entry for June 1, 1834 (*Diary*, 240), Darwin recounts that, just before reaching Port Famine in South America, his ship picked up two European seamen running along the shore. The men had been saved by some Patagonian Indians, after they had run away from a sealer, and had only recently been separated from them by accident. "They had been treated by these Indians with their usual disinterested noble hospitality." Note the use of 'usual'. Darwin knew what some savages were capable of in the way of helping strangers. This passage is not in the first published version of the *Diary* (i.e., in *Narrative*, where June 1, 1834 can be found on 264), but it was restored for the next two editions (*Journal*, 233, and *Voyage*, 197). Curiously, the word 'noble' was dropped for these published editions. Maybe he thought 'noble' was overdoing it, but it is there in the original *Diary*. At least the published editions retained the mention of their hospitality.

A second example from the *Diary* of Natives helping Europeans is in New Zealand where Darwin reported that missionaries "complain far more of the conduct of their countrymen than of the natives. It is strange ... the only protection which they need & on which they rely is from the native Chiefs against Englishmen!" (384; Dec. 22, 1835). This too was forgotten by the time Darwin wrote of savages in *The Descent of Man*. If he would not remember his own examples of the hospitality and generosity of savages, why would he remember anyone else's?

Darwin also recorded an incident of an Indian (he does not say of what nation) saving the lives of a shipwrecked crew of English sailors on the island of Chiloe: "the crew ... was beginning to fail in provisions: it is not probable [that] without the aid of this [Indian] man, they would have been able to extricate themselves" (*Diary*, 281; first bracketed insertion is by editor Keynes, second is mine). Captain FitzRoy in his account of their voyage described the Patagonians as "almost always friendly" with white men (*Narrative*, 2.168). More noteworthy, FitzRoy was told by one old Spaniard in the town of Carmen that he remembered that when they first came as explorers in 1786, "the natives were not only inoffensive, but gave them assistance" (2.299). FitzRoy adds, "How different from the present day! when if a Christian is seen by the natives, he is immediately hunted, and his safety depends upon the fleetness of his horse."

What neither FitzRoy nor Darwin thought about was how much of the hostile behavior they observed in Natives was due to decades of abuse by white invaders. There is always some exception to such a general statement, but basically, they give this little to no thought. One exception is that in New Zealand and the islands of the South Seas, FitzRoy does acknowledge that escaped British convicts from Australia have done much harm by abusing the hospitality of the Natives; "can one then wonder at the natives of some South Sea Islands taking an aversion to white people ..." (2.612.). Here again, FitzRoy is acknowledging that the Natives were originally hospitable. Whether or not Darwin read FitzRoy's volume (he probably did), he certainly would have had many conversations with him about this. Darwin however seems not to have given this much thought at all, certainly not in *Descent*. He never considered that what he witnessed or, more usually, heard about savage immorality, might have been a reaction to decades of European hostility. This was a major scientific error on his part.

Darwin in fact encountered more or less the same point in his friend Charles Lyell's 1845 book *Travels in North America* (2.39). Lyell stated that contact with white Europeans may have caused some tribes to regress and that these tribes would otherwise have attained a more refined civilization. He concluded, "what caution ought we not to observe when speculating on the inherent capacities of any other great member of the human family." What is especially interesting is that Robert Chambers read this too and was so impressed by it that he included a lengthy portion of this in *Vestiges* (I am not sure which edition of *Vestiges* was the first to incorporate it, but see 11th, 244n). Darwin, as far as I know, never considered what Lyell said here. He always rejected more honest and full assessments of savages.

Some of Darwin's low opinion of savages could have been due to culture shock. At the end of *Descent*, he writes, "The astonishment which I felt on first seeing a party of Fuegians on a wild and broken shore will never be forgotten by me ..." He tells us of their naked, painted bodies with long tangled hair and frothing mouths. He goes overboard when he implies that savages generally are lower than monkeys, by saying "I would as soon be descended from that heroic little monkey [described earlier in the book, 126] ... as from a savage ..." (689). This was not his considered opinion of savages. He knew their intelligence exceeded that of apes. Earlier in *Descent* (85, cf. 150), he tells his readers that "man differs so greatly in his mental power from all other animals ... No doubt the difference in this respect is enormous, even if we compare the mind of one of the lowest savages ... with that of the most highly organised ape." In his *Diary* (222; Feb. 25, 1834), he described six Fuegians he had seen in a canoe: "I never saw more miserable creatures; stunted in their growth, their hideous faces bedaubed with white paint &quite naked ...

their red skins filthy & greasy, their hair entangled, their voices discordant, their gesticulation violent & without any dignity … one can hardly make oneself believe that they are fellow creatures placed in the same world" (also in *Narrative*, 235).

In the *Diary* and at the end of *Descent*, he is remembering his shock on seeing the Fuegians. Describing the same experience in the 1862 letter to Charles Kingsley (quoted above) where he spoke of humanity rising higher when all the lower races are exterminated, he said of the idea that we are related to a "naked painted, shivering hideous savage" that "the thought … was at that time as revolting to me, nay more revolting than my present belief that an incomparably more remote ancestor was a hairy beast" (CCD 10.71). Remarkably, he could get used to being related to a monkey but not to a savage.

One could argue that this understandable culture shock shows Darwin to be more a cultural racist than a biological racist. This would be false. Darwin believed that all moral or social or cultural attributes were ultimately grounded in biology, and also, do not forget, that he thought the extermination of the Indigenous was grounded in biology, not in injustice. This had the unfortunate effect of making sure that his prejudices about the character of savages would never change. Everything about savages (and all humans) for Darwin was reduced to the biological. "If bad tendencies are [biologically] transmitted, it is probable that good ones are likewise transmitted … Except through the principle of the transmission of moral tendencies, we cannot understand the differences believed to exist in this respect between the various races of mankind" (*Descent*, 148; when he speaks of transmitted or transmission, it is clear he means biological inheritance). Darwin's racism was both mundane (think of what he said, above, about Indians and the Irish) and deep. But even his ordinary ideas of their immoral character he turned into a deep racism by biologizing them.

This also means that Darwin had a rather strong tendency to blame savages themselves for any trouble they were having—including their impending (so he believed) extermination! In Chapter 7 of *Descent*, there is a section entitled "On the Extinction of the Races of Man" (211-22). He considers the infertility of the women to be one of the chief causes of their extinction. Though he knew that "changed conditions or habits of life" (e.g., 218) (or, as we would say today, stress) was one of the causes of this infertility, Darwin almost never identifies European mistreatment of Natives as the main changed condition of life. He does not see injustice as stressful; he treats stress in the abstract as merely natural. He presents infertility as an unfortunate side effect of civilization—in the same way that many wild animals become less fertile or even sterile in captivity (219-20). He introduces this part of the discussion of the infertility of Native women by referring to "the analogy of the lower animals," which again shows how little Darwin thinks of these people.

Darwin never looks to injustice as a factor. In the contemporary German anthropologist Georg Gerland (to be discussed in Chapter 4), whom Darwin read very carefully, we will see a very different point of view. Darwin never responds to Gerland. Despite his awareness that some scientists like Gerland looked at Indigenous people in a more humane way, Darwin remained a committed (but not loudmouth) racist all his life.

So what does Darwin's racism amount to? The simplest way to put it is that he distinguished between inferior and superior human races just as he saw a hierarchy of groups subordinate to groups in nature in *The Origin of Species*.

What Darwin was doing was subtle but effective and right in line with standard racism. He was saying that while all humans are descended from ancient lower animal life forms, some present human races are more closely related to animals than others. We are all descended from animals, but some are even more so because they have retained those physical and mental connections to inferior animals that either don't appear in white people or that appear in diminished form. And make no mistake about it: Despite seeing a gradation of intelligence from animals to man, as so many others like Chambers did, Darwin did judge animals to be inferior. One of the most fascinating paragraphs in *Descent* (150-51) is where Darwin argues that the highest ape, "if he could take a dispassionate view of his own case," and of course, if he could talk, would have to admit how inferior he is to humans in intelligence (an "immense" difference in mind), in aesthetic appreciation, in communication skills, and in morality. Darwin is playing the racist card of asserting the darker races' resemblance to animals, but doing it oh-so-delicately that you almost don't notice it. The racist effect of his writings is unmistakable and just as deadly damaging to human relations as the more extreme racist nonsense.

This grading of intelligence accurately captures Darwin's racism, yet I think it misses what is most profoundly at stake here and in racism generally. I am not objecting to putting an emphasis on the way racists charge inferiority against certain peoples. That too is certainly what racism is about, although it should be equally emphasized that racists don't believe in inferiority so much as they take actions to make the inferiority "come true" and that their verbal pronouncements about inferiority are part of their system of action. It is less a system of belief than a system to create inequalities. When a racist says "You [or, they] are inferior," that verbal charge is not a statement of belief so much as it is an *action* intended to depress and humiliate a targeted people, and hopefully (from the racists' point of view), make them feel and act inferior.

All that is bad enough, but there is something deeper going on. I did not realize what that is until I read the late 18th century British abolitionist Granville Sharp's first antislavery pamphlet, *A Representation of the Injustice and Dangerous Tendency of Tolerating Slavery* (1769). He was self-educated in the law, and though he never became a lawyer, he organized many cases on behalf of slaves in England seeking their freedom.

Sharp was not a scientist either, but he had something in common with the evolutionary scientists, other than Charles Darwin, who would shortly show up on the scene. He was a holistic thinker. He thought about the whole of society and the common injustices inflicted on many different groups. He saw the interconnections between groups, just as the holistic evolutionary scientists would. Slavery was not just evil because of its abominable cruelties, though he would address that too. He wanted to end slavery not merely for that one reason, but for the deeper reason that it violates the civil and human rights of slaves as human beings. All human beings are entitled to the same rights because we are all fundamentally made of the same material. We are all connected. Sharp understood that racism makes claims about people being disconnected from each other, while antiracism must concentrate on the connections between people, which is exactly what holistic evolutionists would teach.

Sharp was deeply aware that the rights of Englishmen were entwined with rights for all humans: "the spirit and equity," for example, of trial by jury (denied to slaves) would be "entirely lost, if we partially confine that justice to ourselves alone, when we have it in our power to extend it to others" (71; this was presented in a rhetorical question). "The *natural right of all mankind* must principally justify our insisting upon this necessary privilege in favour of ourselves in particular … we certainly undermine the equitable force and reason of those laws, by which *we ourselves are protected …*" if we do not extend them to all men (ibid.; his emphases).

Darwin never uses the language of human rights for slaves. He never argues they are not property or they are entitled to freedom simply as a human right. I think he probably did believe these things, at least to some degree, but it is interesting that he never used such strong language as "divesting them of their humanity" as others did. Thus, Sharp: The Negro "has not been guilty of any offences, that I know of, for which he might *lawfully be divested of his humanity*" (*Representation*, 18; his emphasis). Darwin's focus was almost exclusively on the cruel acts committed by slave owners and not on the basic issue of rights and justice. We should not assume that just because Darwin was opposed to legal slavery that he had the same high-minded ideas as the best humanitarians.

There were two things in Sharp's pamphlet that struck me really hard the first time I read it. One was this: *Twice* Sharp tells us that slavery is "destructive of the human species" (*Representative*, 80, 97). (We have already seen Darwin say almost the exact opposite when it came to exterminating Aborigines; in the letter to Kingsley, he stated his belief that the disappearance of lower races would improve the human race.) Slavery is not just destructive of slaves and detrimental as well to their masters, but it ruins the whole human species. Slavery undermines the common and connected humanity of all people. And Sharp tells us this twice! He strongly believed that the oppression of one part of society, if unchecked, will spread to other parts, particularly to the common people (99). He also notes that the free Negroes, Mulattoes, and Indians in the colonies suffer oppressive measures as a result of the way slaves are treated (99n*). There is implied in this a holistic view of human society. The whole binds all the parts together so that injustice cannot be confined to one part; whatever wrongs are done to one will spread to other parts of the whole. Sharp saw connections where racists and slaveholders saw disconnections.

The second thing that struck me is that long before anyone else was doing this, Sharp saw the connection between the cause of slaves and the cause of Aborigines. In order to explain that a Negro slave can avail himself of English courts, he writes (all emphases are his), "NO MAN of *what estate* or *condition* that he be [Sharp comments there can be no exceptions whatsoever to this] shall be put out of land or tenement ... without being brought in answer *by due process of the law*" (*Representation*, 25). This applied just as well to Aborigines. This becomes clearer as he proceeds. He mentions "the tyrannical constitution of the British colonies (to the indelible disgrace of the British name)" (48), and reviews a number of unjust colonial laws concerning Negroes, Mulattoes, and Indians (using such strong language as the "shameful depravity of mind" [47n*] of legislators in Virginia). Some of these laws applied to slaves (and Sharp also further on reviews cruelties and injustices against free servants). He finally expounds:

> Thus our American provincials (though they pretend to be very zealous in the cause of liberty, yet) make no scruple to deprive the poor Indians of their just rights, who are as much intitled to an equitable and reasonable freedom as themselves. It is a shame to this nation, and may in time prove very dangerous to it, that the *British* constitution and liberties should be excluded from any part of the *British dominions* ... it is the grossest infringement on the *King's Prerogative*, that ... [the protection of the King's laws and courts] should not be extended "*to all his Majesty's subjects*" of every denomination (Slaves as well as others) even in the remotest parts of the *British empire*. [51; his emphases]

Sharp and other humanitarians knew exactly what the implications of their principles were. Human rights apply to everyone, of every race and in every land. They truly believed that an attack on humanity anywhere is an attack on humanity everywhere. Sharp would extend the English Common Law to the whole empire (71-72) and the King's protection under these laws to "black as well as white, bond as well as free" in all the British colonies (72). As for laws protecting aliens in England, he specifically includes savages in this (35). Linking the cause of slaves and that of Aborigines was an idea that came very early. Sharp's antislavery position was that slaves are not unique. When Sharp speaks of the whole human species, he means it.

Saxe Bannister, another British humanitarian who did legal work on behalf of the Hottentots in South Africa and had been Attorney General in New South Wales in the mid-1820s, would make this point again in 1838 (the year emancipation of slaves in the British colonies became fully effective). He considered "the abolition of slavery, a mighty branch of the aborigines' question" (*Colonization*, 85) and expressed "a confident hope that the energy which has effected so much for the slave will now be directed with equal effect to the improvement of the coloured people ... [in] all our own colonies" (97). He also hoped that, after the emancipation of slaves, "it may be expected that the undivided force of public sympathy will henceforth be diverted towards the suffering free coloured tribes ... and it can only be excited by men of letters" (225). Combating racism against colored people *after* slaves were emancipated was crucial to Bannister. He even says that when Thomas Buxton and others were fighting to achieve the emancipation of slaves, they had always had in mind justice for both the free and enslaved colored people (the former being mainly the Aborigines in each colony), "a common cause aiming at universal elevation of the oppressed" (240). Freeing slaves was not the end of the matter, it was part of a more basic quest. There was so much more to do.

Darwin is very far from this kind of thinking. He saw no fundamental quest for human rights in emancipation, only a particular moral concern about cruelty. As we will see in the next chapter, he was a believer in inequality. No brotherhood of man for him. It is not that others did not see inequalities in human beings (differences in abilities, talents, and much else), but they also saw an equality of human rights and social care owed to all. At the end of his great essay/poem *The World, or Instability* (1836), the American (expatriated Italian) naturalist Constantine Rafinesque added some verses in the Additions sections at the end; this one was for the section on "Equality" for verse 3116. (Instability, be it noted, was one of his expressions for evolution; another was constant change.) He acknowledges that human beings are not created equal. They vary so much in size, strength, temper, complexion, and many other qualities. One result is that the strong have made sure that laws "Enacted are to suit the powerful/ And rich …" But Rafinesque proposes, "If men are not of equal frame and mind,/ Yet they are brothers claiming social care,/ And equal laws demanding to obey." The goal, or "constant wish" as he says, is that "equal they become before the law." The last lines in this Additions section are, "Until [equality before the law is] secured, they deem themselves deprived/ Of common human rights or happiness." Human rights not only took precedence over apparent inequalities, they were as fundamental a part of life as other features.

None of this held true for Darwin. For him, we can exterminate Native peoples without moral qualms because they are disconnected from us. He puts the complaint that we Europeans are behaving like savages into a remote future in order to feel disconnected from this complaint. He will connect savages to the world of animals, putting them closer to animals than Europeans are, again to create a feeling of disconnection from other humans. He uses human connections to the animal world to create (or imagine) disconnections between human races. The white man can put a stop to the development of other human groups (as he said in a letter to Lyell) because of that same disconnection. Progress for Darwin, as we'll see in one of his letters, depended on competition and inequality, not on cooperation among disparate classes or races who are seeking bonds. Racism may in one sense be about creating a feeling of inferiority in certain human beings who have been selected for degradation, but it is ultimately founded on claims of disconnection. If racists can convince people we are all of different stock (no matter what our primeval origins are), then the idea of inferiority follows naturally. Darwin's "groups subordinate to groups", one of the premises of *The Origin of Species*, might just as well have been groups disconnected from groups, with the dominant ones set apart and above every other.

If Darwin's system had a purpose, he stated it bluntly in the last paragraph of Chapter II of *Origin*: "throughout nature the forms of life which are now dominant tend to become still more dominant by leaving many modified and dominant descendants"—a Darwinian thought I will have occasion to return to more than once. By affirming dominance as the chief result of disconnections among humans, Darwin was making dominance serve a purpose. He was in effect using dominance to create disconnections.

~ 3 ~

Defenses of Darwin

There are three broad attempts to defend Darwin: 1) Darwin was surely not a racist because he was staunchly opposed to slavery; his abolitionism and hatred of cruelty to slaves reveals him to be a humanitarian; no one who had humane ideas about ending slavery could possibly have held racist views; 2) Darwin could not possibly have been a racist because his theory was about individuals in competition for survival, not about groups; groups such as races had no reality for him, so he could not have promoted the idea that some races were superior; and 3) Darwin was sort of a racist but then everyone in his time was, so he cannot be held accountable for fitting in with his social culture; none of his contemporaries truly appreciated the problem of racism or could define it; there was no genuine antiracist thinking in his time and no movement to expose racism, so why should he be singled out for failing to see things more purely than others did; besides, his "racism" was less severe than that of others of his time.

All three of these defenses are pure fantasy. There is not an iota of truth to any of this. The historical evidence overwhelmingly demonstrates that racism existed in the 19th century, that some humanitarians identified it and even had terms for it, that being antislavery implied almost nothing about one's racial views, that one could oppose slavery and still be highly racist, even opposing civil rights for freed slaves, and that while there was a range of racist ideas, one can identify some racists, like Darwin, who made a deeper contribution to racism than others. Identifying which groups were superior mattered very much to Darwin. Every group must know its place. Darwin was not alone in believing this, he had plenty of company, but that company did not extend to everyone in his society. A hardy minority of humanitarians took exception to racist rankings of human groups.

Obviously, there can be nuances to all three of the above positions, which is why I did not state any one of them in a single sentence. Racism is not always openly violent, but even at its most mild, it lays the groundwork for those who choose to express it more violently. The most difficult thing to confront about racism, to very loosely paraphrase Chester Himes, an African-American writer who lived most of his adult life in France, is that, in racism, it is not the man with the gun who is the most serious problem, it is the man behind the man with the gun. That, in a sense, is Darwin to a T.

(Not to mislead anyone about what Himes precisely said, I have to add this: Now that I have had a chance to look him up again, he complained about "white racists hiding behind the nonracists" and said that the difficulty lay in "persuading the nonracists to take away his gun" [Himes, 27]. I think Himes might have agreed that many of these nonracists were actually racists. But his main point was that it was the ones without guns who posed the greater danger. I think I unconsciously changed it in a way that is still true to the spirit of his original thought. Whichever way you put it, whoever is hiding behind whom, there are people who are more hidden from view and who are pulling the strings. The racists with guns are just the ones most out in front. They do the dirty work. It's the ones behind the scenes or operating more quietly whom you really have to watch out for.)

I will deal with the issue of antislavery first. Everyone knows that Darwin was firmly opposed to slavery. It is one of the most famous things about him. He hated the physical cruelties practiced by slave owners and the emotional cruelties of the slave trade, such as the breakup of families. But that is as far as it went for Darwin. He did not address the economic and social injustice of slavery or promote a brotherhood of man. We too easily assume that if someone was antislavery, then they were also high-minded humanitarians who believed in the equality of blacks or other peoples used as slaves. That is an utterly false deduction. In the 19th century, there are many examples of people who supported the abolition of slavery, but held deeply racist beliefs. Besides Darwin, three more would be Joseph Hooker, Thomas Huxley, and Anthony Trollope. (For the racism of Trollope and Hooker, see *DR*, 167-69 and 197-99, respectively.)

Darwin's friend Huxley can serve as one good example—not only because he was both an abolitionist and a racist, but because he explicitly argued that just because slavery was wrong does not mean that all the arguments brought against slavery were good arguments. He rejected much of what was said in the cause of emancipation. He wished an end to slavery but objected to the idea that blacks were the equal of whites. At the end of the American Civil War, in a lecture entitled "Emancipation—Black and White" (the white part referred to women's liberation which takes up the bulk of the essay), he had this to say (Quashie was a derogatory term for blacks; and I have eliminated paragraph divisions):

> Quashie's plaintive inquiry, "Am I not a man and a brother?" seems at last to have received its final reply … The question is settled; but even those who are most thoroughly convinced

that the doom [of slavery] is just, must see good grounds for repudiating half the arguments which have been employed by the winning side [the abolitionists] … It may be quite true that some negroes are better than some white men; but no rational man, cognisant of the facts, believes that the average negro is the equal, still less the superior, of the average white man … it is simply incredible that, when all his disabilities are removed, and our prognathous [ape-like] relative has a fair field and no favour, as well as no oppressor, he will be able to compete successfully with his bigger-brained and smaller-jawed rival, in a contest which is to be carried on by thoughts and not by bites. The highest places in the hierarchy of civilisation will assuredly not be within the reach of our dusky cousins … But whatever the position of stable equilibrium into which the laws of social gravitation may bring the negro, all responsibility for the result will henceforward lie between nature and him. *The white man may wash his hands of it, and the Caucasian conscience be void of reproach for evermore.* And this, if we look to the bottom of the matter, is *the real justification for the abolition policy.* The doctrine of equal natural rights may be an illogical delusion; emancipation may convert the slave from a well-fed animal into a pauperised man. [Huxley, 115; emphases added].

For Huxley, the moral law is that "no human being can arbitrarily dominate over another without grievous damage to his own nature" (116). The master, he says, will benefit more from emancipation than the slave. That is the reason abolition was the right thing to do and not because blacks are supposedly the equal of whites, which he denies. We did it for ourselves, not for them. We did it to give ourselves a clean conscience and now that it is clean, we can wash our hands of whatever fate awaits the blacks. Note especially how eager Huxley is to proclaim that whatever happens to the Negro after emancipation is entirely "between nature and him." After slavery is abolished, white injustice is no longer an issue for Huxley; it is all nature from this point on.

Huxley's opening line is an allusion to a motto that appeared around the border of a famous medallion made by Darwin's grandfather, Josiah Wedgwood. It depicted a slave in chains and on bended knee, hands clasped, pleading the question about being a brother and a man. It became one of the guiding inspirations of the antislavery movement in Britain. People assume that Darwin, being opposed to slavery, must have subscribed to this sentiment too. In fact, Darwin had doubts about this saying. In Notebook C 217 (around

June 1838), he wrote "civilized Man, May exclaim with Christian we are all Brothers in spirit—all children of one father.—yet differences carried a long way." Those differences were compelling to Darwin, more compelling than the motto on his grandfather's medallion.

Darwin did not favor equality, not the natural kind or the economic or the social. He certainly hated cruelty towards slaves, but slaves (like poor people) should know their place. Slaves who did not observe formalities seem to have bothered him. After describing the New Zealand Maori custom of greeting by pressing noses, he says, "I noticed that the slave would press noses with any one he met, indifferently either before or after his master, the Chief.—Although amongst savages the chief has absolute power of life & death over his slave, yet there is generally an entire absence of ceremony between them" (*Diary*, 387-88; *Narrative*, 505; *Voyage*, 365). This may seem an innocent enough observation, but he follows this with: "Where civilization has arrived at a certain point, as among the Tahitians, complex formalities are soon instituted between the different grades of life [society, in all the published editions]" (*Diary*, 388; cf. 254). Maintaining different social grades was important to Darwin. Slavery should be ended for other reasons, but not for reasons of bringing about social equality. In a civilized country, a slave or a poor man should not know or suffer brutality, but should know where he belongs.

He had firm ideas that equality was bad for society. He did not like what he saw in Tierra del Fuego either. "The perfect equality among the individuals composing the Fuegian tribes must for a long time retard their civilization" (*Voyage*, 193; in *Diary*, 141, the last words are "prevent their civilization"). Even "animals, whose instinct compels them to live in society and obey a chief, are most capable of improvement" and "so is it with the races of mankind" (*Voyage*, 193). Darwin did not like seeing anything in his own society that moved in the direction of social cooperation. He disapproved of trade unions and cooperative societies because they seemed to him to oppose competition. He disliked unions for their insistence that "all workmen,—the good & bad, the strong and weak,—sh^d all work for the same number of hours & receive the same wages. The unions are also opposed to piece-work,—in short to all competition. I fear that Cooperative Societies ... likewise exclude competition. This seems to me a great evil for the future progress of mankind" (CCD 20.323-24).

I don't know if Darwin would have agreed with everything Huxley said in the above blocked quote, but it is more than likely that he did. What I believe they had in common was that both regarded emancipation as the end of the story. They did not care to understand the racism that would dog the steps of freed slaves. Darwin never showed any interest in this. What was a freed slave? Another poor person, the rights of whom Darwin never gave much thought to.

The most positive thing he ever said about slaves was in Brazil. He judges "they will ultimately be the rulers" and draws this conclusion in part "from clearly seeing their intellects have been much underrated" (*Diary*, 80; July 3, 1832; this is not in the published editions). In his enthusiasm for the slaves of Brazil, Darwin made what is probably his most radical statement on behalf of any slaves, in a letter to his sister Catherine, finding himself "almost wishing for Brazil to follow the example of Hayti [where a slave rebellion had occurred]; & considering the enormous healthy looking black population, it will be wonderful [i.e., amazing, unbelievable] if at some future day it does not take place" (CCD 1.313; May to July, 1833). Almost wishing for revolution was decidedly very atypical for Darwin. It sounds more like his grandfather Erasmus Darwin. He also says in this letter that his voyage so far has only given him "a much higher estimate of the Negros character.—it is impossible to see a negro & not feel kindly towards him; such cheerful, open honest expressions & such fine muscular bodies" (CCD 1.312-13).

These highly favorable remarks about Brazilian slaves are in part the result of Darwin's awareness that all species and races have quite a bit of variation in their members. Not all slaves or Africans should be put in the same basket. In Mauritius, he sees things very differently. "With respect to the negroes [in Mauritius], they appeared a very inferior race of men to those of Brazil, & as I believe, of the W. Indies: they come from Madagascar & the Zanzibar coast" (*Diary*, 420). It is also possible that some slaves and Natives were more appealing to him than others, based on how well they conformed to European customs. One of the reasons he liked Patagonian Indians is that they spoke "a good deal of Spanish & some English" and "At tea they behaved quite like gentlemen, used a knife & fork & helped themselves with a spoon" (*Diary*, 217; Jan. 29, 1834). I understand why Darwin felt more comfortable with people who followed customs he was familiar with him. They made him feel at home. But judging other people by the extent to which they have adopted one's own customs makes for bad science. Aboriginals who stuck to their own culture and refused to adapt to European ways posed a great problem for Darwin.

It has to be reiterated (as noted earlier in Chapter 2) that the very positive assessment of Brazilian slaves is unusual for Darwin. This is not how he typically writes about slaves, dark-skinned people, or the Indigenous. There is no pattern of such good assessments in Darwin, only the odd favorable comment here and there. What does form a pattern are all his negative comments about non-Europeans. The inferiority of the Other is how Darwin generally sees the Native populations of the world and he strives to give it scientific underpinning. The occasional recognition of some equality is the exception with him, not the rule. But it should also be said that Darwin retained the capacity to judge individuals as individuals and not as members of a race. He was not the kind of racist who made one blanket judgment of a person depending on their racial category. This does not change the fact that he could still make judgments of entire groups based on stereotypes. He really did think some were inferior to others, even though he allowed for certain exceptions.

With the emancipation of slaves in the British colonies taking partial effect in 1834 and full effect in 1838, many supporters of abolition moved ahead to the cause of fighting for Aboriginal rights. Darwin did not. Many humanitarians saw colonialism as another form of slavery. Darwin did not. Some turned their attention to illegal forced labor which really was the *de facto* equivalent of legal slavery. Darwin did not. On the whole, it is fair to say that Darwin was antislavery in a very limited way. He was a low level humanitarian regarding slavery. Nor did he focus on the underlying racism inherent in slavery. It was the open cruelty of it that bothered him. That was the extent and the limitation of his opposition to slavery. Social and political inequality were acceptable to him.

Following are four examples of Darwin's contemporaries who saw the similarity between slavery and colonialism. The first one Darwin was probably not aware of. The second he possibly could have been, as the *Report* I reference (see Bibliography) was published and available to the public. The third he definitely knew of, as it is quoted in James Bonwick's 1870 book which Darwin read and cited several times in the second edition of *The Descent of Man* (1874). The last example is actually not from a contemporary but from Darwin's grandfather, though Darwin's colleague Alfred Wallace helps to drive home the point.

Alexander Maconochie, who served in the Royal Navy and was later the first professor of geography at the University of London, was an early humanitarian who was deeply impressed by all the testimony taken in hearings held by the House of Commons Select Committee on Aborigines from 1835 to 1837, which culminated in the *Report*. Maconochie wrote his own report on better treatment of Aborigines which he sent to the Colonial Secretary in 1837 and which was printed in *Murray's Review* in January 1838. He summed up what he got from the Committee's hearings: "it has been seriously and in truth, rationally and justly represented … that even the slave trade, with all its horrors has not been such a scourge to humanity as the English colonizing system" (Plomley, 1003).

My second example comes from the *Report* (1837) issued by the Select Committee. Much of the testimony before the Committee, particularly by Dr. Thomas Hodgkin, and from others as well, touched on the twin evils of slavery and colonialism. Thomas Fowell Buxton was chairman and may have been the primary author of the *Report*. He had been the prime mover of the antislavery bill through Parliament in 1833 (having taken over from William Wilberforce who had stood down in 1826 due to illness) and the following year called for that Select Committee. His correspondence with various activist missionaries and officials throughout the British empire had taught him a few things. In the Conclusion of the *Report*, he reminded everyone of how Britain had recently "made some atonement" for slavery (Darwin made the same point about expiating our sin in the 1845 edition of his journal, *Narrative*, 500; also in *Voyage*, 431). Some apology could be made for the evils of slavery and the slave trade, Buxton argued, chiefly in that "they were evils of an ancient date." He implies that the more recent development of colonialism's ills is less excusable. He continues in the Conclusion by comparing the treatment of slaves and Aborigines: "An evil remains very similar in character, and not altogether unfit to be compared with them in the amount of misery it produces. The oppression of the natives of barbarous countries is a practice which pleads no claim to indulgence" (*Report*, 75). How can we *indulge* one evil (mistreatment of Aborigines) which is very much like another (slavery) which we just did something about, the *Report* pleaded, just as Darwin would reprove Lyell for being *placid* about slavery's cruelty.

The third example is from James Bonwick's *The Last of the Tasmanians*. Bonwick quoted from the journal of a Quaker, George Washington Walker, who commented on the treatment of Tasmanian women by white men:

> … we cannot regard the situation of the aboriginal females amongst that class of men [the sealers] as differing materially from slavery … The object of these men in retaining the women, most of whom, it is asserted, were originally kidnapped, is obviously for the gratification of their lust, and for the sake of the labour they can exact from them. In resorting to coercion in order to extort the services of these poor defenceless women, great cruelty appears to have been used by their unfeeling masters, with a few exceptions. [Bonwick, *Last*, 304]

This was *de facto* slavery, as slavery was never institutionalized as a legal system in Tasmania or in most of the colonized countries. Walker got this information by speaking directly with the women, one of whom described in detail the beatings she received.

Darwin was thus made aware that their situation did not differ materially from slavery. Bonwick could also write, on the first page of Chapter II, that white men "came not to share the soil with the dark men, but to appropriate it" and that "The wild men had two courses before them. They could prostrate themselves beneath the feet of the usurpers, and *quietly submit to slavery*; or they could refuse to sell their birthright of freedom and take the consequences" (emphasis added). *De facto* slavery almost everywhere you looked.

I should take the opportunity to observe that Bonwick was apparently one of those people from that "remotely distant future," mentioned by Darwin, who could see savagery in Europeans. He approvingly quoted one unnamed author (*Last*, 376): "He who talks of a necessity that uncivilized man must perish away before civilized … is, with respect to the nobler qualities of man, barbarous and uncivilized himself." According to this unknown author, the spokespeople for western civilization were the real savages when they insisted on the inevitability of wiping out other races. This would apply to Darwin. The author quoted by Bonwick admits that "almost all historical experience is on the side of the exterminating politician … to the shame of our race and of our country" but goes on to protest, "we indignantly deny that the circumstances which impel the civilized race to root out the uncivilized are inevitable."

Bonwick was capable of denouncing the hubris of imperialism in his own words. In response to a Buffalo newspaper which had boasted that Americans will explode in population and soon take over the globe, Bonwick commented, "It is this heartless egoism of our common race of Britain and America that so shocks the benevolent mind, and chills the aspiration for a better policy toward the native peoples" (*Last*, 380). Darwin does not seem to have been too shocked or inclined to object to the chilling effect of this egoism. In what might have been a direct rebuke to Darwin, in his later book *The Lost Tasmanian Race* (1884; two years after Darwin died), Bonwick wrote in the preface:

> Are all *Dark Skins* to perish, like the unhappy Tasmanians, before Europeans? Have we not often been, in our civilizing processes, more savage than the Savages? If the Natural *Law of Selection* necessitates the destruction of inferior races, as History has illustrated thus far, is there not in Humanity a *Higher Law*, happily better recognized in our day, which should and could be employed, by moral force, to resist this fearfully selfish struggle for existence? [his emphases]

But on to my fourth example of someone who saw the connection between slavery and colonialism and Charles Darwin failing (or refusing) to see it. When Darwin quoted some antislavery lines from his grandfather's poetry, he chose *Loves of the Plants* in which a condemnation of slavery stands alone (quoted in Darwin's biography of him, "Preliminary", 47, in Krause). There is another criticism of slavery in *The Economy of Vegetation*, which Charles Darwin did not quote from, in which Erasmus Darwin's criticism is set in the context of a critique of imperialism (for the lines on slavery in this poem, see *Economy*, II, particularly lines 421-24). The antislavery section is preceded by a section on Spain's empire—"Spain's deathless shame! The crimes of modern days!/ When avarice, shrouded in religion's robe,/ Sail'd to the west, and slaughter'd half the globe" (II, 414-16)—and followed by a critique of ancient empires, with admiration expressed for Hannibal who "shook the rising empire of the world" (line 536). Clearly, Erasmus was repelled by any voracious empire and aimed to expose imperialism's brutality and greed. Hannibal was not a rebellious slave so much as a rebellious colonized subject.

The lines Charles Darwin quoted from *Loves of the Plants* end with "… hear this truth sublime,/ He, who allows oppression, shares the crime" (III, 457-58; the last line is originally in all caps). What is so interesting is that Alfred Wallace quoted these very same lines (except changing 'He' to 'They') in *The Wonderful Century* (375), but to a different purpose. The lines as written by Erasmus Darwin applied only to slavery, but Wallace used them to shame colonialism. He made them his final comment on the political and economic injustices of British colonization. Specifically, it was Britain in India that caught his attention here. The "discontent, chronic want and misery," among other things, of the British government in India "must surely be reckoned among the most terrible and most disastrous failures of the Nineteenth Century." A few pages earlier he called European colonialism in Africa (which induced such injuries as seizing lands and cattle, and the "great demoralization both of black and white") "a modified form of slavery" (372). Wallace understood that Erasmus Darwin's denunciation of slavery applied just as much to colonialism. The grandson repressed any such awareness. Charles Darwin had a hard time taking in wider humanitarian concerns. He heard them and turned his back on them.

So much for Darwin's antislavery position. Now to take up the objection of Darwin's defenders that his science was about fitness and competition among individuals, not among groups. This is the kind of thing I am disputing: Adam Gopnik says Darwin's "evolutionary theory is a long explanation of why only individuals have a real existence, while races and species, far from being fixed and authoritative, are just convenient temporary designations of populations whose only real rule is that they vary" (Gopnik, 159). Stephen Gould called Darwin's theory a "theory of ultimate individualism" (in Glick, 154; Glick presents a long selection from a 1995 Gould essay, "Spin Doctoring Darwin"). Gould also said, "Natural selection may lead to benefits for the species … [only as] side consequences …" (in Glick, 153). Is that what *The Origin of*

Species is really about? Is the origin of dominant and weak species a mere side consequence? Does that capture Darwin's essential belief? Who is doing the spin doctoring?

Such defenses of Darwin are nonsense on their face and nonsense when we look deeper. This is so for two reasons. First, Darwin talks about the fitness and competitive advantages of groups all the time, as we will shortly see. It is not the origin of individuals that interests him, it is the origin of species. Species are very real to him. He says so. It is almost as if he wanted to leave behind a record that would fly in the face of the nonsense that his theory was not primarily about groups, like species and races. Just recall how seriously he took the existence of human races and said they should more properly be called sub-species, "the more appropriate" term (*Descent*, 204, 210).

Second, if Darwin believed there are laws governing which individuals are better adapted to their environment, it makes sense that there should be the same or similar laws when we consider the groups to which individuals belong. It would have been impossible for Darwin to believe that laws apply to individuals but somehow groups develop with no rhyme or reason. He would have thought such an idea idiotic. In fact, he stated his belief in the comparability of laws for individuals and groups in his *1844* essay. "Groups therefore, in their appearance, extinction, and rate of change or succession, seem to follow nearly the same laws with the individuals of a species" (*1844*, 199; cf. 155, n2). While I am not aware of Darwin repeating this exact same thought in his later works, he never, as far as I know, contradicts it in *Origin* or anywhere else in his writings. Rather everything comports with this idea.

At the end of the *1844* essay, he also likens 'the production and extinction of forms' to 'the birth and death of individuals' (253; this idea goes back to his grandfather). This too is in the earlier Notebooks, both before and after his inspiration from Malthus: "... a *generation* of *species* like generation of *individuals*" (B 63; his emphases) and "The similarity of child to parent appears to follow same law in two of the *same* variety, as in *two varieties* ... The laws, therefore, of likenesses of fathers to children of mankind, no doubt are applicable to likenesses, when species & races are crossed" (E 77-78; his emphases; cf. E 83).

There is more continuity of thought from his Notebooks and two early essays (*1842* and *1844*) to *Origin* and later works than there are any sharp breaks. This is especially true of the similarity between individuals and groups. In Notebook C 152, probably between mid-May and mid-June 1838, he wrote, "A species is only fixed thing with reference to other living being ... As species is real thing with regard to contemporaries—fertility must settle it." (Further on, at C 161, he explains that his working definition of species is "simply, an instinctive impulse to keep separate, which no doubt be overcome, but until it is the animals are distinct species.") Species are not so walled off from each other that they have no genetic relationship, but they are distinct members of one large family of life.

One might say the whole purpose (or, if not purpose, then result) of evolution is to create distinct species. Darwin tells us so in the last chapter of *Origin* (470): "New and improved varieties will inevitably supplant and exterminate the older, less improved and intermediate varieties; and thus *species are rendered to a large extent defined and distinct objects*" (emphasis added and right on point). In other words, as he said in the earlier Notebook C 152, above, they are "real thing." The Darwin of *Origin* and the Darwin of the Notebooks are exactly the same on this point. I am always stunned how a writer like Darwin who explained himself so clearly could be so misinterpreted by well-known writers.

His book is not called The Illusion of Species. And for good reason. They were very real to Darwin. He will use natural selection to explain not only groups but the scientific classifications of groups. He did not think scientists were wasting their time classifying illusory objects. Darwin approved of the classification system. "... natural selection, which results from the struggle for existence ... explains that great and universal feature in the affinities of all organic beings, namely, their subordination in group under group" (*Origin*, 433; cf. 59, 411). You will never see Darwin explaining a system of individuals subordinate to individuals. It is *only* the subordination of groups that interests him.

Throughout *Origin*, Darwin performs what I call a jitterbug, bouncing back and forth between talking about competition between individuals and competition between groups. He sees fierce competition in both departments of life. Thus, on 344, we have "the species of the less vigorous groups" and on 468, "the most vigorous individuals". If you want an example of Darwin's bounce being closer together, take a look at the following quotes. In Chapter III of *Origin*, Darwin states that "... the struggle almost invariably will be most severe between the individuals of the same species" (75). That should make admirers of the iconic Darwin very happy. Then on the next page, Darwin gives us "... the struggle will generally be more severe between species of the same genus" followed by the example of "... one species of rat taking the place of another species under the most different climates!" In Darwin's view, groups compete just as surely as individuals do.

He will even perform this back and forth jitterbug in the same sentence. At the end of Chapter III, he writes, "The land may be extremely cold or dry, yet there will be competition between some few species, or between the individuals of the same species, for the warmest or dampest spots" (78). In the last chapter too, he encapsulates in one sentence the idea that competition applies to both individuals and species: "As the individuals of the same species come in all respects into the closest competition with each other, the struggle will generally be most severe between them; it will be almost equally severe between the varieties of the same species, and next in severity between the species of the same genus" (467-68). The truth is that Darwin saw individuals and groups in the same way, struggling and competing with each other, almost mirroring each other. He never confined his thinking to individuals. To claim that he did is pure fabrication.

This is also obvious in the language he uses. When Darwin uses words like 'beat' and 'dominant', he usually applies them to groups. In *Origin* (279), he gives us "… intermediate varieties … will generally be beaten out and exterminated during the course of further modification and improvement." Compare that to this comment on 110: "rare species … will consequently be beaten in the race for life by the modified descendants of the commoner species." And at 471, "… the more dominant groups beat the less dominant." On 428, he expresses the same thought without 'beat': "dominant groups … supplant many smaller and feebler groups." I could go on listing examples like this almost *ad infinitum*. That is certainly the impression Darwin gives. Of the fifteen uses of 'beat' in *Origin*, only two (at 83, 472) could possibly apply to individuals. For the rest, each occurrence is clearly in reference to groups. I believe all the uses of 'dominant' are for groups. This might surprise many people. But it makes sense, once you really get to know Darwin's work. Groups become dominant. That's what he sees and what he is interested in explaining.

At the end of Chapter II of *Origin*, Darwin tells the reader, "throughout nature the forms of life which are now dominant tend to become still more dominant by leaving many modified and dominant descendants" (*Origin*, 59; in context, it is clear that by 'forms of life' Darwin is talking about groups, as he references species, varieties, and genera in the immediately preceding lines). The same spirit informs *The Descent of Man*. "A tribe rich in the above qualities [such as fidelity and courage] would spread and be victorious over other tribes: but in the course of time it would, judging from all past history, be in its turn overcome by some other tribe still more highly endowed" (*Descent*, 155; note how Darwin emphasizes conquering and victory; he never considers negotiation and peacemaking part of human life). You can even see Darwin doing the same jitterbug in *Descent* as he did in *Origin*, bringing individuals and groups together in the same dynamic. "Individuals and races may have acquired certain indisputable advantages, and yet have perished from failing in other characters" (*Descent*, 167). Competition, life, and death are characteristics of both individuals and groups like species and races.

To quote again Darwin's rhetorical question in the letter (January 1873) to his cousin Francis Galton, "Would it not be truer to say that Nature cares only for the superior individuals and then makes her new and better races?" (ML 2.44). Individuals may be the means for creating groups, but both are very real to Darwin. Groups are in a sense the product of individuals and, for Darwin, it is not too much to say they are practically the purpose of individuals. I hope it is excruciatingly clear how important groups were to Darwin because the evidence is clear, not to mention abundant. There is no basis whatsoever for claiming that Darwin's theory was a theory of individualism. Individuals were a means to Darwin, not the end. A concern for races and species dominates Darwin's outlook and thinking.

Now on to the third defense raised on Darwin's behalf. Was everyone a racist in Darwin's time? Hardly. Just as there were profounder antislavery activists in Darwin's time than Darwin was, there were humanitarians who disputed the racist thinking that was so dominant in that era. Stephen Gould said he could not blame Darwin "... for repeating a standard assumption of his age ... for a largely passive acceptance of common wisdom" (*Mismeasure*, 418). We have already seen that Darwin's acceptance of racism was not so passive. My current point is that this "common wisdom" was not universal. Exceptions abounded. Many humanitarian opponents identified racism and disowned it. They are quite a contrast to Darwin. Uncommon they may have been, but they did exist. I'll start with Charles Napier who published his thoughts on this while Darwin was nearing the end of his *Beagle* voyage.

Napier was a British officer. As he explains in the prefatory Notice in *Colonization* (1835), he was offered the Governorship of the new colony of South Australia, but when he put two conditions on this (a sufficient monetary reserve and enough troops to insure against any troubles the new colony might run into), the offer was withdrawn. Napier can sing the praises of colonization, thrilled by the discovery of new lands and new forms of nature. But he can also damn the cruelty of it towards the Natives. He presents a sustained critique of both racism and genocide.

Napier tells his readers that Natives are "by nature, equal to all other men ... as good as ourselves" (94). "[C]ruelty, and kindness ... exist, pretty nearly in the same proportions, in all states of society; only taking different forms" (180). He praises one traveler for understanding that "... whether the parties are black or white, wear clothes or go naked ... though there may be no clothes like ours, or even none at all, *over* the skin, there are feelings, exactly like ours, *under* it!" (176; his emphases). Many of his comments are about Australian Aborigines of whom he says "they are as highly gifted by the Creator, both in body and mind, as we are ourselves" (169). The "Creator has cursed no particular nation, or tribe, with intrinsic inferiority of body, or mind" (151). Isn't that as clear an expression of antiracism as you can get?

In contrast to this, Darwin like others of his time wondered which human group was the lowest. He was not alone in choosing the Fuegians. "I believe, in this extreme part of South America, man exists in a lower state of improvement than in any other part of the world" (*Narrative*, 235n; *Voyage*, 194; the note in *Narrative* was incorporated into the text in *Voyage*). He considers how they compare to the Australian Aborigines (in *Voyage*, 194, he acknowledges that he is basing this on what he has read about the Australians). The Australian has more acquirements (boomerang, spear, hunting techniques, etc.), but "it by no means follows that he should likewise be so in capabilities [mental capacity, in *Voyage*, 194]. Indeed, from what we saw of the Fuegians … I should think the case was the reverse" (*Narrative*, 235n). He was having a hard time deciding who was the lowest. Never mind that others who had spent much more time close to Aborigines had a very different, higher opinion of them.

The last chapter of Napier's book contains extracts from authors who had given some idea of the true characteristics of Natives. The following heading introduces these extracts (all caps in his text): "… To prove that the finest qualities of the heart, and mind, are to be found among the aborigines of Australia" (125).These "anecdotes disprove the irrational assertion of those who condemn the natives of Australia as a race degraded by nature, and incapable of civilization" (ibid.) It is "stupidity … [to] pretend, that these people are below the rest of the world in the scale of intellect" (154). It wasn't stupidity to Darwin who offered the Australian Aborigines as a candidate for the lowest race on earth.

What particularly incenses Napier is this intellectual game that so many people played to the point of obnoxiousness (as would Darwin, as we just saw) of trying to determine which human race is the lowest. Napier is especially outraged by the suggestion that the Natives of Australia are "a race which forms the link between men and monkeys" (94; cf. 146). This may serve as a reminder to us that the controversy of the biological relationship between humans and monkeys was going on well before 1859. Only individuals, Napier vehemently argues, can be graded (see immediately below), not races or nations—another exceedingly clear statement of antiracism. Many people might ardently wish that Charles Darwin had said this, but he didn't and actually believed just the opposite. No man can prove, Napier says, that "the Aborigines of this country [Australia] occupy the lowest place in the gradatory scale of the human species" (as one writer he quotes claimed) and which we must never "take for an admitted fact" because "the Creator has cursed no particular nation, or tribe with intrinsic inferiority … this 'gradatory scale' is one composed of individuals; not of nations" (151). Tell me that is not a passionate antiracist statement—made in 1835!

Those who assert that Australian Aborigines are the lowest in intellect Napier compares to a "sack" or "a sort of *human bag*" (his emphasis) that eats and "performs various animal functions" and "gives opinions, as if … it had brains" (Napier, 155). They repeat their absurdity of grading races so often that many have come to believe it (156). It is repetition, not sound argument, that has established this truism. Among these sacks, one may find "sometimes a colonial secretary—sometimes a colonial governor—sometimes a colonist" (155). Too bad he did not add "and sometimes a scientist or philosopher." They form their opinions of savages based on how well the savages serve the needs of the invaders of their country. Napier is so true to his principle of judging only individuals, not larger groups, that he will also apply it to these human sacks: "There *are* sacks, but they are *individual sacks*, not *races of sacks*, not *nations of sacks*" (156; his emphases).

Napier wonders why so many Europeans fail to see that Native people are human beings just like us with the same degree of intelligence. I detect four reasons uncovered by Napier, though he only offers one as a reason *per se*. As a soldier, Napier is especially alert to the virtues in savages he admires most: courage, loyalty, patriotism, humane treatment of the enemy, and the ability to limit one's own violence (kill only when you really have to); in short, heroic actions. He is ecstatic when he comes across these in anecdotes about savages. But so many take note only of the bloodthirstiness of savages, while "the good, and heroic actions are very rarely recorded" (180). Why rarely recorded? Because these heroic deeds of savages "are, generally, done to oppose our injustice, and cruelty; and, of course, we do not proclaim our own villainy" (ibid.). We would have to admit our misdeeds in order to see the heroism of savages which is exercised against our cruelties, and this we are reluctant to do. Racism is a cover-up of our injustice.

A second reason according to Napier is that the human sack's "whole idea of intellect in others is confined to its estimate of their [the savages'] capacity to supply its wants" and therefore the sack "settles that any savages, who will not patiently endure its amiable practices, and administer to its refined appetites, are below the rest of God's creation" (155). What seems to underlie this reason for making low judgments of savages is that savages will not amiably go along with their own dispossession and being treated as inferior, and thus they must be exceptionally unintelligent. The third reason is that "They received us kindly, when we first invaded their country; we took their women … we tortured them, and they only made partial resistance to our cruelties; we then took their infants … [and finally] they declared war for ever against the 'CIVILIZED' *whites*" (95; his emphases). Forbearance at first, as he says, and then unqualified vengeance (94). Either it is our reaction against the eventual justifiable, violent Aboriginal response to white aggression or it is our guilt over the fact of their original kind treatment, while we went on to take advantage of their kindness—either way, we've turned their humanity into inferiority to escape our own guilt.

The fourth reason which I think can be drawn from Napier's musings is the compulsion to put national wealth ahead of everything else. He refers to it as "that damnable thing called 'national wealth'" (179) and that "false and stupid expression, '*national wealth*'" (33). National wealth is both one of the sources of our cruelties and also one of the means we use to disguise cruelty. "We call them *savages*, because they 'shrink under our courtesy,' and we denominate ourselves a *civilized* people, because we set up what we term 'national wealth,' as our God" (96; his emphases), and it blinds us to everything that does not contribute to national wealth. That would include blindness to many savage virtues. We do not value anything in savages that does not serve us, that does not "supply [our] wants ... [and] refined appetites" (155).

Racism is essentially about greed. Napier laments that national wealth blinds us as well to our own happiness which depends on religion and justice, not wealth (101). (I am so glad he put justice before wealth in the scheme of things; he complains, "we treat the natives as it suits our convenience; not according to the dictates of justice," 171.) National wealth makes us both self-destructive and destructive of others. "I see no reason why the savage should not choose his own way, as well as other people" (99). But national wealth won't allow any other way. It is all-consuming—consuming our appetites, our vision, and scientific inquiry ("science ... is a very pretty pastime; makes men rich ... it increases '*national wealth*'" [100]). Napier is "aware of the ineffable contempt with which all that I have said will be received by men of science, and political economists" (101).

The tragedy of all this is that the colonial system "will end in war, and, consequently, in the extermination of a fine race of men" (147). We are just as cruel as some savages are. The difference is that "their manners are rude; ours are polished" (125). We are better at hiding what we do under a scheme of polish. We prefer to kill in less obvious ways, "not being so evident, so nasty, and so *offensive to the sight*" (179; his emphasis); "we *dilute* our cruelty; we don't dabble in blood, quite so openly; our *new drop* is more cleanly and civilized ... and that is pretty nearly as much as we can say, I think, in favour of our boasted humanity" (180-81; his emphases).

Napier was clear that one of the ways we kill Natives is by dispossessing them of their land, actually robbing them: "we rob the aborigines of Australia ... when we oblige them to concentrate their population, they must perish ... This is not JUST—our first act is one of progressive extirpation, and, therefore, of great injustice" (102; his emphasis). At the very end of the book, he accuses Parliament of having told a lie when, concerning Australia, it "calls this territory '*uninhabited*,' when it is well known to be *inhabited!*" (213). His final comment is that we have "deprive[d] an inoffensive race of people of their property, without giving them the slightest remuneration—so much for parliamentary TRUTH and JUSTICE!" (ibid.; all his emphases).

Napier's book is a great one and if we had any sense at all, we would have a university course on the history of humanitarianism in which Napier would be given pride of place. I have presented him at length because I want it to be very clear that he did not just make one offhand antiracist remark. It was an important subject to him and he gave it the space it deserved.

Constantine Rafinesque was not a General like Napier. He was a naturalist and his observations told him that evolution, the gradual changing of species into new species, was real. From this, he drew the conclusion that racial differences were trivial, and from this, he drew the further conclusion that all deserved equal treatment under the law. One of Napier's goals was also "treating the natives as human beings, like ourselves, and making savage and civilized equal in the eye of the law" (103). He proclaimed, "if *I* am [appointed Governor of this new colony in Australia], I will not leave England without laws, that shall give the same protection to the savage as to myself, and those who go with me … we must not then have a *monopoly of justice*"(96; his emphases).

I previously quoted Rafinesque's lines, "If men are not of equal frame and mind,/ Yet they are brothers claiming social care,/ And equal laws demanding to obey." The "constant wish" is that "equal they become before the law" (from the verses added at the end of *The World, or Instability*, for the Additions section on "Equality" around line 3116). In Note 48, he writes, "Nature only acknowledges individuals, and vary them constantly." In the body of the poem, he says,

> … these colors stain
> The skin, but hardly penetrate beyond.
> They form no test, and only split mankind
> Into slight varieties, that change and blend
> With easy mood …
> [lines 2834-38]

He compares racial differences to the differences we meet in any family. "This is the human physical display,/ Of changeful nature …" (2863-64). The very first line of the poem is "I wish to sing the changeful ample world," which is his way of framing and celebrating evolution. One of the blessings of evolution is that it gives us variety in many details that do not create deep differences. Evolution should teach us tolerance of diversity. The wooly hair of Negroes, Rafinesque tells us, is no more significant than the wooly fleece of sheep (2866-67). Though he does not spell this out, the implication is that deeper qualities, like intellect and morality, are spread equally throughout all the so-called races of mankind. The lesson for Rafinesque is that an antiracist anthropology necessarily leads to equal rights under the law.

Was Rafinesque also an anti-colonialist or at least anti-colonial abuses? Most likely, though I cannot say for certain. "Upon all conquerors my virtuous scorn/ I throw, and all their dreadful deeds despise" (3333-34). Would he have been on the side of Indigenous people? Probably. "None but defenders claim our thankful praise" (3300). In some verses added at the end of the poem, Rafinesque declared, "Columbus found a world, but to enslave!" (in the Addition for the section on "Angels and Devils" around line 2520). He goes on to praise several figures who were known for their tolerance and kindness towards the Natives—Las Casas, Roger Williams, and William Penn.

While Rafinesque was thrilled by civilization and its good benefits, such as agriculture—"Blest be the man who did invent the plough,/ Was first to till the ground, increasing food/ And wealth ..." (3028-30)—he could also say, "Curst be the man who first enclos'd a field, And said this is my own ..." (3933-34). He links enclosures or fence-building to greed and inequality in wealth, and even to murder by identifying Cain as the first to seize land like this and the first to murder (3939-40). "Curst be the bards who sing the deeds of war" (3325). "Instead of praising conquerors," it would be better "to stain with infamy their deeds" (3329). It would be hard to extract a positive attitude towards colonialism from Rafinesque's writings. He is very far from finding anything admirable in a suggestion like Darwin's in his *Diary* that butchering all the Indians will give us increased production in corn and cattle.

William J. Darling, a British naval officer in charge of the Natives on Flinders Island (1833-34), who had been exiled from their home in Van Diemen's Land, wrote to the Colonial Secretary in February 1833 to tell him that these Natives (who will later be called the Tasmanians) have unfairly "been called *bloodthirsty* and *ferocious* Savages" (Plomley, 998; his emphases). If they have been violent, he argues, it is only because of "the brutal treatment which it is beyond a doubt has been practised upon them [the Natives] by *civilized savages* ..." (his emphasis). In Darling's opinion, they are "a *brave* and *patriotic* people" (999; his emphases; in *Descent*, 157, Darwin considers these important elements in human societies).

What is interesting is that Darling clearly identifies from whence derives this constant characterization of so-called savages as bloodthirsty. It is pure racism: "all these acts of cruelty towards them, have no doubt been looked upon by the perpetrators, as acts of *necessity* or at all events *justifiable*, as being practised upon *ignorant blacks* while their's [the Natives'] towards us have been attributed to a delight in bloodshed; that such is very far from being their disposition I have had full opportunity of judging" (999; his emphases). Racism (i.e., their presumed ignorance and inferiority) is used to justify violence towards black Natives and it is used to misjudge them as vicious practitioners of violence. Some people were acutely aware of racism and how it was used to batter Natives by misrepresenting their character and subjecting them to unequal treatment.

Language is one sure sign that some people were aware of the reality of racism. They had not invented that word yet, but they had equivalent terms. None of them became standard terminology (probably because of the majority's resistance to acknowledging let alone exposing racism), though one term came close and, of course, there were always words like 'prejudice' and 'contempt'. They knew what they were talking about and tried to invent or bend language to their purpose.

The word 'complexional' figured in some of these expressions (see below). When Britain's Colonial Office was transitioning the colonies from slavery to emancipation, from 1833 (when the abolition statute was passed) to 1838, officials were very concerned that racism not retard the progress of blacks, especially in Jamaica which already had a long history of free people of color campaigning for their rights. British officials wanted emancipation to be a success, meaning that ex-slaves would join the labor market and word hard to improve themselves and acquire luxuries. Upper movement was extremely important. Officials realized it would not happen if racism prevented former slaves from bettering themselves.

Lord Glenelg was Colonial Secretary at the time and James Stephen was an under-secretary; both wanted to get rid of laws inhibiting the upward movement of what would be the black working class. Glenelg wanted to eliminate all racism from colonial laws, even the covert racial references—all laws, as he said, that made "innumerable distinctions of the most invidious nature in favor of Europeans and their descendants, and to the prejudice of persons of African birth or origin" (in Holt, 71). He was very serious that black Jamaicans should enjoy equal protection of the law (179) and supported education for the newly created class of apprentices (72). I think it is fair to say that these insights of Lord Glenelg demonstrate an awareness of the existence of racism.

In order to remove racially oppressive features in the laws, "Glenelg invited representatives of abolitionist societies to the Colonial Office to scan West Indian laws, an invitation readily taken up by many of them" (Holt, 184). James Stephen also closely examined legislation for this purpose. Secretary Glenelg understood that racism infected the laws and that it was used to keep the people of color down. If he and a few others were making a conscious effort to get rid of racism, it was not a chimera they were battling. Recognizing the existence of racism in laws was not a new insight. As early as 1773, Benjamin Rush of Philadelphia in his antislavery pamphlet urged, "… let not the Journals of our Assemblies be disgraced with the records of laws, which allow exclusive privileges to men of one color in preference to another" (Rush, *An Address*, 25). In a note on this, Rush said legal equality should be reached by gradual alterations in the law, but some things, like trial by jury, should be immediately extended to Negroes. Such longstanding humanitarian concerns obviously influenced British colonial officials in their combat against racism.

The marquis of Sligo (Peter Howe Brown), Governor of Jamaica (1834-36) during the first years of the apprenticeship period, was particularly active doing his bit to end racism. His predecessor as Governor, Lord Mulgrave, had begun appointing free men of color to public office (Holt, 99) and was the first governor to invite people of color to dinners and other public events at the governor's residence (Heuman, 75). Sligo continued both these practices. He did not warm to the idea at first, but once he got going, he appointed many coloreds as stipendiary magistrates and to other positions, and encouraged them as well to run for the Assembly (Heuman, 99). Richard Hill was the first colored stipendiary magistrate in Jamaica. Governor Sligo appointed him Secretary of that department. (I am using the racial language that was common at the time. In Jamaica especially, everyone was very color conscious; besides black, brown, and white, the three basic color distinctions, they had many other shades which they gave names to. See Heuman, xix-xx, also 16 n12, 27, 76; for an example of people of color petitioning for their rights, but neglecting to include free blacks, see 46.)

In his enthusiasm to promote people of color, Governor Sligo anticipated too much, too soon, and eagerly imagined, as he said in a letter to the Colonial Secretary, "on *the part of the whites* all feelings of complexional distinctions had been done away [with] and except in two instances, the Browns seemed disposed to accede, and meet them half way" (in Heuman, 75; emphasis in original). That he was wrong about these feelings disappearing so quickly is less important than the fact that he was certainly aware that racism ('complexional distinctions') existed and held back the progress of blacks and browns. It is important to remember that they had their own words for racism. An even more evocative expression was used earlier in 1823 by Richard Hill to describe what we would call racists. He called them 'complexional misanthropes' (Heuman, 35). "The complexional misanthropes … sap the vitals of the Country raised into a sort of Complexional aristocracy" and "endeavour to perpetuate our misery and degradation by joining the cry for the perpetuity of that policy, which having excluded the people from all political importance, makes themselves rich and powerful, and keeps us poor and wretched."

Sligo was succeeded as governor in Jamaica by Lionel Smith. Smith complained to the Colonial Office that Sligo's policies towards people of color were ruining Jamaica: "It requires no prophecy to shew Your Lordship [Lord Glenelg], what a few Years more would have produced, under the old Laws [of Sligo's administration]—Every White Gentleman and White man of property would have been turned out of the House [of Assembly]" (in Heuman, 104). Numbers alone demonstrated that in a democratic society the browns and blacks would soon rule in the legislature. Glenelg's private response to Smith was that Sligo's appointment of coloreds reflected a "just and enlightened view of the subject" (in Heuman, 105). The home Colonial Office thought Sligo had done a good job, specifically with his policies to end race as a bar to holding official positions. Antiracism existed in the 19th century because racism did.

In 1816, when free coloreds petitioned the Jamaican House of Assembly to further extend their rights, John Campbell submitted a memorandum in support to the Colonial Secretary and described the situation of the browns: "… although they have sprung from the Whites, are they exposed to every indignity, to every illiberality; so much so, that the White Parents in public, will scarce notice his coloured Son or Daughter, which, in private are perhaps his only care and companion" (Heuman, 30). Even a white parent would keep his or her distance in public from their colored offspring so as not to share in the humiliation their children suffered. Degradation was a part of racism and at least some people were quite conscious of that.

All this goes to show that racism was a recognizable phenomenon in the 19th century. It also shows how lively language can be before terms like racism become standardized and ossified. 'Complexional misanthropes' captures racism as well as, and even better than, most other expressions. Others reached for different language. Goldwin Smith, an Oxford professor of history, understood that emancipated slaves would have a terrible time of it, if racism continued after freedom. Richard Hill also grasped this. In 1865, Smith wrote to an American friend, pondering the future of freed American slaves: "How can there be real political equality without social fusion; and how can there be social fusion while the difference of colour and the physical antipathy remain?" (quoted in Semmel, 63). Physical antipathy to color of skin may be a cumbersome way to put it, but there is no doubt this was an attempt to identify racism. Georg Gerland, to whom I devote the next chapter, also saw it. In North America, emancipation was made "infinitely more difficult" (*unendlich erschwert*), he observed, by white society "strictly [or, rigidly] shutting itself off from" (*strenge verschliesst*) people of color for whom it felt "the most bitter contempt" (*die bitterste Verachtung*; Gerland, 134). He sometimes referred to racism as "racial arrogance" (*Raçenhochmuth*;

112, 130). As we will see, such arrogance did not fit with his conception of evolution.

One expression that perhaps had a chance to gain wider currency was 'color-phobia'. American author Charles Stuart, who was concerned not only about slavery in the United States but also about the situation of free blacks, in his 1836 biography of Granville Sharp quotes from one of the letters collected in Prince Hoare's earlier 1820 biography. The letter is dated January 15, 1789 and is from Samuel Hopkins to Sharp; Hopkins was an antislavery advocate and pastor at a church in Rhode Island. Hopkins in part says this about blacks in Massachusetts, which had already freed its slaves:

> But the circumstances of the Freed Blacks are in many respects unhappy, while they live here among the Whites; as the latter look down upon the former, and are disposed to treat them as *underlings*, and deny them the advantages of education and employment, &c. which tends to depress their minds, and prevent their obtaining a comfortable living, and involves them in many other disadvantages. [Hoare, 341; Stuart, 70; emphasis in original]

And the cause of all this to which Stuart wished to bring attention? Racism, or as Stuart put it, *color-phobia*. It is a term he uses quite a lot in this section of the book (about 6 times, and further on, at 91, he uses *color-phobiasts*).

The United States, he says, is "Full of color-phobia! The land is full of it. It is exhibited in legislation, in custom and in feeling. The man is deemed a fool or villain, who is free from it" (76). Stuart mentions a kindly white couple with whom he is boarding, who express their color-phobia in their outrage at the idea that a colored person could be considered equal to themselves. He also calls it "the insane and cruel prejudice against color in the United States" (81). He considers it worse in America than in any other country in the world: "This color-phobia; this *distinguishing characteristic* of the United States, from which *all other civilized people* are free …" (77; on the next page, he notes that we treat colored people well only when we need them in emergencies; one could say that he almost foresaw that during World War II, a federal equal opportunity employment act would be passed because they needed everyone to work in the factories). Stuart also calls color hatred *mother-hatred* (74; I could not quite grasp why he says this, but I think it had something to do with blaming people for being born of a mother who was oppressed; also see 76).

While he describes color-phobia as being culturally widespread, he also considers it a minority problem. Only one-tenth of the planet is white, he believes, and only one-tenth of this one-tenth "is afflicted with the *color-phobia* … and *then*, *he*, in his hallucinations, dreams that *his* feelings are the law of *nature!*' (78). Whether his numbers are right or not, he correctly sees that racism is hubris on the part of what is really a small part of mankind. Keep in mind that Stuart is writing all this just over two decades before Lincoln's Emancipation Proclamation, as if he were already warning his country that freeing the slaves will not be enough, as the experience in Massachusetts had already demonstrated.

'Color-phobia' may have been a term peculiar to American writers. Joanne Melish gives a couple of examples from the first half of the 19th century in her book (Melish, 250, 254). Margot Minardi gives another example of its use by William Cooper Nell in his *The Colored Patriots of the American Revolution* (1855) (Minardi, 150). Black writers seem to have been fond of this expression. That no term caught on is probably due more to recalcitrance on the part of whites to face these issues than to any defect in the terms used.

There is another interesting point in Stuart's book that contrasts with Darwin's view of things. Think back to what Darwin said about gaining more land for cattle and corn production by butchering all the Indians. Here is what Stuart had to say about the meaning of increased production of corn and other benefits (the antecedent for *their* in the following is white colonists):

> Strangers come, and he [the Native] is swept from the land of his forefathers—*their* fields wave rich with corn—*their* trees hang heavy with fruit—*their* church spires pierce the skies … commerce, arts, arms flourish—literature is rife, and palace-like are the dwellings which adorn the land … [Yet] slavery is nursed in the lap of republics,—and the aborigines have perished; or linger in oppressed and scattered remnants, a memento to armed colonies, of the cruel iniquity of their heart, and of the daring hypocrisy of their boastings. [Stuart, 69-70; his emphases]

Stuart could see the benefits of colonialism as well as Darwin or anyone else, but he would not lightly dismiss the immoralities that brought us these gains. He sees what Indigenous peoples have lost. This was published only three years after Darwin's *Diary* entry on butchering the Indians. Again, many people may wish that Darwin had written something like this, but he did not. Note well that Stuart implicitly connects, as many humanitarians did, slavery and the abuses of colonialism as twin evils. Darwin seems to have had a very hard time seeing this. So many people were capable of linking colonialism and slavery (including his own grandfather) that it sometimes seems that Charles Darwin was the only one who did not get it.

Dedicated humanitarians may have been in the minority in the 19th century (as attested by their limited ability to affect the language of discourse about racism), but they were there and in enough numbers to have a robust presence on the scene. The sad truth is that Darwin was not among them and, in many ways, stood opposed to them.

~ 4 ~

Georg Gerland:
Who Rejected Whom?

Gerland is important for so many reasons. He wrote one of the great works of anthropology. It is as humane and as carefully reasoned as we would hope the best books of anthropology could be. Even by today's standards, it stands out as a supreme accomplishment. It is one of the saddest disgraces of academia that his book, *Über das Aussterben der Naturvölker* (1868) (On the Extinction of Primitive Peoples), has never been translated into English. His work puts everyone else in the 19th century to shame. That may be why current scholarship wants nothing to do with him. Darwin as an anthropologist pales beside Gerland. Who wants that more well-known? If it were not for the French edition, I would not have been able to grapple with the original German (all page references are to the German edition).

Another reason why the book is so important is that Darwin read it, in fact read it very carefully, and proceeded to ignore almost everything he had read. He cites Gerland a few times in *The Descent of Man* but never for his humanitarian points. Darwin had difficulty with German (see letters in CCD 19.698 and 20.578). For this book, he had a helper. I don't know who it was, possibly his daughter Henrietta. (There are also six separate sheets of paper, 12 numbered pages, with Supplemental Notes on Gerland's book; four of these pages appear to be in what I think is Darwin's own hand and the rest in possibly Henrietta's.) Whoever it was, this helper made translations of key sentences in the margins, so we know Darwin would have paid attention to this much. Whether the assistant read her translation aloud to Darwin, as she (or he) went along, and Darwin picked out which sentences he wanted written down, or the assistant herself decided which sentences to translate in the margin, Darwin would have had a good understanding of what Gerland was saying about the mistreatment and misrepresentation of Indigenous people by westerners and how Gerland linked this racism to his understanding of how the meaning of evolution was being perverted. As far as I can tell, none of this meant anything to Darwin. He simply refused to consider or address this kind of humanitarian science. But he was confronted with it.

Like another professor, Herman Merivale at Oxford, whom I discussed in *Darwin's Racism* (especially 291-94), one of Gerland's major objections to standard writing on the Indigenous was the way so many scientists and assorted writers (Darwin among them) casually assumed the inevitability of the disappearance of Native peoples from the earth. It was horrible and it was unscientific. It was also self-serving on the part of westerners to make this prediction and amounted to a self-fulfilling prophecy. European colonists might try to make it come true, but it had no natural facts behind it. Racial inferiority was not a fact, it was a European judgment that was cruelly used to sanctify extermination.

According to Gerland, "in addition, they [westerners] feel no scruples about hastening to help along by all means the downfall, to which these races were now doomed anyway, and thereby on their ruins the superior races can develop a better life" (9; *da man denn sich auch weiter kein Gewissen machte, den Untergang, welchem diese Raçen nun doch einmal geweiht seien, damit auf ihren Trümmern sich das bessere Leben höherstehender Raçen entwickeln könne, mit allen Mitteln beschleunigen zu helfen*). Westerners have selfish motives in interpreting the lives of the Indigenous. In a similar manner, Gerland also argues that "the frequently made claim of their savage bloodthirstiness is nothing but a fable" (*Ihre vielfach behauptete wilde Blutgier ist nichts als Fabel*) which was "doubtless concocted for an obvious reason [or, motivation], indeed for the purpose of treating them callously [or, recklessly, ruthlessly]. This has happened many times" (*wohl aus dem naheliegenden Grund erfunden, um nun gegen sie desto rücksichtsloser zu verfahren. Und das ist reichlich geschehen*"; 113).

Gerland was a sharper anthropologist than Darwin. He knew how self-serving the European estimation of Native peoples could be. Compared to most contemporary anthropologists, he was in a class by himself. He specifically advised that caution should be exercised when reading texts that claimed Natives were "extremely treacherous" (140n; *höchst verrätherisch*). (Recall Darwin's remark, "Never, never trust an Indian.") In that note, Gerland points to the bias resulting from the mercantile interests of the colonizing trader and the failure to consider the viewpoint of Natives who had suffered injustice, theft, and brutal violence. Also recall Chambers's insight that deception was a survival tactic for an oppressed people. Darwin had at least two people telling him he was wrong to assume treachery was an immoral characteristic of Natives. A third was Charles Lyell who pointed out that white people often had a negative impact on Native peoples. Darwin ignored them all.

Among the points Gerland makes in Chapter 2 of his book, he is highly suspicious of the claim that a race can be deemed inferior just because it has been devastated by a disease it did not have time to become habituated to. The expression "inferior [or, low] race" (*niedere Raçe*), Gerland says, explains nothing (12). His point, I believe, is that this is anti-scientific; it does not make the phenomenon explicable (*nichts … der Erscheinung erklärt*), it is too simplistic or empty a summary (*blosse Zusammenfassen*) (ibid.).

Later on, at the end of Chapter 13, Gerland confronts a similar problem: What happens when a people face a sudden disruption and upheaval of their culture (which had stabilized over thousands of years), as a result of being invaded by a more powerful race? In both cases (disease and cultural disruption), Gerland argues (though in the case of disease, it is more of an implied argument) that it is not disease alone that threatens them with extinction and it is not culture shock alone that upturns their existence. The more significant factor is that it is disease *combined with the hostility of the invaders* and it is cultural upheaval *combined with the same hostility* that poses the real danger. *The elements of hostility, arrogance, and hatred are crucial in determining the fate of primitive peoples.* Disease and social disruption alone are not sufficient explanations. Though Darwin or his helper took note of some of these points in the margins of Gerland's book, he turned a deaf ear to all of it in his own work.

Inferiority, according to Gerland, is not an explanation for anything because inferiority (or concepts of higher and lower) is not a cause of anything. Inferiority is a European judgment. The causes of extinction could only be concrete things like germs or bacteria, or bloody violence, or dispossession, or starvation, or an atmosphere of hostility. But it cannot be inferiority because inferiority is not a real thing. "Inferior races" is an empty (*blosse*) expression, meaningless. Keep in mind that Gerland was taking this position when most scientists of his time, including Darwin, believed that inferiority indeed helped to explain the troubles facing Aboriginal populations. But Gerland knew it explained nothing and he was almost alone in this. Furthermore, he understood that belief in this imaginary idea blocks us from seeing the real causes.

In both the cases of disease and the collision of cultures, Gerland draws a comparison to Europe's own history. Europeans experienced epidemics which they gradually became inured to. Savages too need time. For cultural conflicts, Gerland gives the example of ancient German tribes confronted with Greco-Roman civilization (see last paragraph of his Ch. 13). Gerland identifies several factors that made it easier for the Germans to adapt. Two of these were: 1) the new civilization was *gradually* introduced over many centuries; the Germans did not have to make sudden, catastrophic changes; and 2) it was not forcefully imposed on them; for Germans, classical civilization "did not come in such a hostile degree as modern civilization has for so-called savages" (89; *kam sie nicht in solchem Grade feindselig, wie die moderme Kultur über die sogenannten Wilden*). Take a moment to relish that "so-called savages" (*sogenannten Wilden*) because you won't see it used too often in the 19th century.

Gerland was one of those rare, honest scholars who understood that the invasion of one culture by another was more a historical problem (or social or political) than a biological one. He could thus look for other historical parallels and ask why things had turned out differently for other peoples (he also does this in Ch. 19). The facts, the details—the external circumstances of each people—made it different and *not any inherent qualities or deficiencies in them as human beings.* Gerland simply will not buy the argument that primitives are less well organized (biologically speaking) than white Europeans and that this destines them by nature for destruction and succumbing to the whites (122; cf. 110 where he specifically rejects the argument of less well organized for the Mariana Islanders who had been treated cruelly by the Spanish). By taking the biological approach and indulging in the empty nonsense of inferiority, too many natural scientists of the time had dehumanized the modern-day, so-called savages. Gerland did a good job of exposing this. He also explicitly called it a false view (*wie irrig die Ansicht ist*) that "vanishing peoples were dying out as a consequence of the inferiority of their race" (125; *dass die hinschwindenden Völker in Folge der Inferiortät ihrer Raçe ausstürben*). But in the English speaking world, we have erased Gerland from history.

A similar point about the deeper reasons why disease was so deadly to Indigenous populations was made by James Bonwick, whose 1870 book Darwin also read—and ignored. As Gerland saw the connection between disease and hostility, Bonwick saw the connection between depression and disease. Whether depression caused disease or made people more susceptible to sickness or exacerbated disease, some people like Bonwick, Gerland, and others realized that it was not disease alone that was so devastating to Native peoples and that it was not inferiority that was killing them—it was the hostility and demoralizing actions taken by colonists which depressed the hell out of Natives; this depression *combined with* disease was the real cause of the devastation they faced. I want to dwell on this for a bit because even today, there are defenders of imperialism who argue that the main cause of the deaths of Indigenous people was disease and that these diseases were not brought intentionally by Europeans for the purpose of killing them. Imperialists want disease to appear to be a very innocent factor. But contemporary observers like Bonwick and Gerland saw that it was not so innocent.

Bonwick came very close to saying that depression causes disease, expressing the relationship by noting that it predisposes people to illness. He quotes a missionary who said that civilization "has thrown them [the Blacks] back into a sort of despair." Bonwick continues with what I would call a description of depression:

They are oppressed by our weight, and sink under the burden. This leads them to drink, as affording them a relief from their sense of abasement. This renders families unfruitful. *This lowers the nervous tone, predisposing to disease, and arresting the progress of recovery.* [*Last*, 342; emphasis added]

With this kind of knowledge about what depression does, one cannot say that colonists unknowingly brought Aborigines misery and death.

Here is Bonwick relating in his own words what the captain of a ship who transported one of the last tribes of Van Diemen's Land to the Bass Straits told him: "it was pitiable to witness their distress. Their moaning was sad indeed. They appeared to feel themselves forsaken and helpless, and abandoned themselves to despair" (*Last*, 230). The immediate cause of their distress was seasickness, but the captain seems to have realized that losing their home greatly exacerbated their condition. Bonwick then recounts that he himself had seen the Aborigine children who were separated from their parents and placed in the Orphan School near Hobart Town (to civilize them). "Most of them struck me as being sickly and depressed, and I wondered not at the terrible mortality that had thinned their numbers" (231). This connection between despondency and death carrying off so many Natives had become almost a truism for those who paid attention to the consequences of colonialism.

Further on, Bonwick writes, "No means existed for the arrest of the terrible *home sickness* which was carrying off so many of the Natives" (245; his emphasis). John West in his 1852 three volume history of Tasmania also considered homesickness a major cause of death (West, 2.74, text and note where he references a doctor who said that "a desire to return to their own country" produces a stomach disease). After mentioning that they were often "deeply melancholy" gazing at their homeland in the distance, West states, "They suffered much from mental irritation: when taken with disease, they often refused sustenance, and died in delirium" (2.74). Disease alone did not kill the Natives.

Bonwick too rolls up depression, disease, and death into one ball of wax. He tells us that on surveying the sterility of their new home, the Natives were "uttering melancholy moans, and, with arms hanging beside them, trembling with convulsive feeling ... With their health suffering from chills, rheumatism and consumption diminished their numbers, and thus added force to their forebodings that they were taken there *to die*" (*Last*, 247; his emphasis). Nearer the end of his book, Bonwick quotes another writer, Mr. Brace, who referred to Europeans as a "grasping race" and noted "the effect on the spirits or temperament [of the Natives] which the contrast of a different and more fortunate people causes" (390). Bonwick follows this with his own comment: "The iron entered into the souls of these sensitive men [the Tasmanians]. They sank under the burden of the thought." This comment is followed by more thoughts on heart sickness and home sickness.

If 19th century writers did not always understand depression as causing disease, they certainly believed the two together were a more lethal combination than disease alone. What they saw was that deep despair aggravated illness, making it more deadly. In their view, dispossessing Natives of their land, which was indeed intentional, caused death in two ways: It deprived Aborigines of their food sources and it knocked the spiritual wind out of them, leaving them defenseless under the onslaught of disease. Whether depression and death were understood as cause and effect or just bound together in an intricate web of factors, they knew that dispossession and exile were increasing despair and the mortality rate. Bonwick provided this remark from an unnamed source: "*Progress* is a taking word, and civilization, like a cardinal's red hat, covers a multitude of sins and crimes. It is a tinkling cymbal, which drowns the noise of all other discordant things" (342). Disease too has been used by some scholars as "a tinkling cymbal" to cover up "a multitude of sins and crimes."

Darwin brings up "depression of spirits" once in *Descent* (214), an expression he puts into a quotation from Bonwick in which it does not originally appear, at least not in those exact words: "Another careful observer of the natives, Mr Davis, remarks ... [on their increased deaths and fewer births due to] '... their change of living and food; but more so to their banishment from the mainland ... and consequent depression of spirits' [quoting from Bonwick, 390; though Darwin includes those last words as part of the quotation, they are actually his rewriting of 'expressions of the deepest sorrow depicted on their countenances' in the original quote in Bonwick]." But Darwin drops it as quickly as he brings it up. He does not make as much of this as writers like Bonwick and Gerland would.

Another point related to the intentions of colonizers is this: Even if diseases were unintentionally brought to these new countries, the same cannot be said of the failure to provide medical help. Saxe Bannister had pointed out in 1838 that the whole question of medical aid to the Natives had been much neglected and required further examination (*Colonization*, 262). He considered it a serious defect in the *Report* of the House Select Committee that it did go into the question of medical aid to the Natives (259) and he railed against the failure to take "ordinary precautions" against the spread of disease (260-61). Just a few years later, Herman Merivale called for "time [to] be given him [the Native] to become fortified against the virulence of epidemic diseases" (Merivale, 2.208). That patience was never forthcoming. It was deliberately withheld.

As for disease not being intentionally used to further the cause of colonization, it did not look that way to a contemporary observer like Bannister. Commenting on the situation of Aborigines in New South Wales, Bannister wrote, "instead of medical aid being imparted to them, our imported diseases were spread abroad without any precautions, as if it was our purpose to depopulate their country for our own advantage" (*Humane* [1840], viii). That 'as if' seems to identify a hidden intention. Such failures (both to provide medical aid and to take precautions) in the first few years could be called unintended. But when this is repeated over many decades, to call it unintentional is deceptive.

If Gerland and Bonwick were not more successful convincing others of their arguments, that was not their fault. The blame is entirely on that sense of entitlement in Europeans which blocked them from seeing the rationality of their ideas—and Merivale's and Napier's and Rafinesque's and Bannister's and Wallace's and a handful of others. All the inferior, less developed capacities which mainstream scientists saw in savages should have been a matter of historical-political debate and should have been questioned as self-serving arguments by westerners; they should not have been biologized which is just what Darwin and so many others did.

Gerland admired the resilience of the Natives in most countries—their life force (*diese Lebenskraft*), as he said, which he believed all cultures possessed, and was perhaps a little stronger among the Indigenous (Gerland, 120). He pointed out that Natives resisted European aggression quite well and that it was only in the confined space of islands (he named Tasmania, the Mariana Islands, and the Antilles, as examples; see 118) that extermination had come close to being a reality. In wider spaces, like the continent of Australia, Europeans failed to complete their extermination of the Indigenous. Europeans weren't all that superior. But Gerland was not a romantic about Native peoples. In the last chapter of his book, while he does briefly state that Indigenous cultures have something of value in them and serve the whole of nature, earlier in his book he discussed the vices of Natives that were negatively impacting their lives. Here is where one slight contradiction creeps into his work.

While Gerland very much admired the life force of primitives and did not think them in any way biologically inferior to whites, he also thought they had a number of vices or self-destructive tendencies. They were indolent, rigid in their habits, and under the domination of nature (36-38 for the first two; 84, 121 for the last). This in itself is not necessarily a contradiction. All he is saying is that the life force of any people has its limitations and may not be completely resistant to every vice or evil that comes along. "However it is well to take note that the indestructibility of these toughened peoples has its limit" (121; *Doch ist wohl zu beachten, dass auch die Unverwüstlichkeit dieser härteren Völker ihre Grenze hat*).

Among the vices, or immoral excesses (*Ausschweifungen*), which Gerland saw were drunkenness (some tribes had their own native intoxicants) and sexual immorality. He maintained an awareness that some European reports of these vices were exaggerated and self-serving (in order to justify enslaving or eradicating natives, or to cover up European brutality), yet when these false reports were removed, some genuine problems remained, or so he thought. The main drawback in the life of Indigenous peoples was that they were rigid in their ways and unable to rise above nature (84, 121). "They have not achieved any rule over nature which surrounds them" (121; *Sie hatten sich keine Herrschaft über die sie umgebende Natur errungen*).

Gerland never explains how the self-destructiveness jives with the vitality. Granted that the life force does not make any people all-powerful (I think Gerland would apply this to Europeans too). In and of itself this makes some sense. The contradiction appears in the following way. Gerland believed that the internal self-destructive tendencies in primitive peoples were serious enough that this was leading to their extinction, slowly but surely, sooner or later (the last paragraph of Ch. 18). Earlier, he said, "It is no exaggeration to maintain that, even if they were alone in the world without any outside hostile influence, and considering their actual development, or better, their hardening, they will still little by little fade away and die out" (37-38; *es nicht übertrieben, zu behaupten, dass, auch wenn sie allein auf der Welt wären, ohne jeglichen feindseligen Einfluss von aussen her, sie dennoch, wie jetzt ihre Entwickelung oder wohl besser ihre verhärtung ist, nach und nach langsam vergehen und erlöschen würden*).

What Gerland avoided thinking about is how it could be that the same nature that sustained these Native peoples for thousands of years would all of sudden, without any radical change in their environment (putting the arrival of Europeans to the side), turn on them, in a sense, and lead them gradually into oblivion. For thousands of years, the Aborigines of the world had lived with the balance always having been in favor of their vital force. There were no radical disturbances or developments in nature to change this. Now their affirmation of life was over, no longer strong enough to repel the usual inimical forces of nature? It is a very odd position to take and yet many European authors believed that this was precisely the predicament faced by Indigenes. Their own defects were leading them to ruin.

It was especially odd in Gerland's case to have believed in the gradual self-extermination of Native peoples—he who was otherwise so generous in his understanding of Natives and so aware of how self-serving were the negative depictions Europeans made about them. I can only explain it by referring to British botanist Agnes Arber's insight that "the general intellectual atmosphere of any given moment has an effect upon this history [of science] which is compulsive to a humiliating degree ... we are always too much bedazzled by contemporaneity [to notice the tyranny of the *Zeitgeist*]" (Arber, 7-8). We are compelled to fall victim to "reverting to the familiar beaten paths" (8) and it is humiliating. This has become a western intellectual tradition. No one completely escapes the overreach of the general intellectual atmosphere. Since everyone was making the point that Natives were doomed, it seems that Gerland felt obliged to follow suit in his own way. If, like Gerland, you give in to it only for a brief moment in a way that does not affect the entirety of your thoughts, count yourself very lucky indeed.

That contradiction aside, Gerland believed that their vices or defects would only very gradually extinguish the Natives. The main problem now was the purposeful rapid extermination by Europeans, and that, Gerland insisted, was *not* inevitable. He especially objected to the idea that mere contact with western civilization somehow generated a poisonous breath that Natives could not withstand. One source for this idea was the German naturalist Pöppig (often spelled Poeppig by English writers). Darwin too had expressed it in his published travel journal in 1839. Later in *Descent* (212, text and n34), although he emphasized the search for causes of the demise of Natives, he favorably alluded to Poeppig (212 n34); he seemed to think there was still a little bit of truth to the idea of a poisonous breath. But many people had been affected by what Darwin had said much earlier in his career in the published journal and still quoted it, even after *The Origin of Species* had been published. Gerland quoted from it in 1868, so too James Bonwick in 1870 and Merivale in his 1841 lecture. I have quoted bits of this before, but here is the extended selection from Darwin:

> Besides these several evident causes of destruction [alcohol, European diseases, extinction of wild animals, nomadic life style, high death rate among infants], there appears to be some more mysterious agency generally at work. Wherever the European has trod, death seems to pursue the aboriginal ... The varieties of man seem to act on each other; in the same way as different species of animals—the stronger always extirpating the weaker. It was melancholy at New Zealand to hear the fine energetic natives saying, they knew the land was doomed to pass from their children. [*Narrative*, 520; *Voyage*, 375]

In *Descent* (212), Darwin would say "It further appears, mysterious as is the fact that the first meeting of distinct and separated people generates disease" and in a note to this sentence (n34), he favorably quotes Poeppig's remark of the "breath of civilisation as poisonous to savages" and perhaps implies that Gerland approved it too (or it is possible he was only citing Gerland for the Poeppig reference).

What Darwin did not do was tell his readers how much Gerland disapproved of this idea. Gerland, at the end of Chapter 16, uses the "breaths of civilization" (*Hauche der Kultur*) ironically by putting it in quotation marks after he has discussed at length and in detail the oppression of Mexican Indians by the Spanish (106-07). Darwin breathes not a word of this or any of the following material in Gerland's book. In Chapter 2, Gerland is critical of Darwin and others for expressing the idea of a mysterious agency at work in the contact between Europeans and Natives. He criticized Pöppig too. The disappearance of Natives is not a mystery, Gerland argues. He points out that in New Holland (the original Dutch name for Australia), New Zealand, Africa, and America, the Europeans have been taking over all the best, most fertile, and usable land, and declaring that all the land is their property, and every day are pushing the Aborigines further and further back into the forests and wildest places, all the while destroying their food sources (opossums and kangaroos), "so that it is then not surprising that the natives by this means alone are decaying [or withering away] 'as if touched by poisonous breaths' (or so the cliché has it)" (87; *so dass es den gar kein Wunder ist, wenn die Eingeborenen schon hierdurch allein »wie von einem giftigen Hauche berührt« (oder wie die Phrase lautet) verkommen*; he is obviously referencing Pöppig whom he had quoted earlier in Chapter 2 on page 8). Gerland is mocking the idea of a mysterious poisonous breath. There is no mystery to what dispossession is and what it does; the resulting disappearance of people follows from that and not from magical breaths.

It is not clear if Darwin was aware of Gerland's point, but likely he was. In Darwin's copy of the book, it is difficult to read all of the translation in the left-hand margin (closest to the spine) on 87, as the book was not pressed down flat enough when it was scanned, but I could make out snatches: 'increase pasture' and 'spreading [out?] of the whites' and 'natives [several words illegible] wilderness'. In the right margin, we get "they were soon in a very miserable condition owing to destruction of wild animals." Then at the bottom, the translator writes, "that is is not strange that they here disappear as if from a poisonous breath." Was the translator aware that Gerland was mocking or disputing this claim of a mysterious breath? The words 'not strange' and 'as if ' seem to indicate such an awareness, and if so, Darwin did not take in Gerland's point, as he continued in *Descent* to approve of this idea that the mere meeting of civilized and savage can produce a poisonous breath and disease, though he gave it a smaller role (see above).

When discussing the Spanish oppression of Indians in Mexico, the real wonder or miracle (*Wunder*), as Gerland says, is not that entire groups of Natives have expired due to the "breaths of civilization" (*Hauche der Kultur*; this is where he uses quotation marks), but that in spite of all the evil (*Leiden*, suffering, affliction) done to them, they have not been entirely eliminated (106-07; cf. 94). The tenacious endurance and survival of Indigenes against great odds is more astonishing than their disappearance

On 88 of Gerland's book, Darwin's translator also renders one brief part of Gerland's long quotation of a Cherokee Chief, taken from a book by Gerland's teacher Theodor Waitz, one of whose books Darwin also read (Darwin cites Waitz several times in *Descent*, but not for his humanitarian points). The Chief remarked on how the white man has made himself a great father to his red children whom he loves and has many fancy speeches for his red children, but the white man's words boil down to this: "You must go a little further out of the way [from me] so that I will not tread on you by mistake" (88; *ihr müsst ein aus dem Wege gehen, damit ich nicht von ungefähr auf euch trete*; on the same page, this thought is repeated, followed by "you are too near me;" *ihr seid mir zu nahe*). In Darwin's copy, the annotated translation is: "The Indians say all the speech of the whites is—'go a little further out of the way'." So Darwin knew that Gerland was well aware of the continual pressure that dispossession put on the Natives and that Gerland gave this far more importance than mysterious breaths.

Gerland understood how profound was the disturbance, dismay, and despair caused by the prospect of annihilation, following first contact, and that Europeans were often guilty of taking advantage of that initial despair. But he also saw how strong was the vital life force of many Native peoples which enabled them to overcome this disadvantage. In the right-hand margin on 131, Darwin's helper condenses Gerland's first two sentences of the last paragraph of Chapter 20: "All these examples prove that savages are not by nature doomed to extinction. So soon as civilization presents itself peacefully they prove capable of elevating themselves." And at the bottom of 131, the helper's annotation runs: "But almost everywhere civilization has presented itself in an inimical form." It was western civilization's hostility, and not its breath, that was destructive, according to Gerland. Despite these notes and many more, Darwin refused to consider any of this in his own work.

In denying that the cause of the extinction of primitive peoples is mysterious or due to poisonous breaths, Gerland was following Waitz who said that "... we cannot subscribe the mystical and especially in America, popular theory, that the aboriginal race of the new world would, even without drunkenness, war, or imported diseases, have become extinct by the approach of civilization as 'from a poisonous breath, because nature has devoted it to destruction' [citing Pöppig in a note]" (Waitz, 147; this is from the Waitz book which Darwin read). Gerland (on 9 in his book) quotes this passage from Waitz:

> The extinction of a people once healthy and vigorous cannot be explained by a denial of viability, or an original defective organization, or by the assumption of some mysterious cause; we must investigate and search for natural agencies, though we may be obliged to confess that our endeavours to trace them have hitherto not been perfectly successful. [Waitz, 157]

Gerland then goes on to demonstrate that we can be more successful in tracing the causes. This was precisely Herman Merivale's point (more on Merivale shortly). (It's interesting that Waitz would single out America as a source for the mystical idea of a poisonous breath. There is an 1813 essay by Washington Irving, "Traits of Indian Character", and later included in *The Sketch Book*, which mentions "withering airs" to explain the effect of white society on the Indians; see Irving, 227. Had Waitz read Irving?)

I think Darwin was aware of Gerland's opposition to mysterious ideas like a poisonous breath, but his or his helper's remarks seem to be on both sides of this. In his Supplemental Notes on Gerland's book (on pp. 1-2 of the Notes, covering Chapter 2 of Gerland's book, in what is possibly the handwriting of Darwin's daughter Henrietta), we have "His theory to account for this [spontaneous illnesses among savages when meeting civilized races]—is not that there is some noxious influence emanating from the civilized races caused by their being shut up in ships etc." These Notes then go on to explain that Gerland believes Europeans have become inoculated since childhood "with the germs of all kinds of infectious disorders ... [which we] are able to process these germs in a latent state—These same germs being quite able to infect savage races." On the other hand, on p. 9 of Gerland's book, Darwin's translator has in the margin, "Unprejudiced naturalists see something mysterious in this disappearance ..." as if Gerland approved of this. But Gerland did not intend that as a stand-alone point. Did Darwin realize that Gerland was here setting up a contrary view for the purpose of arguing against it?

Darwin's assistant also has in a translation on the same page that "there has been no pressure by the whites" in Polynesia (no such pressure at all) and in Australia (very little). Omitted is that Gerland was relating the opinion of Waitz (from Waitz, 156-57), not his own, and as becomes clear, Gerland does not agree with it. The marginal translation in Darwin's copy takes no notice of this. In fact, it does not even represent Waitz's full opinion. The word translated as pressure is *Druck*, which can also mean oppression; this was more likely the meaning intended by both Gerland and Waitz. The English translator of Waitz's book (read by Darwin) uses oppression (Waitz, 157). Despite what Waitz says (on 156-57) about "no pressure", he goes on to describe some of the actual oppression of the Aborigines in Australia (165-67), which Waitz believed was taking place.

Waitz mentions that one limited law in New South Wales accomplished almost nothing: "their oppression is but little mitigated by the favour accorded" (165). He also mentions "great injustice" (165) and takes note that the Natives are friendly and peaceful when treated well (166), that "cruelties were committed on women and children" (166), "the crimes committed against the natives by the Whites" (167), that the "English Government has repeatedly in official documents acknowledged the wrongs done to the natives" (ibid.), and perhaps most shockingly, "In several parts of Australia a larger number of natives are said to have been poisoned when it became known that they would for the future be protected against oppression" (ibid.; that is, literally poisoned, not magically by breaths). Since Darwin read Waitz's book, it is surprising that he would not show more awareness of this and Gerland's similar stress on the cruelties committed by Europeans. "No pressure by the whites" is not an accurate representation of the complete beliefs of either Waitz or Gerland. It looks like Darwin was a little too eager to latch onto any statement denying white oppression as a major cause of the demise of Natives.

The fuller truth is that, based on his readings of Waitz and Gerland, Darwin had the information to know better. He knew that some major scientists disputed both the inevitability and the mystery of Aboriginal disappearance and that these scientists instead singled out the injustices, cruelties, hostility, and oppression committed by white invaders as the major causes. Darwin may also have been aware that 25 years before Gerland's book, Herman Merivale had been critical of the idea that the extermination of Native peoples was mysterious and inevitable. If their extermination were really a puzzle, then "this is an anomaly in the laws of Providence ... wholly at variance with all the other laws by which animal life, and human society, are governed" (Merivale, 2.206). Merivale too singled out Poeppig and Darwin for censure (2.204-05, 209). There was no mystery to the supposed extinction of Natives, argued Merivale. We know the causes: hostile aggression, destruction of their food sources, European fire-arms, alcohol, disease, sudden change of habits, and confinement to smaller spaces to live in (2.207, 208). And if we can pinpoint the causes and control them, then the annihilation of Aborigines is not inevitable: "if all these causes of death are removed, must he still perish?" (2.208).

"We are then not their pre-destined murderers, but called to assume the station of their preservers," Merivale concluded (2.212). If we can control or eliminate the factors of destruction he listed (see above) and the Native population increases or at least remains stationary, "then the supposed law of Mr. Poeppig and Mr. Darwin is imaginary" (2.209). But it did not matter how persuasive Merivale was, and Gerland 25 years later, or Waitz for that matter. A withering colonialism would proceed apace—with or without, I should add, the support of people like Darwin.

If dispossession (often physically violent and still more often accomplished by cheating and deception) was one cause of destruction emphasized by Gerland, another was hostility, and he did not hold back from identifying that hostility as racist. Towards the end of the last chapter, I quoted his opinion that it was the whites' "most bitter contempt" (Gerland, 134; *die bitterste Verachtung*) for people of color that would render the emancipation of slaves meaningless and pointed out his use of the expression "racial arrogance" (*Raçenhochmuth*; 112, 130). The English, Gerland notes, are known for their "rigid, racial arrogance" (130; *starren Raçenhochmuth*; cf. 112). And not only the English. "The English and Dutch have distinguished themselves by indescribable [or, unspeakable] arrogance and hatred towards all people of color, which has been no less harmful to primitive peoples than overt hostility" (134-35; *Die Engländer und Holländer zeichnen sich durch unaussprechlichen Hochmuth und Hass gegen jede farbige Bevölkerung aus, durch welchen sie den Naturvölkern fast nicht mindern Schaden gethan haben, als durch offene Feindseligkeiten*; cf. 91, 93). The arrogance of caste (*Kastenhochmuth*) of white people is another term Gerland uses (98). The translation by Darwin's helper of the above sentence (lower left-hand margin on 134) is as follows: "The English and Dutch are distinguished among all others for their [scorn?] & hatred & [this second & might be crossed out] which has worked as much harm as their more open enmity." Darwin knew how much Gerland pointed to racism as the crucial factor in the destruction of Natives.

Here too Merivale deserves some credit. He realized that the chief obstacle to different races becoming harmoniously conjoined ('amalgamated' was the word he and others used), including intermarriage and full civil rights (2.179, 201), was racism, which he referred to as "that mutual repulsion which arises merely out of prejudices of colour ..." (2.201).

Even in the best of circumstances, Gerland explained in Chapter 15, adapting to another culture is exhausting and debilitating. Racism and hostility made it so much more difficult. Had Europeans approached Indigenous cultures in an amicable manner (and Europeans were anything but amicable), it would have been hard enough to take to another language, another way of life, new mental concepts and intuitions, new modes of commerce, legal ideas, and religion (Ch. 15). As it was, the difficulties were increased enormously not only by the physical brutality, but by the constant attacks on the minds and spirits of these peoples. Demoralization and melancholy come up a lot in several chapters (the helper's annotations in Darwin's copy acknowledge this by using 'demoralisation' in the marginalia on 94 and 95). Gerland stresses how often and deeply Europeans wounded the pride and sense of right of primitive peoples (see the last few pages of Ch. 14). Darwin's helper translates on 94, "One of the characteristics of savages is their pride & injury of their pride is the hardest thing they had to bear. Not less remarkable is their feeling of justice." Pride was wounded mainly by the destruction of their culture which leads to "endless humiliation" (see immediately below) and to depression (98). It was also wounded by racism accompanied by dispossession.

At the end of Chapter 15, Gerland gives two examples (from different countries) of Natives who were well educated in western ways. One became a lawyer, the other a doctor. Both suffered from melancholy. The doctor eventually threw off all traces of civilization and returned to a savage way of life. The lawyer, a Choctaw Indian, committed suicide. While others would attribute the suicide to his melancholy nature, Gerland remarks that the melancholy was in part due to the "arrogance of caste" (*Kastenhochmuth*) of North-American whites (98); in other words, racism ('arrogance' is the key word he often used to identify racism). Gerland considers "endless humiliation on one side and overexertion on the other" (*die ewige Demüthigung auf der einen, die Ueberanstrengung auf der anderen Seite*) to be twin causes of their demoralization (98; by 'overexertion' Gerland is referring to the enormous mental effort it takes to adapt to another culture, especially when that culture has been introduced too quickly; the end of Ch. 13 is another place where Gerland stresses how devastating is the sudden upheaval of everything one has known).

"One cannot emphasize strongly enough this destruction of the entire spiritual [or, mental] and ethical life of nations, if one wants to find the reasons for their extinction" (Gerland, 94; *Diese Vernichtung aber des gesammten geistigen und ethischen Lebens der Nationen kann man gar nicht stark genug betonen, wenn man die Gründe für ihr Aussterben aufsuchen will*; it is a point he returns to fairly often, e.g., at the end of Ch. 16). This was noteworthy enough for Darwin's helper to translate (on 94): "This destruction of their spiritual and ethical life cannot be overrated in considering the grounds for their extinction. Nothing is as depressing as a sense of powerlessness & desolation."

Gerland quotes another writer who was quoted by his teacher Theodor Waitz to the effect that a people can only disappear when its courage, energy, and self-respect have been ruined by oppression, slavery, and vice. As summed up by Darwin's helper in the marginalia on 94 (lower left), "Every race must perish says Waiz [*sic*] when their self esteem is gone." In his own words, Gerland says that nothing oppresses the spirit of a people (*den Volksgeist*) more than "the feeling [or, self-consciousness] of its own powerlessness and lostness [or, forlornness]" (94; *das Gefühl der eigenen Ohnmacht und Verlorenheit*; in Darwin's copy, the helper's choice of 'desolation' for the last word, see above, is very good, I think). Europeans have done their utmost to carry out this horrible cruelty:

> On the other hand, Europeans bear the heaviest responsibility here for they have intentionally trampled underfoot the rights of these peoples; they look at primitive peoples as hardly human, not even willing to allow them their human self-confidence, but also trampling it underfoot through political steps, as the United States did, and the French in Tahiti and the English in Australia; and by means of a boundless arrogance and hatred, they further trample these peoples underfoot by excluding them from all community and, by that, from all civilization, subsequently depriving them continually of land and sources of food. [Gerland, 93]

And here is the German:

> Theils aber tragen auch hier die Europäer die schwerste Verantwortlichkeit, denn sie haben die Rechte dieser Völker absichtlich mit Füssen getreten, sie haben, da sie die Naturvölker kaum für Menschen ansahen, nicht einmal ihr menschliches Selbstbewusstsein ihnen lassen mögen, sondern auch dieses, und oft von Staateswegen, wie die Vereinigten Staaten, wie Frankreich in Tahiti, wie die Engländer in Australien, mit Füssen getreten; und man tritt es durch den grenzenlosen Hochmuth und Hass, mit dem man diese Völker von aller Gemeinschaft und damit von aller Kultur ausschliesst, nachdem man ihnen häufig Land und Lebensmittel genommen, auch ferner mit Füssen.

All the Natives can do, Gerland adds, is respond with sporadic violence. Note the use of that word 'arrogance' (*Hochmuth*) again, for what we would call racism.

Perhaps Gerland's most eloquent statement of this was the following: "They [savages] have not rejected civilization, [rather] civilization has rejected them (Gerland, 114; *Nicht sie haben die Kultur, die Kultur hat sie von sich gestossen*). Who rejected whom? Who decided the other was not human or less human? Gerland answers that western civilization rejected primitives, not the other way around. But in the English speaking world, the choice has been not to translate Gerland.

While Gerland may have become caught up in a bind of being unsure whether vitality or self-destruction was more true of Natives (as discussed above), he never lost sight of the fact that their main problem now was the racism, hostility, and dispossession by whites. And whatever self-destructive tendencies Natives may have had, he understood that, rather than take advantage of this, Europeans should assume a positive role in their lives. It cannot be stressed enough that Gerland in the main insisted that biology was not the cause of the major problems the Indigenous were facing. It was not biology that was forcing Europeans to destroy Native peoples. It was a moral choice, it was excessive greed.

Was Darwin aware that there were some writers who were arguing openly or implicitly that the extermination of Indigenous peoples, not to mention countless other injustices and injuries they faced, was *not a biological problem* because it was a moral problem? I think he was, but he did not show it in his published writings. Some writers were certainly clear in making their point that what Europeans were doing was a moral choice, not a biological necessity. I think Darwin suppressed an explicit realization of what they were saying. What we can be sure of is that Darwin frequently read such authors, some of whom were perhaps only hinting at this argument. Not many put it that starkly that biologizing every human development was a radical distortion of human reality. But consciously or otherwise, Darwin constantly faced this difference between himself and certain other writers—and he chose not to think about it.

One such writer was Thomas Robert Malthus. In the first few pages of the first volume of the sixth edition of Malthus's *Essay*, which inspired Darwin to come up with the theory of natural selection, he was also reading Malthus's point that while the population principle applied biologically in a pure way to the world of animals and plants, it could not apply to human beings in the same way and, furthermore, it would be absolutely unthinkable to apply it to the European extermination of Native populations. When it came to Europeans exterminating savages, Malthus stepped back: "the right of exterminating, or driving into a corner where they must starve ... will be questioned in a moral view" (1.7). He observed that the continued population increase of Europeans in America would have the result that "... the Indians will be driven further and further back into the country, till the whole race is ultimately exterminated ..." (1.8). He was quietly appalled.

Malthus *never* looked at the spread of the European population and its effect of exterminating Natives and said to himself, Yes, this is entirely in accord with my theory. As far as he was concerned, his population principle in no way endorsed the genocide of faraway peoples or rationalized it. If we fail to remember that, we do a disservice to historical study.

Man's ability to reason and to make choices which animals would never make, said Malthus, removed him from the strict application of a biological process: "plants and irrational animals … are all impelled by a powerful instinct to the increase of their species … interrupted by no doubts about providing for their offspring … [But in the case of man] Impelled to the increase of his species by an equally powerful instinct, *reason interrupts his career*, and asks him whether he may not bring beings into the world, for whom he cannot provide the means of support" (6th, 1.3; emphasis added). He might as well have said (had he known about Darwin's future theory), reason interrupts natural selection. But Darwin in his eagerness for colonial conquest ran right past these warning posts and treated *everything* about humans as biological.

Thirty years after Darwin's reading of Malthus, the same warning trilled from the pen of Georg Gerland. In the last paragraph of his book, Gerland argued that the development of mankind has long been "under natural law" (*unter naturalistischem Gesetz*), and this is "the 'struggle for existence' in which the stronger conquers" (*Der »Kampf ums Dasein«, in welchem es der Stärkere ist, welcher siegt*), but this should not be applied to the extermination confronting Indigenous tribes. He believed that the stronger human races do not have to wipe out the weaker or "destroy [them] with pleasure and for no reason [literally, without serving any need or necessity]" (*mit Lust und ohne Bedürfniss zerstörend*). They can instead lift (*emporhebt*) the weaker to their own level. For Gerland, "the moral choice of mankind must rule" (*die sittliche Wahl des Menschen herrschen*). "Man," he says, "is capable of reason and love" (*Mensch ist der Vernunft und der Liebe fähig*). By choosing these qualities, "the collective [human race] will have taken another big step on the road it must travel towards the liberation of the spirit from the cruel shackles of external nature" (*die Gesamtheit hätte einen grossen Schritt weiter gethan auf der Bahn, die sie gehen muss, in der Befreiung des Geistes von den rohen Fesseln der äusseren Natur*).

Darwin paid enough attention to have his helper translate this, scribbling it at the bottom of page 144 and continuing on the top of 145, and even though this just repeats what I have already indicated, it is worth seeing exactly what Darwin read with his own eyes:

> Till now the development of mankind depends upon natural laws—the struggle for existence shows itself all powerful— But man is capable of reason & love, & shd show his

strength in elevating the weaker races to his level instead of exterminating them—then would the spirit & moral choice of mankind rule, & the totality would have made a great step forwards on the road of this emancipation of the spirit from the rough fetters of the external nature.

In this last paragraph, Gerland came as close as anyone of his time did to pointedly declaring that biology and morality (or culture) are very different things. Human beings do not have to be stuck with irrational nature (*unvernünftgen Natur*) or "the cruel chains of nature" (*den rohen Fesseln der äusseren Natur*) or even simply stuck "under natural law" (*unter naturalistischem Gesetz*) and "the struggle for existence" (*Der »Kampf ums Dasein«*). Human beings can choose reason and love (*der Vernunft und der Liebe*) over brutal nature and in making this moral choice (*sittliche Wahl*), we also choose the elevation, not the extermination, of Native peoples. This means that the extermination we witness in our time is a choice, not a natural, biological outcome.

Though Darwin clearly heard this argument, he turned his back on it by not even acknowledging it in his published work. He chose to ignore every humanitarian approach to human nature and evolution. Even when Malthus warned against applying the population principle (sexual reproduction outstrips food production) to humans in the same way it applies so intensely in the wider world of nature, Darwin refused to listen.

When Europeans do choose the worse path (such as exterminating the Indigenous), we should remember that this is a choice and not the outcome of natural forces. In between Malthus and Gerland, Darwin would have read this warning too in a book by John Lort Stokes, who had been his cabin mate for part of the *Beagle* voyage. They must have had many conversations in their roughly two years together, but whether they talked about the fate of Native peoples, I have no idea. Darwin's letters are not very revealing on this. But Darwin did read Stokes's 1846 book *Discoveries in Australia* and had even done some of the proofreading for him (see CCD 3.362). In it, Stokes had this to say:

> most men seem willing to content themselves with the belief that the event [extinction of the natives] is in accordance with some mysterious dispensation of Providence; and the purest philanthropy [i.e., humanitarianism] can only teach us to alleviate their present condition, and to smooth, as it were, the pillow of an expiring people [the pillow metaphor became a common one]. For my own part *I am not willing to*

believe, that in this conflict of races, *there is an absence of moral responsibility* on the part of the whites; *I must deny that it is in obedience to some all-powerful law,* the inevitable operation of *which exempts us from blame,* that the depopulation of the countries we colonize goes on. There appear to me to be the means of *tracing this national crime to the individuals who perpetrate it*; and it is with the deepest sorrow that I am obliged to confess that my countrymen have not, in Tasmania, exhibited that magnanimity which has often been the prominent feature of their character. They have sternly and systematically trampled on the fallen. [Stokes, 2.463-64; all emphases added]

I quote at length from such sources to make a point of how much extended thought some people gave to these problems and to emphasize that Darwin was thus made very aware of these thoughts. Stokes also said, "I must say I regret that that page of history which records our colonization of Australia must reach the eyes of posterity" (2.462). Note that Stokes's concern about what future generations will think was very different from Darwin's dismissive attitude about a remote future. Many colonists, Stokes lamented, "cannot conceive how any one can sympathize with the black race as their fellow men. In theory and practice they regard them as wild beasts whom it is lawful to extirpate. There are of course honourable exceptions ..." (2.459).

Darwin chose a different path. The constant biologizing of every feature of Indigenous people, which Darwin along with so many others engaged in, is comparable to the habit of using euphemisms. Just as euphemisms cover up a harsher reality, so biologizing blocks us from seeing the cultural problems of racism and injustice. "Great is our sin" if we turn man-made problems into natural ones (see *DR,* 338-44). The purpose in both cases is to make us not see. And both euphemisms and biologizing thereby become silent admissions that something is being covered up.

Darwin did not just biologize genocide, he biologized everything about the Native peoples of the world. In theory, Darwin believed that it was all biology for all peoples in all places and all times. But he was reluctant to carry out pure biological thinking on the home front, while he had no hesitation doing it to the Other from another land. Perhaps it is this more than anything else that captures his racism. And not so much doing it to the Other as assuming it and making a host of assumptions without the data to back them up. Darwin was eager to use the biological inferiority of Others as his preferred explanation for their supposed failure, their perceived immoralities, and their inevitable extermination when confronted by western powers.

Biologizing savage traits was a relentless activity among European writers. Darwin was no different. He biologized moral, intellectual, and every kind of characteristic one could think of. To repeat a quote from Darwin I presented in Chapter 2, "If bad tendencies are [biologically] transmitted, it is probable that good ones are likewise transmitted … Except through the principle of the transmission of moral tendencies, we cannot understand the differences believed to exist in this respect between the various races of mankind" (*Descent*, 148). In his way of thinking, the immoralities that Darwin perceived in Natives were a biological inheritance.

A humanitarian like Gerland would look deeper and see racism as one of the underlying factors of the melancholy situation of savages, where others saw only implacable biology. As one specific example of this, everyone else found the wandering lifestyle of many Indigenous peoples objectionable and lamented their refusal to settle down like civilized people do. (I cannot let this pass without mentioning that, in many cases, their nomadic lifestyle was greatly exaggerated; westerners simply overlooked all the farming they did.) Western scientists usually considered this one of the most inferior things about savages, and perhaps a sign of their inherent, biological laziness. Darwin made several disparaging references to it in *Descent* (158, 162, 168, 211). "Nomadic habits … have in every case been highly detrimental" to the development of civilization (158); he called it a "relic of barbarism" (162).

This was part of a general trend among western writers to depict western civilization as bringing only good things to these primitive peoples and the savages rejecting them because they were too inferior (too stupid, too lazy, too ignorant) to appreciate the benefits. In their view, Natives rejected civilization because they were less human. Gerland saw it differently. Civilization had rejected the Natives. Whatever nomadism they did practice was not a relic of barbarism, but was often a consequence of European injustice. Western civilization did not treat savages as human beings entitled to equal rights and actually offered savages very little (little more than slavery by another name). In the case of nomadic habits versus a more settled life, Gerland asked: Why should they settle down? When they do and take jobs, they are paid very little and always less than Europeans for the same work. "Naturally, they would rather go about wandering and begging" (Gerland, 114; *Natürlich schweifen sie lieber bettelnd umher*). They continued to be treated as inferior people, as if they were wild animals, regardless of their lifestyle, regardless of whether they led a settled life or a wandering life.

Gerland was no admirer of the primitive way of life. He was not a romantic. He did not admire their superstitions and their own cruelties. He did not think their subjection to the whims of nature was a good thing. Above all, he thought thousands of years of little development had left them stuck in harmful habits.

His main point here was this: Nature by itself was not an educative force and offered them no way out. What primitives needed was "a swift kick" (122; *ein plötzlicher Anstoss*) to jolt them out of their rigid habits. For that jolt, "the action [or, intervention] of civilization is necessary" (ibid.; *es war das Eingreifen der Kultur nothwendig*). Although he does not spell it out in this passage from the end of Chapter 18, he likely had in mind very positive contributions like teaching them about medicines and more productive agricultural skills. Unfortunately, what civilization had brought so far was "much blood and misery" (ibid.; *das viele Blut und Elend*). The great sin would be if Europe did not change its violent activity and continued to contribute to the ruin of Indigenous people so that it came sooner rather than later.

Gerland could deemphasize his own point about the faults in Indigenous peoples because of his holism. He understood nature and evolution as affirming each group and sub-group in nature, including the Indigenous. Everything strives for life and security. Gerland sets forth his beliefs about holism in the first couple of pages of the last chapter. He sees the wholeness of nature as "striving for greater perfection, strength [or, stability], and security of existence" (*eine grössere Vollkommenheit, Festigkeit und Sicherheit der Existenz anstreben*). He calls this the "the law of evolution" (*Das Gesetz dieser Entwickelung*) and it operates not only in nature as a totality but in each individual and each group as well. Everything in nature and the whole of nature itself aims for the ultimate goal which is simply "preservation and advancement" (*Erhaltung und Förderung*). Everything wants to live and advance. This includes the sub-parts of nature. Nature can be broken down into individuals subordinate (*unterordnet*) to species, species to genus, and genus to family. In general, each limited part is subordinate to, or subsumed under, the greater or larger part, and in a sense, the limited entity can be sacrificed (*aufopfert*) to the interests of the greater part.

At first glance, these last thoughts look like Darwin's "groups subordinate to groups" all over again, and that business about sacrifice, *if taken out of context*, might make it seem all the more Darwinian. But banish any thought that Gerland is expounding a system of domination. Gerland's fundamental point is that all individuals, species, etc., are subservient to the whole of nature and to the law of development or evolution. In other words, if a weak species is subservient to a dominant species, the fuller truth is that both weak and dominant are subservient to the whole of nature. In Darwin's view, the dominant do not serve anything except themselves. Not so for Gerland. The term *aufopfert* can also mean devoted to. Each part of nature is devoted to, or integrated in, the interests of the sub-whole just above it and all the lesser wholes devote themselves to the completeness of nature and to the striving for life which each fulfills as best it can.

Nature wants to create life, not death, and absolutely not any inferiority of life resulting from one group being forced to serve a supposedly superior form of life in another group. *You do not elevate the whole by degrading any part of it.* I believe that is a firm rule with Gerland. Nature strives to elevate all to the final goal of advancement for all—to achieve security, strength, safety. Each blessed part of the whole shares in this goal.

Human beings are a part of nature, a part of the same whole that every other organism is a part of, and therefore, the same law of evolution applies to us. We humans are not a law unto ourselves. We don't get to establish another law just for us. "We stand under the same whole as all other organisms, except that we are in a distinct position" (142; *dass wir unter ganz denselben stehen, wie die übrigen Organismen alle, nur dass unsere Stellung verschieden ist*). If nature wants preservation and advancement for all, we don't get to cut that off for some parts of nature in our own selfish interests. This is by no means a stretch of what Gerland means, as his next remarks demonstrate:

> Now indeed the chief purpose of nature is the preservation and advancement of the whole, so must it also be for us human beings, namely, above all the preservation and advancement of human society, for our primary sphere of activity is naturally among our own particular race. Yet it would be a very bad way to serve the whole, if we wished to crush [or, stamp out] similar viable germs [buds, sprouts], simply because they have not developed [evolved] the same spring [bloom, prime] and the same race [behavior, character] as we have. Who knows towards what final purpose of nature they also can serve! [Gerland, 142]

And the German:

> Wie nun also der Natur Erhaltung und Förderung des Ganzen Hauptzweck ist, so muss er es auch uns Menschen sein, und zwar zunächst Erhaltung und Föderung der menschlichen Gesellschaft, da unsere Thätigkeit zunächst unserer eigenen Gattung naturmässig gehört. Das aber heisst schlecht dem Ganzen dienen, wenn man lebensfähige Keime desselben, bloss weil sie nicht im gleichen Lenz und nach gleicher Art mit uns sich entwickelt haben, zertreten wollte. Wer weiss, zu welchem Endzweck auch sie der Natur dienen können!

We should be very clear that Gerland was not comparing primitive peoples to germs (*Keime*) in the sense of bacteria. The word means buds, sprouts, the first shoots of life. He is also comparing Indigenes to spring (*Lenz*). I believe his overall meaning is that just because Native peoples have not blossomed in the same way we have, that gives us no right to stamp them out (*zertreten*). I also believe, though I am not entirely sure about this, that by 'human society' he means all human beings on the planet, so that it is regard for the whole race of human beings that we have to pay mind to and not just our part. There is in this a real humility that is absent from Darwin's system of thought. Next to a holistic thinker like Gerland, Darwin is as arrogant as western civilization ever gets.

Gerland's entire thought process seems to be this (expanding only ever so slightly on his words by reading between the lines):

We should not overrate the importance or naturalness of extinction. Especially in cases where we, the western civilized nations, are playing a role in the extermination, it is presumptuous of us to declare that extinction is a natural outcome—and this is because the ultimate purpose of nature, both for itself as a totality and for all within it, seems to be preserving life rather than destroying it. (Darwin would probably have agreed with this last statement, but not with what follows.) The ending of life may sometimes happen, but it should never be taken as a final goal in itself. (Darwin refers to extinction and extermination so often in *Origin*, they appear to be major results that nature is driving towards. Gerland does not specifically criticize Darwin here, but he is definitely concerned to oppose this point of view which is represented by Darwin among others.) Life rather than death should be our guide.

It is the life of the whole that matters, as if all of nature constituted a single organism. That is nature's primary object. Because each part of nature contributes to the whole and because we are more ignorant than wise about the whole and the interconnectedness of everything, we have no business deciding that the function of any one part or another has expired. What I like about Gerland's evolutionary thinking is that it tries to incorporate ignorance into the system. We don't understand all that is happening, so let us err on the side of life, not death. Whereas the approach of Darwin and most scientists of the time was guided by the idea that however ignorant we may be, we can be sure that nature wants us to be on top and wants inferior parts to be eliminated.

To condense and rephrase in smoother English the last two sentences in the previous blocked quote from Gerland: "Who knows but that primitive peoples, sprouting life in their own right, do not also serve nature's ultimate goal!" That is a holistic thinker for you. (Any suggestion that dying can be a contribution to the final goal would be a complete perversion of Gerland's meaning.) We don't get to put an expiration date on anything. That would be sheer arrogance. Does nature want anything to disappear? We should not assume so. We should always assume nature needs each part for some purpose and wants to preserve life as much as possible. This contradicts some of what Gerland said previously about primitive peoples having serious defects which were slowly leading them to extinction. He was not perfect. I think he made a mistake there and went off the rails. But those earlier thoughts do not go to the heart of what he was aiming at. The real essence of his thinking was captured by something I heard in a film or TV show I saw not too long ago (I cannot remember which one): Every child that is born God wants to be born. You could say the same of species and races.

Gerland's thoughts continue: We in the more advanced nations have a responsibility to imitate nature in this respect. All human races, actually sub-races, together on this planet should be looked on as one whole race. We ourselves are only a sub-race. We are not the whole thing, and we are certainly not the whole of nature. We should help our fellow human beings to achieve the best life they can because it serves the whole race of humans. If we are going to appoint ourselves leaders, we should lead the whole towards more life, not towards destruction. Gerland actually says, "the sole task before civilized nations, when faced with the uncivilized, can only be to carry civilization to them too, and not to exterminate them by ample and effective means" (Gerland, 143; *die einzige Aufgabe schon civilisirter Nationen uncivilisirten gegenüber kann nur die sein, die Civilisation auch zu jenen hinzutragen, nicht aber durch die reichlicheren und wirksameren Mittel derselben jene vertilgen*). Or as Herman Merivale said, we are not predestined to become the murderers of Indigenous peoples.

When we take it upon ourselves to exterminate another people or facilitate their destruction when other causes are in operation (like the infertility of the women, which Darwin made so important in *Descent*), we stand outside the laws of nature and especially the law of evolution. Again, this is real humility and it is, I think, why western scientists have traditionally found holism an unacceptable approach. It does not support the west's arrogance towards nature and other peoples, and its quest for power.

If there is one concrete suggestion that was shared by many humanitarians, it was the idea that western civilization should proceed more slowly in the new countries it attempts to colonize. We are rushing things, which is very harmful to Native groups. Saxe Bannister said we need to give the Natives more "breathing time" to adjust to European civilization (*Colonization*, 12; cf. "our cupidity gives them no breathing time" in *Humane* [1830], 104n). They were being subjected to immense pressure to change overnight—if only "we will abstain a short time from abusing our power" (*Colonization*, 12). Herman Merivale argued that the demise of Aborigines does not have to happen: "if he [the native] can be placed in safety from hostile aggression; if a sufficiency of food can be secured for him; if *time can be given him* to become fortified against the virulence of epidemic diseases … if all these causes of death are removed, must he still perish?" (2.208; emphasis added).

Time is what Aborigines need. Napier believed in winning over the Natives peacefully and with persuasion, so as to achieve "a very gradual intercourse: at first, confined, reserved, and made extremely profitable and pleasant *to them*" (Napier, 106; his emphasis). Recall too what Gerland said about German tribes having had many centuries to adjust to Greco-Roman civilization. They were not forced to change overnight as modern-day savages are. It is also true that even these great humanitarians shared a common fault in their acceptance of the superiority of western civilization and its colonizing efforts. But they had the decency to know that the extreme greed of westerners was wrong, that Indigenous rights must be established and respected, and that lines must be drawn to limit western conquest and destruction. All this was unacceptable to the gung-ho imperialists.

In Chapter 6, we will see Langfield Ward go even further and suggest that Natives could learn some things from western civilization that will enable them to slow down and perhaps even defeat colonialism. What all these humanitarians were in effect arguing for is that Native people should dictate the pace of western civilization, or even whether it invades their nations at all. In Chapter 3, I quoted Napier, "I see no reason why the savage should not choose his own way, as well as other people" (Napier, 99). Napier was afraid that our obsession with national wealth prevented us from seeing that.

Justice demanded that colonialism acknowledge the Native voice in its own affairs. It was their land after all. Saxe Bannister urged the Select Committee on Aborigines that "perfect equality of rights should be declared by law and enforced in the courts for the natives" (*Report*, "Minutes", 19, #6). Rights were just step one. He anticipated that eventually Natives should be allowed to serve as judges (ibid.). He also suggested that since the Colonial Office had a conflict of interest in representing both the colonists and the Natives, an independent body should oversee the Colonial Office and look out for the interests of the Natives, and this body should include colored people (15). Recognizing the difficulty of enforcing rights in a hostile society, he proposed, "When judgments cannot be executed against oppressors of the natives, the governors should indemnify the oppressed" (18). Almost all these recommendations and more were repeated in his 1838 book *British Colonization and Coloured Tribes* (273-98). In the book, he compared the problem of protecting Aborigines to that of protecting "the emancipated negroes" (284). Emancipation was only the first step of what should be done for the slaves. Giving them a voice in their own affairs was the bigger step that awaited completion.

It is not clear whether Bannister would have supported full autonomy for Natives (I think he would have), but at the very least he supported that Natives have more of a voice in their own governance. This is implicit in many of the humanitarians.

The humanitarians were probably overconfident that Natives at all times and in all places would appreciate and want the benefits of the west. But the crucial point is that some of them saw that Natives should be more in control of if, how, and when western civilization made inroads into their cultures. If there was no progress towards implementing or respecting Native autonomy, it was because there was no dialogue about it, and if there was no dialogue, it was because the supporters of imperialism made sure it was dead at birth. Under-secretary James Stephen suggested that Bannister "was suffering from mental aberration!" (Uys, 26). That's a good way to shut down dialogue.

Stephen was not a half-bad humanitarian himself when it came to emancipation of slaves and combating the racism that would prevent the full success of emancipation. But when it came to Aborigines in all lands, Stephen was inclined to accept the prejudices of colonists. In some instructions to a naval officer in New Zealand (in 1840), he expressed a defeatism about the efficacy of humanitarian ideas: "... neither penalties, nor regulations, nor the teachings of Christianity would restrain settlers from oppressing the Maoris" (quoted in Ward, Alan, 37; also see Reynolds, *Indelible*, 88-91, for Stephen's very deep pessimism that anything could be done to prevent the extermination of the Indigenous). The general tendency was to cave in to settler hostility and to respond to Native antagonism with armed force. Stephen believed that the only way Natives could be saved from total destruction would be to supply them with weapons and ammunition, "an act of suicidal generosity which of course cannot be practised" (in Reynolds, *Indelible*, 89). Stephen's example is a reminder of how difficult it was to be a consistent humanitarian in that time (or any time). The ones (like Napier, Bannister, Gerland) who stood up for Aboriginal rights and respect for their voice, if not for full autonomy, deserve all the more credit. They were sure that at the very least colonialism must slow down.

To anticipate a remark I will return to in Chapter 8, Walter Bagehot, editor of the *Economist* and a disciple in a sense of Darwin, said in 1868 in response to an old Native who had disparaged western civilization, "we need not take account of the mistaken ideas of unfit men and beaten races" (Bagehot, 209). This is very much Darwin's language and reflects Darwin's belief in the west's complete takeover. As far as I know Darwin never engaged in dialogue with any humanitarian, not with Gerland or anyone else, not even with one who was very close to him, Alfred Wallace (see last chapter for more on Wallace's humanitarianism). He contributed to the almost complete shutdown of dialogue. For Darwin, every species is destined either for dominance or "the high-road to extinction" (*1844*, 149-50). There is nothing in between in his view. Native autonomy would have made no sense to him, or at best it would have represented a temporary respite from their real manifest destiny.

Even if I am mistaken about some of the steps in Gerland's reasoning, I am certain of his conclusion. He considered that "an essential task of civilization [is] the preservation of less developed peoples" (142; *die Erhaltung der minder entwickelten Völker für eine wesentliche Aufgabe der Kultur*). Any attempt by the civilized to rush Native peoples towards annihilation would mean we ourselves have returned to a state of barbarity. Darwin certainly understood at least this much of what Gerland was saying, even if he chose not to respond to it.

The last lines of the translation in the marginalia on 143 of his copy of Gerland go like this: "Now nothing is more degrading to civilised than to sink back into savagery & the destructive exterminating [exterminatory?] wars of the nations & degraded [them?] generally. There is here another reason for the preservation of savages." And on 142, the annotation is: "But it wld be very bad for humanity to tread out germs capable of life only because they are not of the same nature with us." As explained above, 'germs' (*Keime*) here does not mean bacteria, but seedlings, buds, sprouts. On 135, the translated summary by Darwin's helper reads: "The Inhuman and bloodthirsty way in which savages have been treated shows that the gulf which separates civiliseds and savages is not so great as has been thought—for these are essentially savage traits."

Gerland wanted to remind people of the easy slide from civilized to savage. Like a true holist, he was always looking for the connections between human beings. Gerland understood how important this was for human rights. He pointed out that colonized primitive peoples will continue to be in trouble "as long as civilized peoples imagine themselves to be made of completely different material than those 'savages' to whom are surely accorded the form but by no means the rights of being human" (Gerland, 141; *so lange wenigstens sicher als die Kulturvölker sich von ganz anderem Stoff dünken, als jene »Wilden«, denen man wohl Gestalt, aber keineswegs die Rechte eines Menschen zugesteht*). Gerland knew that racism was about creating a belief in disconnection, a belief that some groups are made of completely different material than our group, thus leading directly to a denial of human rights. This is the fundamental assertion of racism that the human races are disconnected from one another, which Granville Sharp saw as early as 1769. For Gerland, his knowledge of evolution demanded that he be an antiracist.

Darwin in his own work was more concerned to emphasize the disconnections, and from that comes his racism. If Darwin had ever really believed (which is highly unlikely) his remark to Lyell in that 1860 letter about

European savagery being a judgment from a *remote* future, here was Gerland in 1868 forcefully reminding him that the future was now. Whatever awareness he gained from Gerland, he would submerge it again under the euphemisms in *Descent*.

Based on all we know about Darwin's writings, it is pretty obvious that he did not share Gerland's views. He never expressed any such ideas in *The Descent of Man*. In Gerland, Darwin came face to face (by virtue of the translations in the margins) with an evolutionist whose understanding of the main causes of the impending extinction of Indigenous peoples was different from his own and whose sense of man's relation to the rest of nature, especially to Native peoples, was more humane than his, and yet, what is truly stunning, Darwin never acknowledged these differences nor the different approaches to evolution from which they stem. Readers of *Descent* would have had no clue about any of this. Gerland believed that the extermination of savages or Native peoples by civilized powers is a violation of the fundamental law of nature to preserve and elevate. It is not natural and it is not a mysterious poisonous breath. No matter how many causes seem to be contributing to this, it is not inevitable and the part played by European countries is not one of the laws of nature, it is a moral choice. The greed and bloodthirstiness that brought Europeans to these other lands is not part of the natural struggle for survival. If anything, it is a struggle for luxuries and status that has nothing to do with survival of the fittest. It is closer to survival of the shittiest. And it raises the question of who are the real savages.

~ 5 ~

I Weep for You,
I Deeply Sympathize

In Chapter 2, we found Darwin writing placidly (to use his expression) in his travel *Diary* about the genocide of Aborigines and even about their children being sold into slavery. Some of this indifference carried over to his later published work in *The Descent of Man*. In the section "On the Extinction of the Races of Man" in Chapter 7, he is quite unconcerned as he discusses what he believes are the causes of their annihilation. Here is a representative selection from what he says about the Tasmanians (who may or may not have become extinct in 1874, but certainly came close to it):

> When Tasmania was first colonised [in 1803] the natives were roughly estimated by some at 7000 and by others at 20,000. [The current estimate is 5,000 to 7,000.] Their number was soon greatly reduced, chiefly by fighting with the English and with each other. After the famous hunt by all the colonists [the Black Line set up by Governor Arthur to sweep across the island], when the remaining natives delivered themselves up to the government, they consisted only of 120 individuals, who were in 1832 transported to Flinders Island ... [which] seems healthy, and the natives were well treated. Nevertheless, they suffered greatly in health ... In 1835 only one hundred were left. As they continued rapidly to decrease ... they were removed in 1847 to Oyster Cove ... But the change of site did no good. Disease and death still pursued them, and in 1864 one man (who died in 1869), and three elderly women alone survived. The infertility of the women is even a more remarkable fact than the liability of all to ill-health and death. [*Descent*, 213]

There is no emotion here, no outrage, and hardly a modicum of caring. The rest of this section is much in the same spirit. Some will argue that this is an appropriate scientific tone. But science does not demand phony detachment. There is a kind of detachment that distorts the evidence—and, it might be said, even lies about the evidence. Such detachment is opposed to good science because it is not really disinterested. It is rather attachment to some cause (in this case, colonial conquest) masquerading as objective detachment.

Isn't that at bottom why Darwin was so upset with Lyell's placid response to the breakup of slave families? It is possible to interpret Darwin's complaint to Lyell in a simpler way. He may have merely been saying that what was done to the slaves is an important issue that deserves more caring. But I think Darwin intuitively grasped a deeper point that Lyell's detachment promoted a lie. At the very least Lyell was understating the suffering of the slaves compared to the treatment of poor whites. There is an imbalance in being distraught over one and not the other. The same can be said of distancing oneself from the disaster visited on Aborigines.

Darwin writes as if the disease, infertility, and death that pursued the Tasmanians were somehow objective facts that hovered in the air, unattached to any injustices on the part of British human beings. His very brief mention of 'fighting with the English' is the *only* time he brings this up and he seems to regard it on the same level as intertribal fighting. In the rest of this section in Chapter 7, he harps on changed conditions of life (his favorite euphemism) producing infertility in savage women—this seems to fascinate him more than anything else ("the most important of all the causes [of population decrease] seems to be lessened fertility;" 216). 'Changed conditions' is his term for stress, but it is also a euphemism for invasion, dispossession, and displacement.

Darwin can actually write "infertility has coincided too closely with the arrival of Europeans ..." (219)—this is comparable to his journal statement "Wherever the European has trod, death seems to pursue the aboriginal" (*Narrative*, 520; *Voyage*, 375)—and he does it so naively that he seems to have no realization of what he just said. What is it about the arrival of Europeans that precipitates infertility among Native women? Might it be violence, rapacity, and hostility (as Gerland believed)—in short, racial arrogance? Darwin does not take a deep look. Most of the time, Europeans and their injustices disappear from his account. He takes note that something is going on, but in effect, he eliminates mistreatment by Europeans as a main cause of the destruction of the Aborigines.

Even that reference to fighting with the English is phrased in a passive point of view. Note well that he did not say 'chiefly by the English making war on the natives and decimating them.' The way Darwin puts it—natives have been "fighting with the English"—allows one to think that if only the Tasmanians had been more peaceful or passive, they could have avoided all this destruction. That is not the way others of Darwin's time saw it. Some of them are quoted in James Bonwick's 1870 *The Last of the Tasmanians*—a book Darwin read, but chose not to pay close attention to.

Or as an editorial writer in a series in an Australian newspaper remarked in 1880, "As a rule the blacks have been friendly at first, and the longer they have endured provocation without retaliating the worse they have fared, for the more ferocious savages have inspired some fear, and have therefore been comparatively unmolested" (in Reynolds, *Whispering*, 110). Not everyone agreed that more passive behavior would have benefited the Natives. Sometimes you only get the respect you demand.

G.W. Rusden's three volume *History of Australia* was published the year after Darwin died, but Rusden still counts as a contemporary whose moral and scientific approach is very different from Darwin's. He was writing about mainland Australia, but this history is similar to what happened in Tasmania. Rusden rails against the inhumanity practiced towards Aborigines and the failure to properly report (which is what real science should be doing) all that had happened: "A supporter of the existing atrocities admitted that it would be fatal to the usefulness of the force if reports were exacted" (Rusden, 3.248-49). "The air of Queensland so reeks with atrocities committed and condoned that the few who plead for justice and mercy deserve the more praise" (3.249). Almost a half century earlier, Saxe Bannister had pointed out that "… every species of neglect and persecution is heaped on the men who, if listened to, could have prevented such doings [atrocities, dispossession, and other notorious acts against the Natives]" (*Colonization*, 259).

Rusden was able to determine that for one year, a good portion of £20,000 "was expended on the ammunition with which the blacks were shot, and on the wants of those who shot them … [while] £100 were allotted for fees for defending aborigines and Polynesians" (3.249). (Darwin's investigation does not go this deep.) Rusden was critical of the statistics kept by the Registrar-General, Henry Jordan, who "finds no place for the aborigines in his account of the population. In his table of 'causes of death in Queensland' in 1878, 'arranged in the order of degree of fatality,' Mr. *Jordan omitted the rifle*" (ibid.; emphasis added). The Registrar also recorded how much had been expended "in importing immigrants. The sums spent in destroying those whom the colonists found upon the land are not mentioned" (3.250). Rusden's scholarship was good science. He was demanding *a full account*, which Darwin had no interest in. A full account often demands passion, not detachment. You cannot and will not see the *whole* story unless you have a passionate commitment to see it.

I will make a general point here. It is impossible to think without emotions. They are always there. Even when we pretend to be placid, detached, and above it all, they are there. That's not a bad thing, or I should say, it does not have to be a bad thing. First of all, it is a fact of life, a medical fact. The emotional part of the brain bleeds into every other part (see the work of Antonio Damasio). It is inhuman and medically impossible to think without tapping into the emotions. Emotions can play the role of saint or devil in our thinking. They can help us see more clearly or they can blind us. When they give us light, revealing more evidence, they are a good thing. When they give us heat, concealing and leading us away from the evidence, they are destructive of good thinking. Whatever reveals is good, what conceals is bad. That is the true test of the value of emotions. And the more visible we make them, the better off we are. Light, more light, always more light.

In fact, one can lay odds on the following: if anyone is pretending to detachment, it is likely they are using their concealed emotions to conceal other evidence as well. In the end, we can put aside all this talk of emotions and evidence, and simply focus on what is being revealed or withheld. Those who reveal the most and conceal the least make the best scientific scholars. The great battle in all fields of science and scholarship, but especially in historical studies, is over who reveals the most evidence and the most telling pieces. Light, always more light.

Rusden's superior approach to science is one way to deal with the misinformation handed out by mainstream scientists. There are other ways. Art and something like satire also help us to face what is going on. When Darwin was trying to convince the public that genocide was natural, other authors gave the public another point of view. You could choose whom to read and whom to believe. You could weigh one against the other.

The first edition of *The Descent of Man* was presented to us in 1871. The same year also gave us Lewis Carroll's *Through the Looking-Glass*, his follow-up to *Alice's Adventures in Wonderland*. *Looking-Glass* contains "The Walrus and the Carpenter". It is a poem about colonialism and genocide. Carroll is comparing imperialists to cannibals, an idea that has a long history to it going back at least to Jonathan Swift (see Boulukos, 109).

For Carroll, this genocide began with "A pleasant walk, a pleasant talk/ along the briny beach." Genocide can begin so deceptively. Deception is a key point in this poem. There were many travel books that could have given Carroll this picture of initial pleasantness. Well before mid-century, plenty of writing about exploration and the colonizing venture (see further on for one example from the French explorer F. Peron) would testify to the original pleasant nature of it before it turned sour. What happened, for example, in Tasmania was well-documented in book after book.

But before Carroll gets to that "pleasant walk", the poem opens with "The sun was shining on the sea,/ Shining with all his might" and what was odd about this, says Carroll, is that "it was/ The middle of the night." The sun never sets in this world. Didn't they used to say that the sun never sets on the British empire? It is literally true in Carroll's poem. "It's very rude of him to come and spoil the fun," complains the moon—echoing the complaints of Aborigines all over the world. (I believe the saying "his Majesty's dominions, on which the sun never sets" was originated in 1829 by Christopher North, pseudonym for John Wilson, in *Noctes Ambrosianæ*, appearing in installments in a magazine; for later book editions, see Bibliography.)

Darwin too expressed this pride in Britain's colonial venture. In his view, Britain is the quintessential non-intruder. It is not intruding because it has a right to be everywhere. He expresses this often in his *Diary*. "Seeing, when amongst foreigners, the strength & power of ones own Nation, gives a feeling of exultation which is not felt at home" (*Diary*, 78; July 1, 1832); and "it is surprising to see how Englishmen find their way to every corner of the globe. I do not suppose there is an inhabited & civilized place where they are not to be found" (145; Mar. 2, 1833); and "little embryo Englands are hatching in all parts" (424; June 2, 1836). At the end of his journey, as they near home in England (in a long section following the entry for September 25, 1836), he summarizes some of what he has learned on this long voyage: "It is impossible for an Englishman to behold these distant colonies, without a high pride and satisfaction. To hoist the British flag seems to draw as a certain consequence wealth, prosperity and civilization" (446; this remains substantially the same in all the published editions; e.g., *Voyage*, 436). What Darwin does not have to spell out for his readers (because they all share this assumption) is that it is wealth and prosperity for the British, not necessarily for the Natives.

I am not criticizing Darwin for his nationalism. He has a right to that. But incorporating nationalist pride and a barefaced colonial agenda into a scientific system is something else altogether. When Darwin fails to engage in any deliberations about whether we should be here at all or whether we owe these people something when we take their land, that is a scientific failure.

Darwin shows little awareness of the way Natives experienced this. Ironically, in New Zealand, as I have previously noted, the complaints that Darwin was sensitive to was that of the missionaries who "complain far more of the conduct of their countrymen than of the natives. It is strange … the only protection which they need & on which they rely is from the native Chiefs against Englishmen!" (384; Dec. 22, 1835; compare this to the Select Committee *Report*, 18, which gave an example of Native chiefs in the Sandwich Islands protecting missionaries). Missionaries sometimes bore witness to the rudeness of the imperial invaders. Would Darwin have been as sensitive to this if the complaining had come from Natives? I really don't know. On the same page as the "little embryo Englands" remark, Darwin calls the Hottentots "the ill treated aboriginals of the country [the Cape of Good Hope]," but he gives no details (also in *Narrative*, 575). This is one exception to Darwin's general tendency to ignore the situation faced by the Indigenous population, but this one general comment tells us very little.

(Most likely, Darwin was referring to the fact that Hottentots were virtual slaves; if so, this is the only occasion I know of where Darwin shows any awareness of forced labor or illegal slavery. Of the Hottentots, the Select Committee said in 1837, "They had fallen, as we have seen, into a state of bondage to the [Boer] farmers, through a system of forced contracts of service, and of apprenticeship of their children" [*Report*, 60]. The *Report* also described them as "the actual, though not the nominal, slaves of the boors" with laws being passed to keep their movements under "rigorous control" [26]. The *Report* attributes this to the Boers' greed to take all their land and cattle. "Avarice is the motive, and its fruits are systematic robbery and murder" [29]. The *Report* here also provides one of the earliest examples of government orders calling for or approving of genocide, though I have no idea if Darwin, or Lewis Carroll, was aware of this. It quotes at length from a statement by a Captain Stockenstrom who said, in part, that "many documents still extant clearly demonstrate ..." that in the late 18th century "extermination [of the Bushmen and some Hottentot tribes] ... became its [the local colonial government's] avowed object ..." [27]. The *Report* goes on to note, "In 1774, an order was issued for the extirpation of the whole of the Bushmen" [ibid.] and further on, from a statement of a Colonel Collins, "The total extinction of the Bosjesmen race is actually stated to have been at one time confidently hoped for" [28]. But this sort of documented evidence for intentional genocide under colonialism is rare. For a full discussion of genocide and why grossly negligent genocide may be a possibility, see *DR*, 650-92.)

If you read French explorer François Peron's account of his party's first encounter with the Natives of Tasmania in 1802 (during his travels from 1801 to 1804, published in English in 1809)—meeting the charming, young, "lively and animated" Ouré-Ouré and her family (Peron, 177-80)—you will see that it was very much "a pleasant walk, a pleasant talk," sharing food, presents, and music. Finally, it came time for these first European visitors to leave: "when we put off, their sorrow was expressed in the most affecting manner: they made signs to us to come again, and as if to point out the spot, they lighted a large fire on the hill ... it even appeared that they passed the night at this place, as we saw the fire till the morning" (180). Less than half a century later, as a result of returning again and again to that place marked by the fire on the hill, European rudeness had spoiled all the fun. Almost the entire population (probably between 5,000 and 7,000 at first contact) had been wiped out.

The two interlopers in Carroll's poem pretend they want to civilize the Aboriginal Oysters. More deception. The Walrus invites them on that pleasant walk and talk. Carroll's whimsical version of the civilizing mission is "To talk of many things: Of shoes—and ships—and sealing-wax—Of cabbages—and kings—And why the sea is boiling hot—And whether pigs have wings." But it's just a ruse. "It seems a shame," the Walrus said, "To play them such a trick. After we've brought them out so far, And made them trot so quick!" Offering civilization was merely a trick, so they could consume them all. The more honest genocidal perpetrator, the Carpenter, will only say, "The butter's spread too thick!" The one time the Carpenter weeps is at the beginning when he sheds "a bitter tear" over their inability to rearrange and improve the landscape (to sweep away all the sand) to suit their needs or whims. Both of them "wept like anything to see/ Such quantities of sand" which could not be entirely swept away.

The Native Oysters who are about to be eaten voice their own lament over being consumed: "that would be a dismal thing to do!" Dismal it was. No one would be trotting home again. That is as perfect a summary of what happened to the Tasmanians as any I have ever seen. I don't know if Carroll read James Bonwick's book, but the Oysters remind me of the orphans Bonwick saw in the school near Hobart Town (see last chapter, near the beginning).

Carroll then gives us the most chilling scene of all. The Walrus holds his pocket handkerchief before his eyes as he bemoans the disappearance of the Oysters and eats them at the same time:

> "I weep for you," the Walrus said:
> "I deeply sympathize."
> With sobs and tears he sorted out
> Those of the largest size,
> Holding his pocket-handkerchief
> Before his streaming eyes.

He laments the fate of the victims even as he exterminates them nonstop. That in essence is European colonialism and genocide—just as Darwin in his published journal could express melancholy over the Natives losing their land (in Argentina and New Zealand) and yet celebrate the complete ethnic cleansing of Natives in Van Diemen's Land or calmly remark on the final extermination of Indians in South America (this last is, I believe, only in the original *Diary*, 278).

In the next and last stanza, the Carpenter invites the Oysters to trot home again (an odd thing to do, as if he had no conscience or awareness of what he and the Walrus had done). "But answer came there none—/ And this was scarcely odd, because/ They'd eaten every one." Total extermination, the victims apparently of impersonal forces. Alice says she likes the Walrus best "because he was a *little* sorry for the poor oysters." To which Tweedledee responds, "He ate more than the Carpenter, though. You see he held his handkerchief in front, so that the Carpenter couldn't count how many he took: contrariwise." The sympathy hides the genocide, contrariwise. As for the Carpenter, "he ate as many as he could get." Carroll is posing this dilemma: Who is worse, the openly genocidal maniac or the one who combines murderous tendencies with sympathy for the victims? Carroll's comment on behalf of Alice: "This was a puzzler." It still is.

The extraordinary thing about this poem is that except for the ending—all the Oysters have been eaten—and a bare hint at the beginning with the sun rudely spoiling the fun, there is nothing overtly brutal in the poem. It's all politeness: a pleasant walk, a pleasant talk, weeping through a handkerchief, delightful conversation about the wonders of civilization, a simple meal of bread, pepper, and vinegar. The ruthlessness is almost entirely hidden. You don't see it, cannot see it, it is so well covered up, but somehow it is there.

Real life colonialism was not quite so perfectly polite. Too much of the brutality was always apparent (like shooting an Aboriginal child on his mother's back to demonstrate the accuracy of a rifle at a great distance—recounted by Alfred Wallace in his 1865 essay "How to Civilize Savages"), but Carroll captures the essential smiling, self-satisfied cruelty of colonialism. In a review of a book on Carroll, Michael Wood writes "how often [Carroll's] Wonderland looks not like an alternative world but a crazed, sardonic representation of our own" (Wood, 15, col. 3). One could also say that sometimes Carroll's world looks exactly like our own. It takes some melancholy reflection to see the abominable behavior in the oh-so-polite Walrus and Carpenter, but it is there. Maybe that's what Carroll was going for. Maybe he wanted us to see it by reflecting. Equally haunting is this: What was Carroll thinking, putting a poem about genocide in a children's book?

Do Carroll's Walrus and Carpenter correspond to real historical figures? You bet they do.

George Arthur, Lieutenant-Governor of Van Diemen's Land (1824-1836), wrote of the colonist John "Batman's sympathy for the Aborigines, but also observed that he 'had much slaughter to account for'" (Boyce, *Van Diemen's Land*, 201). Sounds very much like the Walrus, doesn't it? The same in fact can be said of Arthur himself. He could easily out-walrus the Walrus. He expressed a lot of compassion for the Natives, especially after the few remaining members had been removed from the main island to the smaller Flinders Island, but also earlier when he issued proclamation after proclamation containing pleas for their humane treatment. He did much official weeping. Yet he was the one who declared martial law, who had only some hesitancy using convicts to go after the Natives, who was fully committed to the expropriation of their land without compensation ("Such quantities of sand: 'If this were only cleared away,' They said, 'it would be grand!'"), and who never prosecuted a single white man for the murder of an Aborigine, despite threats to do so. The whole history of Tasmania is one of compassion and extermination, until "They'd eaten every one."

When George Robinson, a kind of self-appointed savior of the Tasmanians, asked if a handful of Natives could be moved back to their homeland, he recorded Governor Arthur's response in his journal (Dec. 18, 1838): "he was sure the [white] inhabitants would raise such a hue and cry against it that could not be withstood ... He said if the natives were brought [back], property would immediately fall in value very considerably ..." (Plomley, 608). That could not be allowed, so they had to continue to colonize until they'd eaten or ejected every one. Lewis Carroll could not have written a more accurate history of Van Diemen's Land (Tasmania), if he had had personal access to Robinson's journals, which was impossible as this part of the journals was not published until 1987; but Robinson did periodically make official reports to the Colonial Office, and local newspapers frequently reported on his activities.

These issues were being debated, facts were being reported. What was happening in many of the colonies was well documented. In an 1841 lecture, Herman Merivale said that "the wretched details of the ferocity and treachery which have marked the conduct of civilized men" can be found "in the accounts of travellers and missionaries, in the reports of our own legislature, in the language of philanthropic [humanitarian] orators and writers" (Merivale, 2.150). He continued, "The general features of the subject are by this time [1841] sufficiently known ..." (2.151). In the same lecture, he also said, "The history of the European settlements in America, Africa, and Australia, presents every where the same general features—a wide and sweeping destruction of native races by the uncontrolled violence of individuals and colonial authorities, followed by tardy attempts on the part of governments to repair the acknowledged crime" (2.153). That is an excellent summary of what was happening.

It was common knowledge. Everyone had the ability to know. Neither Darwin nor Lewis was writing about an arcane subject. The public was getting enough information and viewpoints from many different sources that it could make up its own mind about some of these things.

Lewis Carroll is a famous name, and the reason for revisiting this one aspect of his work is that, having been a famous author, his words, like Darwin's, reached a public arena. Though they may never have met, their views engaged in a kind of public debate that was ongoing. But it is important to remember that there was a real public debate in which members of the public, who are completely unknown to us, took an interest and sometimes took part as well. These issues reached *everyone*.

Thus, in January 1844, a young man, Henry Mort, in Queensland, Australia, wrote home to his mother and sister about a dispute he was having with his friends:

> John and David McConnell argued that it is morally right for a Christian Nation to extirpate savages from their native soil in order that it may be peopled with a more intelligent and civilized race of human beings, etc etc. F. McConnell and myself were of the opposite opinion and argued that a nation had no moral right to take forcible possession of any place. What is your opinion on the subject? Don't you think it a most heinous act of any Nation however powerful, however civilized and however christianized that Nation may be—to take possession of a country peopled by weak and barbarous tribes? [in Reynolds, *Whispering*, 13-14]

It was not only the famous voices that stimulated thoughtfulness and controversy. Society as a whole was confronted with varying opinions by more than just the most well-known voices.

While this is slightly off the point, the public had been heavily invested too in the debate over whether humans were descended from monkeys and whether there were degrees of descent. This was not an issue just for the experts. From 1841, the same year as Merivale's lecture, there is an interesting record from a British missionary society in Manchester. They were trying to convince a young man who is dying and is an unbeliever that he already knows something about faith because he believes many things he could not possibly have seen or have knowledge of. They ask where he came from. He answers from his parents. Where did they come from? From their parents. And where did the first parents come from? He responds, "By some other race of animals—such as baboons or monkeys." And how did they get here? "By some other race of animals." (See Secord, 301-02.) This had, before Darwin and even before Robert Chambers, become a part of the conversation in the streets and in the slums. Recall too Charles Napier in 1835 taking offense at the suggestion that Australian Aborigines were "a race which forms the link between men and monkeys" (Napier, 94; cf. 146). The allegation that the Indigenous were a missing link was being used as one justification for their extermination.

I am sure that when the Manchester proselytizers went home, they talked about what the young man had said. Maybe some were influenced and others were not, but by such means, ideas spread. I am sure too that when Henry Mort's mother and sister received his letter, it sparked a lively conversation. Maybe they dragged some of their neighbors into it. People knew what was going on. Genocide was a publicly debated topic. Carroll's poem or Darwin's *Descent* was not their first whiff of this. How they felt about it is something else.

One local newspaper, the Melbourne *Argus*, pointedly commented that the Tasmanians had been "in the most literal sense, 'civilized off the face of the earth' …" (quoted in Bonwick, *Last*, 351; no date given, but Bonwick introduced this article with 'some few years ago'). Note the use of quotation marks, as Darwin did when he said in a September letter to Lyell, "White man is 'improving off the face of the earth' even races nearly his equals" (CCD 8.379). This expression "improved or civilized off the face of the earth" had probably become a well-known euphemism for extermination. In 1872, one of Darwin's correspondents used it in a letter, expressing the hope that a Christian mission in Tierra del Fuego would "succeed in preventing the poor people from being 'improved' off the face of the earth" (CCD 20.49).

No matter how much they wept for the Natives, the logic of greed was more compelling still. They would not stop gorging themselves until the end result was achieved. That's what Carroll's poem presented. Darwin would say it contrariwise (reporting the genocide but denying its immorality) in his summary of what happened in Tasmania (in the long blocked quote at the beginning of this chapter), "the change of site did no good. Disease and death still pursued them … The infertility of the women is even a more remarkable fact than the liability of all to ill-health and death." Darwin makes it seem like it was their own fault, their own inadequacies, that killed them. Carroll is a lot clearer that they were tricked and eaten by the colonizers in their greed to have it all. In 1871, readers had a choice of whom to believe.

~ 6 ~

J. Langfield Ward:
Strangers in the Land of Their Birth

The year 1874 gave readers another choice. That was the year the second edition of *The Descent of Man* was published. In the same year, an obscure book (as most people would call it), yet the winner of a university prize, came out. This was *Colonization in its Bearing on the Extinction of the Aboriginal Races* by J. Langfield Ward. The year before, this long essay had won Le Bas Prize for 1873. This was an annual prize established in 1848 to honor the Rev. Charles Webb Le Bas, a Fellow of Trinity College. No one remembers it now. (I believe, though I am not sure, that it was last awarded in the 1890s.)

We do a lot of forgetting. Memory takes practice. We have to remember that while the humanitarians may have been a minority, there were enough of them (varying from the obscure to the well-known), and enough publications and republications of their work, that the public would have had numerous chances to encounter their ideas. Herman Merivale's lectures on colonization from 1839 to 1841 were first published in 1841 and republished in 1861. The 1789 letter from Samuel Hopkins complaining of the unhappy lives of free blacks in Massachusetts due to prejudice was first published in Prince Hoare's 1820 biography of Granville Sharp and then again in 1836 in Charles Stuart's biography of Sharp, not to mention all the other humanitarian material you will find in both biographies. Not to mention Sharp's own numerous antislavery pamphlets.

I once had a philosophy teacher, Professor Henry Wolz at Queens College in New York, who taught us that it is not always the big name writers, the classics, to whom we should look for truth, but to value the smaller figures for insights and glimpses of precious bits of truth which will surprise us. Many years later, I had an acting teacher, Jane Dentinger at Warren Robertson's Theater Workshop, who made the same point. Don't look down on the lesser playwrights, she told us. They too may have created characters on the page that are worth fleshing out. Forget the word 'lesser'. An actor's job is not to make judgments of artistic worth based on degree of fame, but to find life in the text—*any text*—and bring it out. This should be a golden rule for the study of history as well. Instead, academia gears itself to look for those who achieved renown and glory, and especially for anything or anyone that advanced the quest for power. Any voices in the past that did not do that get lost. These voices were not accidentally misplaced. This was deliberate.

My teachers taught me well. Famous voices aren't the only ones we should be listening to. There are obscure voices that had something worthwhile to say. We should pay attention. Their "obscurity" was not based on anything intrinsic in their work. They were pushed into obscurity by the powers that be precisely because they had valuable and compelling insights to offer. They were a threat to the interests of power or were perceived to be threatening. In the 19th century, anyone who did not give *unqualified support* to imperialism was deemed to be such a threat. And famous voices, like John Locke, whose fame could not be undone and who sided with the obscure, had to be rewritten to disguise what they said (in *DR*, 602-38, I extensively discussed how Locke's opposition to a cruel imperialism was falsely turned by the scholarly world into unqualified support for colonization). It would be a betrayal of everything I learned from my teachers, Wolz and Dentinger, if I did not apply their teaching to history. I have to do this, you understand.

At first glance, Langfield Ward does not give the impression of being a strong humanitarian. Deep down he is. It just takes a little diligence to see it. He generally does not adopt the voice of moral indignation to make his points. He is quite willing to put a good slant on colonialism and see good intentions even when they are dubious. He blames the colonists far more than the government for misdeeds and even then, he often seems to limit the blame to a few bad elements among the colonists. He characterizes the early settlers as displaying "self-denial, courage, and audacity ... [and] perseverance" and praises them for developing self-reliant colonies which will be able to receive the excess population of the mother country (Ward, 4).

This is probably due in part to his desire to conciliate his fellow Britons and reassure them that the British empire is a vast improvement over the Spanish sort with its monstrous atrocities. When the British kill Natives, it is almost inadvertently: "if the aborigines must perish before our advance, it will not be by acts of monstrous injustice, but by the insinuating, though perhaps quite as fatal, causes which civilization brings along with it" (31). The colonists did not seek "perpetual warfare" but slipped into it through inefficiency (46-47). He holds Europeans "answerable" for introducing intoxicating liquors and diseases, but adds, "it is hard to see what more could have been done than has been done [to reduce the resulting harm]" (90).

In all this, Ward is a committed colonialist. He believes Europeans have a right to colonize and cultivate distant lands: "vast tracts of country cannot be abandoned to a few hunters; the world we inhabit was given us for something beyond that" (12). But there is a lot more going on his little book. If Ward is not nearly on the level of a Saxe Bannister or a Charles Napier with their passionate concern for the rights of the Natives, he is not that far behind them. Ward is a committed colonialist in whom humanitarianism has made deep inroads. His conscience nags at him. Native tribes are disappearing and that seems to him catastrophically wrong and preventable. "Is there no power to prevent the extinction of those tribes, whose downfall the colonists have primarily been the cause … Must we unresistingly allow their villages to be deserted and fall in ruins, their languages to be forgotten, and their very names blotted out? Undoubtedly duty bids us use our endeavours to stop this extinction" (100). (I believe that Ward and some other humanitarians were horrified not only by the loss of lives, but by the destruction of languages, as language represents the soul of a people.)

There is in Ward, as in most of the humanitarians of the time, an inherent contradiction. They saw much good in colonialism and believed in bringing a civilizing mission to the rest of the world, though they wanted this done peacefully and only by peaceful means. They assumed the Natives would welcome this, but they never asked themselves what if the Natives did not want the so-called benefits of western civilization. I think most of the humanitarians would have defended the Natives' right to autonomy and right to decide how much of these benefits to accept. Throughout the writings of humanitarians, you can sometimes see them trying to straddle both sides of this. What they were absolutely firm about was that cruelty and injustice, or any sort of force, were entirely out of the question.

While Ward affirmed the right of Europeans to colonize and cultivate land in new countries—"vast tracts of land cannot be abandoned to a few hunters" (12)—he also stated, "It must be conceded that the tribe should be allowed the continued enjoyment of its original mode of life" which meant that there should be "set apart a tract of land sufficient for this purpose" and in addition "a fair price … [offered to] the tribe [for] compensation for loss of territory" (ibid.) As to the very last part of this, it has to be lamented that Ward could add that if the Natives refused the offer of purchase, the colonists would be justified if they take up "arms in vindication of their right of occupation."

That Ward could say such a thing is indicative of the pressure that social conformity exerts (Agnes Arber's compulsive-intellectual-atmosphere-to-a-humiliating-degree). He was socially compelled to state the "rights" of colonists. But this last quoted comment stands as an isolated remark and does not represent what Ward really thinks. It is not typical of his thought as a whole. He may have said colonists are justified in taking up arms to occupy the land, if their offer to purchase is refused, but it is clear that he did not really believe it. Ward's usual mode is to stress peace (74, 134) and insist that one duty of colonists is "to respect the property of the natives" (16). Ward was certainly an imperfect humanitarian. But because he was essentially humane, his sensitivity always comes to the fore, as when he urges the British nation that we have to remain aware of the Natives "as smarting perhaps from a sense of injury" (15). He emphasizes "measures to discourage contentions" and "a peaceful settlement of all questions in dispute," especially regarding "the purchase and tenure of land" (15-16). Resorting to arms would never be his first or even second choice. It might be his tenth choice. Ward is really the epitome of "Give peace and negotiation a chance, and then more chances, and then more." To make him out to be an ardent colonialist would be a severe misinterpretation of him.

Ward understands that there is an inherent greed in colonialism as a whole which is unfair and devastating to the Native population. 'Aggrandisement' comes up a couple of times (18, 102) and even 'cupidity' (110). As long as cultivation is profitable to the colonists, "the natives will be continually dispossessed" (94; cf. 21). Dispossession (or encroachment) is one of the causes of war. A Native tribe "cannot be expected to acquiesce tamely in the gradual appropriation of its territory" (71). Dispossession Ward considers to be an indirect cause of extinction, as it brings on war and aids disease (95), so that "the colonists have primarily been the cause" of the extinction of tribes (100). With great understatement, he says that even in colonies where we have done much better, "we have not always used fair means in extending our territory" (47; cf. 64). He considers "the land question" the most difficult of all (75). He is sympathetic to Aboriginal inhabitants who have been forced to live in a corner of their land and then been dispossessed of even that corner (91-92). By the end of his book, he is recommending as "the things needful ... a resolution to deal on equitable principles with the natives, a willingness to respect their rights, and a determination to avoid all disputes where it is possible to do so" (134; he refers to "human rights" on 102).

Ward can be patronizing when he speaks of civilizing and protecting the Natives, but even so, he comes up with something I have not encountered in any other writer of the time, at least not as explicitly as it appears in his book. For Ward, one of the purposes of civilizing the Natives, or elevating them as he sometimes puts it, is "thereby fortifying them against the impending danger" of extinction which results from colonization (101). As he explains, "the advantage of civilization to the native is that he is thereby enabled to offer more effectual resistance to the too rapid advance of the colonist" (114; cf. 97). Like other humanitarians, Ward realized that one of the main faults of colonization was that it was proceeding too fast (see near the end of Chapter 4 on Gerland for some of those who pointed this out). So here he advises that Natives can use western civilization to slow down the pace of civilization. The

Natives will be better "able to mingle and compete with the Europeans" (124). He even includes in this that they will "keep pace in military knowledge" (97). Ward was arguing that Natives should use civilization to combat civilization and colonialism, and that this would be the best use to which they could put the civilizing process.

This is a daring suggestion on Ward's part—and smart, as he was saying to the Natives that if you want to compete with Europeans, you will have to learn some of their ways. He may not have realized the full implications of what he was saying, but that may be unfair of me. Like Merivale and a few other humanitarians of the time, Ward hoped for amalgamation of the races (which would include intermarriage; see 130). He seems to anticipate that the Natives will not remain "a distinct people" (129) and he clearly thought the arts and sciences of western civilization were superior to Indigenous cultures. Yet in suggesting that learning western civilized ways (including military skills) can serve as "a stronger barrier of defence" (97) against colonization and offer "more effectual resistance" (114), he was implying that Natives can use some aspects of civilization to ward off its takeover and to maintain their own culture. Civilization for them would not be the outcome of colonialism, but a means of resisting and defeating it. To use civilization to defeat civilization—it's a grand thought. Perhaps Ward unconsciously hoped for this result, prompted by a consideration of all the injustices perpetrated against Indigenes.

Those injustices included the Natives being unable to obtain redress in a judicial system that did not serve them at all (at the end, in Note A, he gives examples of white people getting away with the murder of Aborigines). Ward knows that some Natives have been forced into slavery (e.g., the Hottentots; see 53, 138). He is horrified by the extermination of Native children and believes the colonists have thus surpassed the Natives in cruelty (76). When children are involved in or made the special object of extermination, "there is no hope for the nation" (ibid.) because the country cannot recover itself. Ward is clearly addressing acts of genocide, "this extermination, so opposed to all notions of humanity which civilization has introduced into wars," which cruelty he points out has been frequent in the wars against Indians. Further on, he notes that Europeans have developed rules of humane warfare among themselves and asks, "why should not the same rules apply to conflicts with savages as to contests with civilized nations?" (108). Ward anticipated Raphaël Lemkin's warnings about genocide by seventy years.

Ward reads an 1874 report on what is happening in South Africa (in Natal), detailing the enslavement of women and children and the seizure of cattle, and comments, "No one, who hopes for the spread of humanity and freedom, can read this paragraph without pain and humiliation" (140). The soul of Ward's book is contained in that one line. It is "pain and humiliation" more than indignation that prompts him to write. You have to imagine a man who is ashamed of himself and his culture, whenever he hears of the injustices and atrocities it has committed, to appreciate why he picked up his pen at all.

He is clearly no Darwinian. He denies that the civilized or the stronger have a right to take advantage of those they regard as the weaker party or treat them with contempt (100, 102, 114); he sees "the narrow-minded feelings of contempt for savages" (16) which he frequently refers to (44, 72, 114, 130). Of his fellow Englishmen, he says "No colonists have exhibited a greater repugnance than ours, to mingling freely with aborigines" (130).

And he is no Darwinian when he opposes the belief of "some scientific men and travellers in various countries, that wherever the white man is brought in contact with the coloured, the latter gradually but inevitably disappears" (40). It is a fair guess that Ward had Darwin in mind with that reference to scientific travellers. (Merivale too called Darwin a "philosophical traveller" [Merivale, 2.204], at a time when philosophical was often used as a synonym for scientific.) Ward here gives the example of an increase in population of Mexican Indians as a refutation of this belief, and further on (116-18) the growth of the Cherokee population. Some statistics contradict the inevitability. Merivale and Gerland also provided numbers for some Native groups that undermined the notion of inevitable disappearance. Darwin never paid any attention to statistics that contradicted the widespread belief among upper class scientists that Indigenous extermination was inevitable. Merivale specifically cited Darwin for missing this in Tahiti (Merivale, 2.210; the numbers went down for a while, he says, then bounced back up). Merivale also took note of other Aboriginals whose numbers have gone up, as for example the Cherokees and Choctaws in America.

Darwin, it must be said, remained fixed on the idea that declining numbers lead inevitably to extinction, or as he put it in one of his early unpublished essays, "decrease in numbers or rarity seems to be the high-road to extinction" (*1844*, 149-50). He never changed his mind about this. Throughout the section "On the Extinction of the Races of Man" in Chapter 7 of *The Descent of Man*, he is obsessed with tracing the declining numbers of Native populations everywhere, and with lessened fertility of the women, so that he will remark, "even a slight degree of infertility, combined with those other causes which tend to check the increase of every population, would sooner or later lead to extinction" (*Descent*, 218), and then will sum up at the end of this section, "decreasing numbers will sooner or later lead to extinction" (222).

Gerland had also used the Cherokees as an example of a Native population increasing and Darwin's helper took note in the margin on 126 in Chapter 20, translating Gerland's observation that the Cherokee population had increased from 10,000 to 13,500 in the years 1819-1825. Gerland also pointed out that Cherokee villages, economy, and educational efforts were thriving. Waitz too argued (again, in a book Darwin read) that "under favourable circumstances, severely visited peoples may recover their losses" (Waitz, 147) and goes on to give many examples (148-49). But in his own work Darwin ignored such reports. In the same Chapter 20, Gerland also made an important point about Samoa that can serve as a more general insight: if a people can get over the deleterious consequences of the initial impact of colonization, their population can begin to climb again (Gerland, 131). That initial shock, or reaction to it, was all-important in determining how well a people survived.

Ward's different approach from Darwin's can also be seen in his attitude towards infanticide (see further below). Darwin was disgusted by this practice among the Indigenous. He often brings it up in *Descent* and uses it as an example of Native immorality. On the last page of *Descent*, Darwin describes the savage who "delights to torture his enemies, offers up bloody sacrifices, practises infanticide without remorse, treats his wives like slaves, knows no decency, and is haunted by the grossest superstitions." He implies at one point that savages are lower than animals for practicing infanticide (*Descent*, 66). This will be a bit of a detour from Ward, but in what follows, I offer some of what Darwin missed about this issue which other contemporary investigators did notice.

Historian Henry Reynolds points out that even when the Natives were not being killed outright, they had to live on the run in order to avoid white settlers and parties of armed forces: "... how quickly and frequently they had to flee. They clearly lived with constant danger and acute anxiety for months and years on end" (in Manne, 130). That left them in a "constant state of alarm" as one military officer observed in March 1830. This officer continued that "the frequent change of positions rendered necessary to avoid the parties must be very harassing to themselves and their families" (ibid.). Living in flight contributed to their deaths and especially to the deaths of their children. I don't know if Darwin read John West's *A History of Tasmania* published in 1852, as he does not mention West in *Descent*, but there is a pertinent quote from West's book offered by Reynolds which does bear on one point Darwin repeatedly makes:

> Thus, in their harassing life, parents and children had been divided, and families had been broken up in melancholy confusion ... Infanticide and distress, rapid flight, and all the casualties of a protracted conflict, threatened them with speedy destruction. [West, 2.66; quoted by Reynolds in Manne, 130]

(Note the word 'melancholy' put to more meaningful use here than Darwin's perfunctory mention of it in his published journal.) Where Darwin attributes infanticide to immorality, West considers it one of the results of the conflict. West was not the only one to see it this way. Darwin read Bonwick's *The Last of the Tasmanians* which also raised this point. Bonwick says the settlers noticed "a marked decrease of children" among the blacks during their prolonged war with them and attributes this to the tribes being "hard-pressed" in their flight so that sometimes they killed their children to prevent their cries being heard and sometimes to keep them from falling into the enemies' hands (*Last,* 106).

Children could also die from neglect. Bonwick quoted a Dr. Story: "Their being at war with the Whites may have caused the mothers to neglect their children ..." (388). *The especially interesting thing about this last quote is that Darwin omitted it, though he quoted another part of Dr. Story's remarks from the same page in Bonwick* (see *Descent,* 214). This is apparently a case of Darwin erasing a piece of evidence that was right under his nose. It did not help him make a case for the exceptional immorality of the Natives, so he removed it from his awareness.

I don't have all the facts on infanticide; and I seriously doubt that Darwin did either, but he constantly brings up infanticide as evidence for the low morals of savages. He never once advances the possibility that white immorality contributed to the high Native infant mortality rate. Mostly he considers infanticide as something the Natives practice because they cannot support all their children (*Descent,* 65, 141,168, 211, 296-97, 644, and especially 659-61), yet in his last reference in *Descent* to this, he clearly considers it an example of how indecent savages are, practicing "infanticide without remorse" (689). How did he know there was no remorse? Humboldt would have been appalled by Darwin's opinion. Never does Darwin consider that some of this may have been the result of European savagery, driving the Natives to live on the run (the part of Dr. Story's remarks that Darwin did quote vaguely hints at this, but not nearly as clearly as the part Darwin did not quote). For someone who believes in appreciating the complexity of every problem—and Darwin did this better than most scientists—that is a serious omission in this case.

Darwin also read Wallace's *Malay Archipelago* (1869). He would have seen there that Wallace spotted another cause of infant mortality in certain areas he visited. The women had to work on plantations. They either took their infants with them or left them at home in the care of other children. "Under neither of these circumstances can infants be properly attended to, and great mortality is the result ..." (1.257). Wallace suggested that the government and missionaries had a responsibility to improve this. His solution, however, only amounted to inducing the women to becoming more domestic, based on their willingness to adopt European customs.

As for Ward, he simply registered his opinion that infanticide was a slight problem "weighed in the balance against the manifold causes of depopulation which [colonization] has introduced" (Ward, 98). He refused to use infanticide as an opportunity to berate Natives for immorality.

Given all the bad results of colonialism, one can see why so many humanitarians were concerned about a stain on the honor or character of the mother country and worried about a disgrace to the nation. Even officials expressed this. One of the most famous of such remarks was made by Colonial Secretary George Murray in a letter to Governor George Arthur, which Darwin would have read in James Bischoff's history of Van Diemen's Land: The result of the extermination of Aborigines, Murray said, however much desired by the colonists, was "one very difficult to be reconciled with feelings of humanity, or even with principles of justice and sound policy; and the adoption of any line of conduct, having for its avowed or for its secret object *the extinction of the native race, could not fail to leave an indelible stain upon the character of the British government*" (Bischoff, 233; emphasis added). This passage was also given a prominent place in the 1837 *Report of the House Select Committee on Aborigines* (*Report*, 14).

This famous remark by Secretary Murray should be set alongside something else he said which deserves to be just as well-known, but has been completely forgotten. In July 1828, speaking in the House of Commons, Murray said that he shared humanitarian feelings for the Natives, but "it is my duty to respect, not only the interests, but the prejudices of the colonists, their habits, and even the errors into which they have been led" (quoted by Bannister in *Humane* [1830], 179; he italicized most of this). *This is a powerful admission. It reflects the pessimism of all the officials that the prejudices of white society were in charge and that there was little that could be done about it.* (Recall under-secretary James Stephen taking a similar position that nothing could be done about the colonists' destructive attitude towards the Natives; see Chapter 4, near the end.)

Also to be considered is a point I discussed extensively in *DR* (581-92). These officials gave very little thought to securing the legal rights of Aborigines. One such right was the ability to testify in court. Without that right, Natives could not get justice in court, which meant they had to resort to violence for revenge, which in turn prompted more violence against them. Some people of the time thought that the denial of this right contributed to the extermination of Native peoples. To use Murray's language, the inadmissibility of Aboriginal testimony could be said to have had extermination as its *secret object*, and as such, it added to the stain on British honor. (See the above reference to *DR* for more on all this.)

Murray was not the first to raise the idea of a stain. In 1813, Thomas Davey, the second governor of Van Diemen's Land, wrote of the cruelties inflicted on the Natives by settlers, "That he could not have believed that British subjects would have *so ignominiously stained the honour* of their country and themselves, as to have acted in the manner they did toward the Aborigines" (Bonwick, *Last*, 59; emphasis added). Darwin read this too, though much later in 1870 when Bonwick's book was published.

After Murray, another Secretary, Lord Goderich, sent a Despatch to a British officer on January 31, 1832, stating in pertinent part, "There can be no more sacred duty than that of using every possible method to rescue the natives of those extensive islands [Van Diemen's Land, New Zealand, New South Wales] from the further evils which impend over them, and to deliver our own country from the disgrace and crime of having either occasioned or tolerated such enormities." These enormities would have included, as referenced earlier in the letter, "a rapid decline of population, preceded by every variety of suffering" and "the work of depopulation" which caused Goderich to say "I cannot contemplate the too probable results without the deepest anxiety." This too is in the 1837 *Report* of the Select Committee (17). This language of indelible, stain, and disgrace is very old humanitarian language, as demonstrated by Granville Sharp in his 1769 anti-slavery pamphlet: "the tyrannical constitution of the British colonies (to the indelible disgrace of the British name) reduces the freedom of any poor man to so low a value ..." (*Representation*, 48).

The point was getting around on both sides of the Atlantic. In an Enclosure of 15 June 1789 to President Washington, in which he addressed some injustices committed against Indians, Secretary of War Henry Knox said, "A system of coercion and oppression, pursued from time to time for the same period as the convenience of the United States might dictate, would probably amount to a much greater sum of money [as opposed to the cost of a conciliatory system]—But the *blood and injustice which would stain the character of the nation*, would be beyond all pecuniary calculation" (emphasis added). In the same Enclosure, he also said, "It is presumable that a nation solicitous of establishing its character on the broad basis of justice, would not only hestitate [*sic*] at, but reject every proposition to benefit itself by the injury of any neighbouring community, however contemptible and weak it might be either with respect to its manners or power." Recall too Rafinesque's remark in 1836: "Instead of praising conquerors," it would be better "to stain with infamy their deeds" (*World*, 3329).

The idea of a stain on the nation was at the root of the Select Committee's investigation. In his testimony before the Committee (#4367), the Rev. J. Beecham found himself grateful that some "religiously-disposed" individuals in their treatment of Aborigines in the colonies "have to some extent redeemed our national character" (Coates, 91). It was generally acknowledged that there was a stain. The open question was whether and how it could be redeemed.

Indelible stains and honor were the language of humanitarians and it was not confined to cases of approaching genocide. Any gross injustice had the potential to stain. In 1830, Bannister, writing about the Caffres in South Africa, said that if we seize their land without attempting compensation, "an indelible disgrace will be stamped on us" and further down on the same page, "a regard to the national character should urge us to do justice to the rightful joint claimants of this little spot" (*Humane* [1830], 81). For the humanitarians, the honor of Britain was at stake in the colonies.

Ward was no exception to this way of thinking. After recounting the terrible slaughter of the Pequods by the Puritans in the early days of the American colonies and referring in general to the British failure to protect Natives from injustices, Ward worried that "our credit as a nation, and our reputation for justice" were at stake (Ward, 17). He brought up such sins as "the deliberate trampling upon all human rights, and the tyrannical conduct to the weak … and territorial aggrandisement" as examples of what "bring misery upon the natives and dishonour upon ourselves" (102). This was about ensuring the "happiness of the natives … confided to our care" (ibid.; there is some paternalism in this, but it doesn't affect his main insight about justice and moral duty [e.g., 15]). In Note A at the end of his book, Ward gives some examples from the colonies "to show how unlikely a native is to obtain redress from a functionary or a jury interested on the side of the colonists."

In 1833, Darwin used language about slavery similar to Murray's about extermination of Aborigines. Darwin wrote from the *Beagle* to a friend, "I trust they [the Whigs] will soon attack *that monstrous stain on our boasted liberty, Colonial Slavery*" (June 2, 1833; CCD 1.320; emphasis added). Darwin did not necessarily get this language from Secretary Murray, though he was certainly aware of Murray's remark from reading Bischoff. The interesting difference between Darwin's comment in this letter and all the above humanitarian remarks is that Darwin confined himself to slavery, whereas all these other comments were about injustice to Aborigines, or in alternative language of the time, free colored people. Darwin, it seems, was always more narrow in his minimal humanitarian concerns. If Darwin was impressed that exterminating a people or dispossessing them was as stain-making and dishonorable as slavery, he never let on. He never sees or acknowledges the parallel between these injustices. Be it noted that some of these comments on staining British honor or character as a result of how Aborigines were treated came not only from outsider humanitarians, who were probably the source of this way of talking, but from British officials. It seems that Darwin resisted whatever effect this may have tended to have on him, no matter who said it.

I am not claiming that Ward was pure and perfect. Almost all the humanitarians embodied a contradiction stemming from their commitment to colonization. I can offer two contrasting passages from Langfield Ward (in the first I am combining his remarks from two different pages in his book). On the one hand, he can make British colonization seem utterly benign. Our colonists "did not, as the Spaniards did, set out with a purpose to subjugate and bring slavery on every tribe" (46). English colonists often

> have endeavoured to gain possession of the land by fair purchase or barter, have suffered the natives to practice their own customs, have encouraged trading with them in an equitable manner, and have visited any offence against a native with severe punishment [5; this last especially sounds like wishful thinking] ... the simple plan they proposed to themselves was to raise up a settlement, acquire adjacent lands by purchase, leaving this area to be enlarged as the colony increased, and carry on trade with the Indians in an equitable manner, but not to secure more territory than was sufficient for their present needs, and not to interfere with the happiness and contentment of their neighbours. They were exhorted on setting out to practise all possible forbearance to the natives ... [46]

Further on, he says, "the colonists, who in spite of their fierce wars and massacres, had always endeavoured to exercise a benevolent policy to the Indians, while living at peace with them" (61). There is some fantasizing in this. On the other hand, he does see the injustice of all colonization:

> If the unhappy aborigines have been mercilessly chased from one district to another, so that they become strangers in the land of their birth, if they have had to suffer the extirpating effects of wars waged against them while they were defending what they might justly consider theirs, and if they have had to mourn the swift reduction of their numbers by diseases brought in by the colonists, we must expect them, if they have a spark of manliness in them, to make a stand against the usurper's further progress; and if in their endeavours to drive back the invader they commit crimes or acts of treachery ... we must reflect that their minds have been embittered by the

> long series of insults, barbarities, and oppressions, suffered at
> the hands of those who have banished them; we must think
> of them as men who have had hard measure dealt them; we
> must not give way to the desire for retaliation ... we must
> repress vindictive feelings, and as Christians we must be
> compassionate. [98-99; cf. 110]

In sum, Ward is an imperfect humanitarian, but he is a humanitarian of some depth. That last passage was written by a very troubled conscience. Hard measure indeed. He saw what it was to become a stranger in the land of your birth. It was an injustice that gripped Ward. Despite his praise of colonists in the early part of the book, he knew there was no equivalency between the atrocities committed by each side in this struggle. One side had an excuse. Being made homeless in your own land was a tragedy that staggered the imagination. It could make a human being crazy, and the Indigenous were humans just like us, so what should we have expected?

By way of comparison, here is a similar contradiction in Charles Napier. While half his book is a vigorous critique of racism and a rotten system of colonialism, the other half offers advice on how to found a successful colony, which Napier considers a good thing: "... it is glorious to people a new continent, and spread the language, and renown of England in distant regions" (45). Given all he says about how we have robbed the Aborigines, what does a successful colony mean except to make secure and lasting our outright theft?

Napier's is a book in which one can find a marvelous paean to colonization:

> in a colony all is new, all is interesting; we rise, filled with
> curiosity, we half shave, half wash, half dress, and then half
> mad, with high and joyous spirits, we jump on our horses,
> (our breakfast half swallowed), and away we go, the beast
> as wild as ourselves, *crossing the country as we please* [my
> emphasis]; all is new, all is animating ... New beasts, new
> birds, new fishes, are hunted, shot, and caught; we mount
> a new hill, and a new country spreads far and wide before
> us ... my pilgrimage through many countries; all crying
> aloud for *people* [his emphasis]: every where regions without
> people! [78-79]

At the very end of the book, however, he will call it a lie to claim that this land was uninhabited. And on the other hand, we get this heartfelt outcry against the injustice of it all:

We rob the natives of their land, we rob them of *their* food, (the kangaroo,) we then shoot them to protect *our* food (the sheep), and we not only shoot, but torture them for our diversion; and finally, we say, that they are incapable of civilization, because their stupidity does not find out, that we are a delightful people ... We call them *savages*, because they 'shrink under our courtesy,' and we denominate ourselves a *civilized* people, because we set up what we term 'national wealth,' as our God ... In short, we torture and shoot "*savages*," and call ourselves the most *moral*, and the most *religious*, and the most *civilized* people, in the world! ... if *I* am [appointed Governor of this new colony in Australia], I will not leave England without laws, that shall give the same protection to the savage as to myself, and those who go with me ... we must not then have a *monopoly of justice*. [96; all his emphases]

The contradiction in Napier is forgivable considering how unrelenting he is in his criticisms, especially his insistence that injustices against Aborigines must be punished, that violence and theft are out of the question as a means of dealing with the Natives, that "making savage and civilized equal in the eye of the law" (103) should be a main objective, that we must revoke "downright robbery" (103), and that "peaceful intercourse" and the interests of the Natives (103-05) should be the primary concerns.

Napier, Ward, and other humanitarians may have had their faults, but I prefer their contradictions to Darwin's apparent consistency—*apparent* because he had to erase a lot of evidence to achieve his consistently biased approach to Indigenous peoples.

What is significant about Langfield Ward's book is that it comes out in 1874, the same year as the second edition of *The Descent of Man*, and he offers such a contrast in thought. He does not believe extermination is inevitable; he does not exaggerate, as Darwin does, the importance of infanticide as compared to the multitude of causes of depopulation brought by colonization (98); he does not use 'changed conditions of life' when dispossession is the right word. Ward may be imperfect, but he is an example of what a little conscience will do. Look at Langfield Ward in 1874 and at Charles Darwin in the same year. One is famous, the other is not. One writes a celebrated book, the other a forgotten, slight volume. One is touched by humanitarian concerns, the other will not be moved. Darwin does not even come up to Ward's imperfect level of humanitarianism. That is as telling as any other fact I have presented.

~ 7 ~

Connect the Whirling World: More Holistic Evolutionists

In Chapter 3, at the end of the discussion of Darwin's antislavery position, I pointed out that Darwin's positive statements about non-European peoples do not add up to a consistent pattern, whereas his negative comments do. Another way to put it is that his positive assessments of Indigenous peoples do not flow from his system of thinking. They are the odd comment here and there. His antislavery views, as well as his strong feelings about cruelty to animals, are not the result of how he sees the world. They do not fit with the way he analyzes nature. They are rather add-ons to his basic thinking. It is very different with his prejudices about other peoples. They are woven into his scientific system. They flow directly from his deepest beliefs about the way nature works, or else he modeled nature on his prejudices—either way, he gave these prejudices a very deep standing in his worldview.

The exact opposite applies to the holistic scientists. Robert Chambers's antislavery views and his feelings about cruelty to animals probably have more than one source, but one thing we can say about them is that they fit well with his worldview (and they may in part be a result of that worldview). His humanitarianism is incorporated in his efforts to understand life on this planet. He wants to account for it in the system he envisions, not merely add on bits of humane thinking to a system that does not really contain them, which is what Charles Darwin does. Erasmus Darwin, Constantine Rafinesque, and Georg Gerland are like this too. They are all holistic thinkers and they want to fold their love of scientific inquiry and their pursuit of justice into the same mold. They feel the whole of life and try to see it that way in their intellect. Justice and scientific knowledge are not separate things for them.

The disconnection between his theory of the world and some of his humane inclinations is there in the work of Darwin because disconnection itself is a part of Darwin's view of life on this planet. Despite the fact that for Darwin life has a single origin, he sees divergence and disconnection among the descendants. Life now is, and for a long time has been, not about connections but about a hierarchy of groups subordinate to groups. Recall that even though Georg Gerland appeared to say something similar about subordination, the emphasis for him was on the whole of nature in which all groups are subordinated. That is true for all the holistic evolutionists.

This holistic thinking shines perhaps most clearly in Robert Chambers. For him, the world is so interconnected that what happens with each part has repercussions for all the other parts. Hence, justice and his scientific view of the world are intertwined. They are bound together into a single whole.

Chambers concludes his theory of evolution in *Vestiges* by arguing that slavery, war, and one class in society taking advantage of other classes ("if one portion of a nation … grasp at some advantages injurious to the other sections of the people …") are all similar evils (382-83). (Rafinesque drew similar connections when he wrote that "In war began the curse of slavery … may both evils cease together"; *World*, 3291-95; he includes in this train of evil the idea that the weaker are doomed to obey the stronger.) The system espoused by Chambers demands that slavery be seen as an evil. Opposition to slavery is not just a moral position that he tacks on to his intellectual process. It is a necessary consequence of evolutionary thinking. War too he regards as "a tremendous example of evil … waste of human life, and mis-spending of human energies" (365), "purely an evil, even to the conqueror" (366). Evil will always bounce back to the detriment of the perpetrator.

Chambers puts it thus: "an individual, a party, a people, can no more act unjustly with safety, than I could with safety place my leg in the track of a coming train …" (383). For good measure, he adds, "We have been constituted on the principle of only being able to realize happiness for ourselves when our fellow-creatures are also happy" (ibid.). God through his works (that is, nature) speaks this truth to us as truly "as if we heard them uttered in his own voice from heaven" (ibid.). Imagine that: Nature speaks as clearly as a voice from heaven. Chambers had a much firmer grasp on all things being bound in a common net than Darwin did.

What goes round comes round. That's the Chambers theory of evolution in a nutshell. It should make us humble in our relationship to the rest of the world.

This is not a small point. For Chambers, it is a law of nature that the evil a human group does will come back to bite it and all of us in our plumpest region. For Darwin, history goes in a straight line. It leads to the dominant and the dominant rarely, if ever, have to pay a price. Injustice is simply not an issue in Darwin's world. For the holistic evolutionists, injustice and the long-running harm it produces is a law of nature. We could ignore this law, but if we do, it is at our own peril.

Chambers would include animals among our fellow creatures whose happiness we must have regard for. In the fifth edition of *Vestiges* (238), he states: "A deep moral principle seems involved in the history of the origin of man" and since man's relation to other animals "is, after all, one of kindred … he bears from nature an obligation to abstain from wantonly injuring them, and as far as possible to cherish and protect them." In other words, we are all family. Darwin would never say it that way—"cherish and protect"—even though he certainly agreed about not "wantonly injuring them." We get some idea of how important this was to Chambers from the fact that it is a thought he keeps returning to. And so in 1846, in *Explanations*:

> [The development theory, which he calls 'the new view of nature'] extends the principle of humanity to the meaner creatures also. LIFE is everywhere ONE. The inferior animals are only less advanced types of that form of being perfected in ourselves … We are bound to respect the rights of animals as of our human associates. We are bound to respect even their feelings … we shall reap as certain a harvest of benefit to ourselves … Is our own position affected injuriously by this view …? Assuredly not. Our character is now seen to be a definite part of a system which is definite … The place we hold in comparison is humble beyond all statement of a degree; yet it is a certain and intelligible place. We know where we stand, and have some sense also of our chronological place … [and] the stage of his [man's] long descended history. [*Explanations*, 185-87; his emphases]

I am not aware that Darwin ever went as far as Chambers did in declaring that we should respect the rights and feelings of animals. Darwin was opposed to unnecessary vivisection and all cruelty, all wanton injury, but he was not opposed to all experimentation on live animals. He was always very clear that animals serve us. In a letter to a professor which was reprinted in the London *Times*, April 18, 1881 (available at D-O), on the subject of vivisection, he said it is his "deepest conviction that he who retards the progress of physiology commits a crime against mankind" (see Darwin, "Letter on vivisection" in Bibliography). He believed that vivisection sometimes furthers our knowledge of physiology, and in such cases, it would be a crime against mankind to ban it.

To Professor Ray Lankester (March 22, 1871; CCD 19.205), he wrote: "You ask about my opinion on vivisection. I quite agree that it is justifiable for real investigations on physiology; but not for mere damnable and detestable curiosity. It is a subject which makes me sick with horror, so I will not say another word about it, else I shall not sleep to-night." Anesthesia should be used whenever possible, though he gave no thought to how an animal feels when the anesthetic wears off. The purpose of his testimony before a Royal Commission on vivisection in November 1875 (also available at D-O) was to ask them not to recommend an outright prohibition on all such experiments. Chambers's "cherish and protect" is taking it further than Darwin was prepared to go. If Darwin ever did go as far as Chambers, he never expressed it.

Darwin was certainly aware of what he called the "horridly cruel works of nature!" in one of his letters (CCD 6.178), such as the female Ichneumon wasp which paralyzes, but does not kill, the caterpillars in which she lays her eggs, so that the larvae then eat the caterpillar from the inside out (see another letter, CCD 8.224). Darwin's grandfather had already given attention to this wasp in Canto IV, "Of Good and Evil" (in lines 31-36) in *The Temple of Nature*. The last two lines on the wasp are: "The cruel larva mines its silky course,/ And tears the vitals of its fostering nurse." I don't think Charles Darwin believed that nature's "horridly cruel works" gives human beings permission to imitate such acts, but I do think such cruelties meant for him that we sometimes have to tolerate this when human beings do it. Human cruelty just becomes a part of nature's cruel works.

One of the things that troubled Charles Darwin most about animals was their general lack of sympathy or love for other animals. There were some exceptions to this among animals. It delighted Darwin to collect animal anecdotes, especially of dogs and monkeys, showing signs of sympathy, devotion, courage, loyalty, as is obvious in *The Descent of Man*. But he knew that, all too often, examples of the opposite tendency could be given. "That animals sometimes are far from feeling any sympathy is too certain; for they will expel a wounded animal from the herd, or gore or worry it to death." He called this treatment of wounded members "almost the blackest fact in natural history" (*Descent*, 125). It is a sure sign of how much he valued love, caring, and affection—at least to some degree.

But Darwin could also be indifferent to nature's cruelties or even admire them, as in the following:

> It may be difficult, but we ought to admire the savage instinctive hatred of the queen-bee, which urges her instantly to destroy the young queens her daughters as soon as born, or to perish herself in the combat; for undoubtedly this is for the good of the community; and maternal love or maternal hatred, though the latter fortunately is most rare, is all the same to the inexorable principle of natural selection. [*Origin*, 202-03]

Why admire? He could have said this is fascinating to study, as he in effect does with the slave-making ants whose instinct he calls wonderful (*Origin*, 219, 223), meaning amazing. In fact, he connects the instincts of these ants and the wasp "as small consequences of one general law, leading to the advancement [i.e., improvement] of all organic beings, namely, multiply, vary, let the strongest live and the weakest die" (244), as he will also connect the behavior of the wasp and the queen bee (472). The ants, the wasp, the bees all participate in destructive behavior. In the case of the bees, Darwin chose to say we should admire them, which may be implicit in the other cases as well. It is interesting that he chose, as an example of admiration, individuals being sacrificed for the good of the community.

Hardly any extra steps are needed to go from this to Social Darwinism. Darwin was already there. What Darwin sees is a web of violence in nature, making up one great law. And while he may have been timid about applying these lessons at home among the lower classes of his society, he had absolutely no timidity whatsoever about being a Social Darwinist abroad, applying it to those regarded as totally Other, the Natives of other lands.

In Darwin's hands, a review of all these cases of horror—the wasp, the slave-making ants, the queen bees—serves to exemplify that law of nature, "let the strongest live and the weakest die," and ends up making human destruction of humans more palatable. If that is not the only law of nature he sees, it is certainly the only law he cares about.

For the holistic evolutionists, like Chambers and Erasmus Darwin, the cruel works of nature provided no lessons for human behavior. Grandfather Darwin could see the cruelty of the Ichneumon wasp just as well as his grandson and could describe nature as "one great Slaughter-house the warring world" (*Temple*, IV, 66). But, as far as he and the other evolutionists were concerned, this was not the great lesson to be learned from evolution. It was not a web of violence they were interested in.

But it was interesting to grandson Darwin, so interesting that he could latch onto his grandfather's words about the world being a slaughter house and perhaps over-appreciate their significance. He scored these lines in his copy of *Temple* (see Erasmus Darwin's *Temple* at BHL for information about Charles's markings). He also quoted his grandfather from another of his works in which Erasmus also described organic nature as "one great slaughter-house, one universal scene of rapacity and injustice." Charles Darwin said of this observation that it was "forecasting the progress of modern thought" ("Preliminary", 113). Perhaps Charles Darwin was more right than he knew about what intellectuals would consider modern, but it was not ultimately what his grandfather's work was about.

If dominant and weak species were presented to Chambers as important distinctions, he probably would have said they are bound together in one common life force. That commonness was the essence of evolution for him and not their ranking in their ability to destroy. "Constituted as its head … we are yet essentially connected with the humbler vehicles of vitality and intelligence, and placed in moral relations towards them" (*Explanations*, 185). Because he did not buy into the major *Zeitgeist* of the time (i.e., to dominate and to rule), as did Darwin, this became the major reason why he was and still is so disregarded. Flout the dominant worldview of your time and you are destined to be erased.

Chambers also takes it further down the road of humility than Darwin was prepared to go. Writers like Stephen Gould have always emphasized the humbling aspect of evolutionary theory—1) man is a late arrival on the scene, 2) we are part of life with the rest of nature, 3) we are not the end purpose of nature, and, therefore, 4) human beings have no reason to be excessively proud as if all of life were designed for us. But Gould and others are wrong to ascribe this kind of thinking to Charles Darwin. It was Chambers who championed this way of looking at life. It may be implied in some of Darwin's thoughts, but he never made as much of this as Chambers explicitly did. What Gould and others have done is taken Chambers's accomplishment and handed it to Darwin.

We can see their difference on this so clearly in how each responded to the implications of man being descended from lower animals (which was probably the most outrageous consequence of the theory of evolution for its opponents; Chambers and Erasmus Darwin had received plenty of heat on this issue). Both Chambers and Charles Darwin believed that mankind was the highest point of creation. If anyone has any doubts that this was true for Darwin, just look again at the last sentences of *Origin* and the end of *Descent*. In *Origin*, he says that evolution gives us "the production of the higher animals" (and "the Extinction of less-improved forms"). The first sentence of the last paragraph of *Descent* is: "Man may be excused for feeling some pride at having risen, though not through his own exertions, to the very summit of the organic scale." (The caveat "not through his own exertions" means it was due to natural selection, but the end result for Darwin is that there is a summit.)

Chambers's answer to the meaning of our descent from the lower animals is contained in the blocked quote above: "Is our own position affected injuriously by this view …? Assuredly not. Our character is now seen to be a definite part of a system which is definite … The place we hold in comparison is humble beyond all statement of a degree; yet it is a certain and intelligible place. We know where we stand, and have some sense also of our chronological place … [and] the stage of his [man's] long descended history." Man finds his meaning in the whole, "a definite part of a system which is definite." We may hold the highest place, but even the highest place is still just one point in the whole, and furthermore, it is the outcome of a long descent, and therefore it is "humble beyond all statement of a degree." Humility is exactly the lesson that the whole would want us to draw.

Chambers emphasized the humbling conclusion that man is a late development in the history of the earth. This is why the study of earth's organic history was rapture to him. This is what he got out of it: "*A time when there was no life* is first seen. We then see life begin, and go on; but *whole ages elapsed before man* came to crown the work of nature. *This is a wonderful revelation to have come upon the men of our time* [this last sentence is my emphasis; the previous emphases are his] ... [Organic life] observed a PROGRESS" (*Explanations*, 31). Notice in particular what he is calling a wonderful revelation: *Man was not created at the beginning, he is a late arrival* ("whole ages elapsed before man came to crown"). While Chambers may have called man the crown of creation (as Darwin called him the summit), he was very clear throughout his writings that it would be very strange to regard man as the purpose of creation, since creation went on for so long without him. The purpose is the whole, not any one part.

Very different is Darwin's response to the charge that man being descended from the lower animals is somehow demeaning. Just as very few people pay attention to that part of *Descent* where Darwin imagines that an ape would have to admit its inferiority to humans, so too they never pay attention to what he has to say about our lowly origins. In the last paragraph of Chapter 6 of *Descent*, Darwin admits that our pedigree is "not ... of noble quality." Unlike Chambers, he does not look to the whole for solace. Rather, he looks for the fact that there is something lower still: "The most humble organism is something much higher than the inorganic dust under our feet ... any living creature, however humble [i.e., low in form] ... [has] marvelous structure and properties." It seems that Darwin, with his strong sense of order and rank, could not see worth in something unless there was something or someone else beneath it. Hierarchy, groups subordinate to groups, always comes first with Darwin, not connections to each other or to the whole. We may be descended from low forms of life but even low life forms are superior to inorganic dust. If it were proven that mankind is descended from inorganic material, Chambers would likely have celebrated that too. 'It's all good' is his philosophy. Darwin would have to look for something that was even lower than the inorganic, perhaps a vacuum.

I don't think it is possible to praise Chambers too much. In case anyone disagrees with that, I should remind everyone that Chambers assembled much of the same evidence for the general theory of evolution (species biologically descending from previous species) that Darwin would fifteen years later in *On the Origin of Species* (1859). (Darwin had also done it privately in his unpublished essays of *1842* and *1844* before *Vestiges* came out in October 1844.) Chambers may not have been as meticulous and thorough as Darwin, but he saw the large pattern of evidence that proves the development (evolution) hypothesis is far more probable than the special creation hypothesis (each species was created independently of the others). He *proved* it and no one pays attention to that.

Mainstream scientists of the time deployed a phony outrage at the anonymous author of *Vestiges of the Natural History of Creation*, ridiculing him as an amateur scientist who did not understand science—a tactic that was so effective, it clings to him to this day. I call their outrage phony because what truly annoyed them about his work, which they dared not openly admit, was that in fact he had done a great job at assembling the evidence to prove that development or evolution was happening, meaning it was more probable than special creation. He put them to shame and they could not bear to admit it. The one aspect of their outrage that was not phony was how incensed they were that he would not go away. This truly upset them. Despite their attacks and intense loathing of him, his book went through ten editions by 1853 and kept getting better and better. Scientists were fuming.

To prove *that* evolution was happening, Chambers did not have to prove *how* it was happening. Those are logically distinct things. The cause of evolution was an extra that Darwin was going for, but it is not strictly necessary for establishing merely that species are, in some unknown manner, gradually transforming into new species. Darwin understood this logical distinction. "It is one thing to prove that a thing has been so, & another to show how it came to be so" (Notebook E 69). Most scientists felt that the proof for evolution was incomplete until the cause was sufficiently understood. I think Darwin felt this way too, but he never misused this as other scientists did. They promoted the illogical position that understanding the cause was necessary for the full proof. They asserted this over and over to block any attempt to demonstrate that the evidence for the occurrence of evolution was plentiful and right under their collective noses. At least Darwin never followed this.

As for Chambers, he had no interest in the *how* of evolution. In response to a scientist who criticized the author of *Vestiges* for failing to understand that material cause and effect cannot explain everything, Chambers said, "Cause and effect of any such peculiar character are never once alluded to there [in *Vestiges*]" (*Vestiges*, 11th, li). The cause was unimportant to him. He found it exciting enough to know that evolution was indeed happening and, in addition, that this was provable because a large amount of evidence supported it. That was all he needed and he was right. He hammered scientists for their refusal to acknowledge this evidence.

Chambers saw the importance of so many bits of evidence (which I discussed in more detail in *DR*, 402-10), such as geology and fossils (the vestiges referred to in the title of his book), the commonality of structure in various organic beings, intermediate forms and gradations (which he often calls 'links'), variations like monstrosities and sports (individuals born with marked differences from their parents), the variability of organisms in breeding or artificial selection (which, he correctly pointed out, showed that nature's creations were malleable and not fixed), embryos, rudimentary organs, and more. Chambers looked at all this and said, Whoa! He could see that the fact that the embryos of many different adult animals so closely resembled each other pointed to a common ancestor. Rudimentary or abortive organs also showed this. The commonalities between the bones in a human hand and the bones in a bat's wing also signaled a genetic relationship. In the sixth (1847) edition of *Vestiges* (a complimentary copy of which was sent to Darwin by the publisher), Chambers uses the term 'genetic' six times: genetic history (144), genetic system (154), genetic origin (156), genetic line (161; also in *Explanations*, 77), genetic relations (166), and genetic succession (166).

Chambers got it right: "These facts clearly shew how all the various organic forms are bound up in one ... fundamental unity ... one system ... *though it did not all come at one time*" (*Vestiges*, first edition, 197; emphasis added). This is a perfect summation of modern evolutionary theory based on facts and it was published fifteen years before *Origin*. As Darwin said in the conclusion of the sixth edition of *Origin* (637), "It can hardly be supposed that a false theory would explain, in so satisfactory a manner as does the theory of natural selection, the several large classes of fact above specified." The same applies to the general theory of evolution which is what Chambers was fighting for.

Chambers then continues: "After what we have seen, the idea of a separate exertion for each [i.e., creationism] must appear totally inadmissible. The single fact of abortive or rudimentary organs condemns it; for these, on such a supposition, could be regarded in no other light than as blemishes or blunders ... On the other hand, when the organic creation is admitted to have been effected by a general law, we see nothing in these abortive parts but harmless peculiarities of development ..." (197-98). Darwin constantly argues like this from his initial essays (completed before *Vestiges*) to *Origin*: Independent creation cannot explain these wonderful facts very well, but my theory makes perfect sense of them. Chambers was the first to publicly put the theory of independent or special creation on the run.

One might think that Chambers is taking a big leap when he says that the single fact of abortive or rudimentary organs is enough to condemn independent creation as a bad theory. But he is not far wrong. He means it is an extremely powerful objection to that theory. Darwin argues in a similar vein when, at the very end of Chapter XIII of *Origin*, he alludes to the facts he has discussed in this chapter (morphology, embryology, and rudimentary organs) and says they "seem to me to proclaim so plainly, that [the many organic beings of this world] have all descended, each within its own class or group, from common parents ... that I should without hesitation adopt this view, *even if it were unsupported by other facts or arguments*" (457-58; emphasis added). Chambers had made essentially the same argument fifteen years before. He too immediately followed his discussion of rudimentary organs with embryos and recapitulation (*Vestiges*, 198). He links some things in the same way Darwin would because the development hypothesis explains this variety of facts. Chambers seizes on rudimentary organs all by themselves as dealing a death blow to independent creation. Darwin makes the same claim based on a few more facts, but in principle, he is making the same argument as Chambers: Even a small amount of *powerful* evidence can overturn a theory and point to another as the better possibility.

Also, just like Darwin, Chambers saw that organic changes leading to new species would take a great amount of time and that this was a stumbling block for many scientists. "Time is the true key to difficulties regarding appearances of determinateness in species," Chambers wrote in *Explanations* (158). The period in which mankind has been carefully recording natural facts "is not sufficient to allow more than a chance of any transition of species being or having been observed ..." (160). But if we have noticed any changes at all, "may we not well suppose that much greater have taken place in the course of the vast series of ages here described?" (161). He had made the same point in the very first edition of *Vestiges*: "... the gestation (so to speak) of a whole creation is a matter probably involving enormous spaces of time" (*Vestiges*, 210). In historical time (which is "only a small portion of the entire age of our globe"), "the limits of species have been, to ordinary observation, rigidly adhered to" (211). Like produces like—that's what we observe in our small space of time. It would take an immense amount of time to see feet developed, internal lungs come about, tail erased. "Precisely such may be our difficulty in conceiving that any of the species which people our earth is capable of advancing by generation to a higher type of being" (211).

By comparison, here is Darwin in the concluding chapter of *Origin*: "But the chief cause of our natural unwillingness to admit that one species has given birth to other and distinct species, is that we are always slow in admitting any great change of which we do not see the intermediate steps ...

The mind cannot possibly grasp the full meaning of the term of a hundred million years; it cannot add up and perceive the full effects of many slight variations, accumulated during an almost infinite number of generations" (481; almost the same exact words, from 'we are always slow' to 'number of generations', can be found in the *1844* essay, 249). Here again is Chambers: "… the stages of advance [from species to species] being in all cases very small … so that the phenomenon has always been of a simple and modest character" (*Vestiges*, 222; cf. 276, "the external world goes through slow and gradual changes …"). I stress this because Chambers was falsely accused, even by current scholars, of promoting spontaneous change as the means of evolutionary transitions. While he did suggest that sometimes spontaneity played a role, his basic argument relied on gradual change. The fossil history showed him that.

In short, Chambers is important and he got it right (at least as far as the general theory of evolution goes). He was as incisive as Darwin (though not as meticulous) and obviously did his work independently of Darwin. So when someone like Chambers explains evolution and yet keeps racism out of it, that is significant. Not that Chambers did not occasionally make a racist comment, but it never becomes systemic in his thinking.

Like others of his time, including Darwin, Chambers had feelings about the superiority of Caucasians. He can make the occasional comment in support of that (most of this is in *Vestiges*, 306-10). "The Negro exhibits permanently the imperfect brain, projecting lower jaw, and slender bent limbs, of a Caucasian child …" (307) and so too the other races which are in the stage of the arrested development of infants. "In the Caucasian or Indo-European family alone has the primitive organization been improved upon … [all the other races] comprehending perhaps five-sixths of mankind, are degenerate" (309). The Caucasian race is the highest type (307). There is also an endorsement of imperialism as the Caucasians "fill up the waste places … [and] supersede the imperfect nations already existing" (310; cf. 367).

But Chambers was not stuck there. He was also capable of saying things that would upset a racist. He believed that facts showed "the possibility of a natural transition by generation from the black to the white complexion, and from the white to the black" (279). More significantly, the external conditions in which people lived greatly determined their appearance so that "elegant and commodious dwellings, cleanly habits, comfortable clothing … co-operate with food in increasing the elegance of a race of human beings" (281). If they are forced to live miserably, they will assume a degraded appearance. Skin color and other physical characteristics "are of a more superficial and accidental nature" (278; Darwin agreed with this). Take note that Chambers is not internalizing or biologizing racial differences as Darwin would. Chambers sees the possibility that an apparently degraded people will no longer be degraded if given the right environmental conditions.

In later editions of *Vestiges*, Chambers took this further and changed his mind about the presumed inferiority of savages. "The state of our knowledge of uncivilized nations makes us liable to error on this subject [how capable savages are of advancing towards civilization]" (11th, 243). He observes that all Native races should not be classed into one group. He again emphasizes that the conditions of life make a great difference and that even European civilized people will revert to barbarism under the right conditions (11th, 245). As I pointed out in Chapter 2, he approvingly quotes a long passage from Charles Lyell in which, among other things, Lyell states that contact with white Europeans may have caused some tribes to regress and that these tribes would otherwise have attained a more refined civilization (11th, 244n; from Lyell, *Travels*, 2.39). Darwin read Lyell too, but only Chambers took these words to heart. (I could not find the 10th edition of *Vestiges*, which Darwin read, so if Chambers included the Lyell passage in the 10th, then Darwin had a second chance to be impressed by Lyell's comments.) Given the bad influence of white people, Lyell concludes, "what caution ought we not to observe when speculating on the inherent capacities of any other great member of the human family." Chambers concurs with the entire passage. That would not sit well with any die-hard racist.

One could say that Chambers is not a consistent racist, or equally, that he is not a consistent antiracist. But the most important thing about him is that *he is not creating a system in which racism plays an integral role*. What racism we do find in him comes as a surprise. *Vestiges* is otherwise so large-spirited and so good-willed a book that we don't expect this harshness. Not only do Chambers's occasional racist remarks feel out of place, they are indeed out of place. They do not fit into his system of thought. They are from another world, another way of looking at things, and he is willing to give them up when he acquires more information.

In Darwin's case, his racism does fit his general scheme. It feels very much like he is building racism into his system of groups subordinate to groups. More information would not help Darwin, it would only interfere with the system he is building. *Origin* prepares us for the imperialism and extermination we will encounter in *The Descent of Man* (to be fully explained in the next chapter). In Chambers, racism seems like an accident. It does not match his general optimism and benevolence for all creatures of God. You get the feeling he could easily remove it and end up being more consistent, if you pointed out to him the facts of Native life and the justice of letting them live their own lives. As we just saw, Lyell's comments caused Chambers to reconsider his attitude towards other races. One could argue that Chambers is more flexible than Darwin, but I think it is rather the case that his system of thought won't allow racist ideas to last for long.

As usually happens, it was the consequences drawn from a theory that got investigators like Chambers (and Erasmus Darwin and Rafinesque and others) into trouble. His emphasis on holism, in which all have a humble place, and a world of rolling change (which was taken to be a threat to established social order) doomed Chambers to be a forgotten man, whereas Darwin twisting the theory to support the *Zeitgeist* of racism and colonial conquest ensured his more favorable reception.

Constantine Rafinesque's work is as large-spirited as Chambers's, but his focus was on the consequences of evolutionary theory, and not so much on the theory itself, which he took for granted. He had one evolutionary insight—species give rise to new species—which he repeats in several places in his writings (Darwin quoted one in the "Historical Sketch" which was added to *Origin* from the 3rd edition on), but Rafinesque never showed an interest in proving it or even carefully explaining what facts led him to this conclusion, which he took to be obvious.

When it comes to evolution, Rafinesque always says the same thing: Varieties become species and every species was once a variety. That's all he has to say about it. That's what he said in the quote offered by Darwin. It is what he says in Notes 22 and 48 of *The World*. Thus: "Every species was once a variety, and every variety is the embryo of a new species" (Note 22). He did not even think this was a new discovery. "The constant gradual progress of mutations and changes all over the world, *has long been surmised*" (*World*, Note 2; emphasis added), though I wish he had given examples. In another book, he includes an extract from a letter he wrote in 1832 to Dr. John Torrey (who would later be one of the executors of his will) in which he says:

> There is a tendency to deviations and mutations through plants and animals by gradual steps at remote irregular periods. This is part of the great universal law of PERPETUAL MUTABILITY in every thing. Thus it is needless to dispute and differ about new G. [Genera] Sp. [Species] and varieties. Every variety is a deviation which becomes a Sp. as soon as it is permanent by reproduction. [*Herbarium*, 11; his emphases]

In a narrow sense, that is pretty much the extent of Rafinesque's contribution to evolution. He never shows any interest, for example, in Lamarck's suggestion (made in 1809) that changes in external circumstances, the environment, somehow precipitate changes in organisms as they adapt to the new conditions.

Perhaps Rafinesque never made a bigger scientific deal of it because he knew how opposed the scientific establishment was to this. A year after he died, in an 1841 essay, American botanist Asa Gray, who would later become one of Darwin's closest friends and supporters, was revolted by Rafinesque's idea of new species deriving from existing forms (see Fitzpatrick, 54). Like everyone else, Rafinesque felt a need to put down Lamarck (*World*, 1191-1203, even misspelling his name Lamark). Chambers too was harsh towards Lamarck (*Vestiges*, 230-31) and Darwin was always unkind to Lamarck in letters to his friends and colleagues, making it up to him only in the "Historical Sketch" (in which he also partly corrected his original misjudgment about *Vestiges*). Promoting evolutionary theory was not a career-maker in the first half of the 19th century, which was probably the main reason Darwin delayed so long in publishing his work.

What Rafinesque was more keen on investigating were the consequences of this new view of nature, as Chambers later repeatedly called it. The first line of *The World, or Instability* is "I wish to sing the changeful ample world." When he compares racial differences to the differences we meet in any family, he says, "This is the human physical display,/ Of changeful nature ..." (2863-64).Words like 'instability', 'changeful', and 'mutability' (see above blocked quote) were Rafinesque's way of referring to evolution. Change was a good thing, and change for Rafinesque meant primarily this: It should teach us tolerance and love.

A world that did not constantly change would be "gloomy uniformity" for Rafinesque (*World*, 2262), or "dullest uniformity" (254), or "one dull mass" (257). It was "endless monotony" for Chambers (*Vestiges*, 385). The evolutionists believed the creative power of nature or God was ongoing. The unstable nature of the world is a sign that creation is still taking place in our time. Creationists believed creation happened only once and spent itself a long time ago. The new naturalists believed creation is a force so strong and so intrinsic to nature that it does not stop. Creation happens slowly over a long period of time, not all at once by a fiat that exhausted itself in one shot. The energy of creation has staying power. The world is still being transformed because everything in it is unstable or mutable. It was precisely *that* which frightened professional scientists of the time. If human cultures were an outgrowth of nature, then this meant that culture and social classes were not fixed and final either.

Rafinesque nailed it with his lines explaining that God "Ever gives new forms" (*World*, 1963), "the endless time ... never feels inaction" (3566-67), and "... the power divine inactive/ Can never be, creation still proceeds" (2245-46). That's a good way to put it. Divine power or nature's power, whichever way you choose to look at it, never becomes inactive. Why would it? Why would God or nature burst forth once in a fit of creative energy and then shut down? It makes no sense as a premise from which to study and understand the world. No wonder Chambers (and others) insisted that this new view did more justice to God's divinity and sublimity. It's also an amazing, brilliant idea.

On "endless time", compare this to Erasmus Darwin's comment, "Nature rises on the wings of Time," (*Temple*, II, 36) so that, as he said a little earlier, "the long line of Being never ends" (II, 20). Robert Chambers pointed out that organic life did not come all at once but "observed a PROGRESS" (*Explanations*, 31). This continuing creativity, or as Erasmus might have put it, this progressive formation of the earth and nature's productions, is "consonant to the dignity of the Creator of all things" (*Temple*, note on II, 122).

Where Rafinesque proposed that divine power can never be inactive, another writer, quoted by Chambers, called it "unremitting energy." In a long section added to the 1853 tenth edition of *Vestiges*, offering various authorities in support of his views, Chambers quotes a naturalist named Doddridge who refers to "a perpetual divine agency" and proposes that "… an unremitting energy … greatly exalts our idea of God, instead of depressing it; and, therefore, by the way, is so much the more likely to be true" (quoting from 11th edition, ii). That is exactly what Chambers thought. A continually creating God is more sublime, not less, and more realistic.

Darwin affirmed this idea too when he wrote that independent creation "makes the works of God a mere mockery and deception" (*Origin*, 167) and when he included in the second edition of *Origin* some comments which clergyman Charles Kingsley had made to him in a letter (CCD 7.380; Nov. 18, 1859; in *Origin*, see 2nd, 481; in 6th, 638). Darwin was thrilled to have received this. In a letter to John Lubbock, Darwin called it a "grand letter from Kingsley with a capital sentence on the theological bearing of such notions as mine" (CCD 7.433). Kingsley, having read the first edition of *Origin*, expressed his belief that it was a more noble conception of God that he created the world by beginning with a few "primal forms capable of self-development" rather than that God "required a fresh act of intervention" for each subsequent form (CCD 7.380). (Never mind that Erasmus Darwin and Robert Chambers had already promoted this idea.) As Darwin made clear to his publisher, it bothered him very much that there were people "who may … say that my Book is irreligious" (CCD 7. 410).

For those evolutionary thinkers who came before Darwin, continuing creation is connected to their sense of holism. They see all of nature as a whole organized being, set in constant motion. This is Erasmus Darwin's "webs with webs unite" (*Temple*, I, 244), "Life's subtle woof in Nature's loom is wove" (I, 252), "Rings join to rings" (I, 255), "the living web expands" (I,

259), and "connect the whirling world!" (I, 20). This is Rafinesque's earth as an "organized animal rolling in space" (in Sullivan, 188). As Chambers had it, "LIFE is everywhere ONE" (*Explanations*, 185). One life force and one set of organic laws running through everything and creating not a hierarchy but an equality or at least a profound brotherhood and sisterhood of being, because we are all connected.

'Connect' appears occasionally in Rafinesque's poem *The World, or Instability* (and just as a reminder, that last word 'instability', in Rafinesque's vision, stands for evolution and the constant creativity of nature). He imagines a common bond or substance in all things: "The latent fire is spread in ev'ry pore/ Of matter" (815-16). It pervades all bodies "To plants and animals, to man himself" (831) and finally "in all shapes, connections, e'er the same" (833). You can find it in the winds which "waft across the seas the floating vessels/ Connecting of mankind, the tribes remote" (730-31) so that oceans have divided us "in vain" (732). When Rafinesque speaks of humans connecting, he means the opposite of conquering and dominating. He means humans recognizing their common humanity. His vision for the future of the "Vast human family" is that we "By mutual trade,/ and many other links, will be united" (5305-06).

Naturalists like Erasmus Darwin and Rafinesque have often been accused of sentimentalism. That is unfair. They were realists peering into a human reality that Charles Darwin ignored. Life is not always about war and death. The more typical human experience is about peaceful connections and negotiation, what John Locke had called "mutual consent." The English, being a nation of traders and merchants, knew this in their bones. Long before they sailed far overseas, they had explored a sea much closer to home—the North Sea—and the peoples on the continental side of that sea were doing their exploring and trading too. The sea provided the means of "connection, not the barrier," Michael Pye tells us in *The Edge of the World* (36; cf. 38). "It was easy for Scandinavians to be in York, Frisians in Ipswich, Saxons in London, and the fact is so unremarkable that it is hardly recorded" (39).

The English traded and bartered and negotiated. One had to bargain over many things: the use and ownership of land, the value of goods, the costs and benefits of being an ally in peacetime and war, the trade-offs in politics, and information leading to any and all of the above. 'Negotiate' comes up only five times in Pye's book (the first one not until 150, and the others on 236-79), but it is implied everywhere. The North Sea brought "a constant flow of foreigners and foreign ideas that citizens needed some constant way to sort life out" (154). The British took their negotiating skills and, more important, their belief that peaceful negotiations come first, with them to new worlds over the vast oceans. Britain's initial contacts in its far-reaching colonialism were often of the peaceful variety.

So it was in Australia, as Lisa Ford tells us. "Though no treaties were signed between Aborigines and the colonial state, diplomacy, gift-giving, and negotiation formed the substance of their nonviolent interactions well into the nineteenth century" (Ford, 44; cf. 30-31). One result of this recognition of the independence of Aboriginal culture was that, on a regular basis, Aborigines were regarded as exempt from British criminal jurisdiction. So it was in Africa, as George Boulukos tells us: "seventeenth- and early eighteenth-century European travelers to West Africa looked at Africans first as potential trading partners, and therefore assessed the black people they encountered in terms of civility, religion, and willingness to trade" (Boulukos, 45; also, see 46-51). It was only as the British and other Europeans began to realize that they could enslave and dispossess Indigenous peoples, *and get away with it*, that they came to have racist ideas about the deficient humanity of the Other.

Conquest and racism was not on the mind of Erasmus Darwin. He was trying to give a scientific underpinning to what was originally the very English and human experience of living in the world through peaceful connections. In his huge medical treatise *Zoonomia* (Charles wrote the title on the front page of his Notebook B), his evolutionary ponderings are concentrated in section XXXIX.4.8 of Volume 1. Chapter XXXIX is entitled "Of Generation", the word used at that time for both individual reproduction and what we would call evolution. Charles read it carefully, underlining many parts. In his *Autobiography* (43), he states that on reading his grandfather's book "a second time, I was much disappointed, the proportion of speculation being so large to the facts given." There is a little truth to that, but only a little and it leaves out a lot. (His own speculations on Indigenous inferiority did not bother him, be it noted.)

The problem is that Charles Darwin set an example and the tone for how the history of evolutionary science should be studied. Because of his comments, Erasmus Darwin is remembered today as someone who had semi-mystical ideas about evolution but no real hard evidence. That is a falsification of the real history. Erasmus did not offer a lot of evidence, but he did offer some significant pieces and, perhaps just as important, he acknowledged the scantiness of his evidence and explained very carefully why this was not a bad thing. Moreover, his grandson was very aware of the reasoning he provided. In an Apology which prefaced *The Botanic Garden* (and which Charles quoted from in "Preliminary" [103], his biography of his grandfather), Erasmus ventures "to apologise for many of the subsequent conjectures ... as not being supported by accurate investigation, or conclusive experiments." But, he continues, "Extravagant theories ... where our knowledge is yet imperfect, are not without their use; as they encourage the execution of laborious experiments, or the investigation of ingenious deductions to confirm or refute them." All speculation is useful because it can lead to confirmation or refutation—that is, provided no one tries to pass off the speculation as fact. Charles Darwin pointed out in *Descent* (676) that even false theories (or views) can advance the cause of science (the full quote is provided two paragraphs below).

Here is a pertinent example of this: The presumed inevitable extermination of Indigenous people was a theory, not a fact. The humanitarians treated this so-called inevitable extinction of Native peoples as a theory and presented evidence to refute it. They were following Erasmus Darwin's advice. But that is not what Charles Darwin and other scientists were doing with the claimed inevitability of the extinction of allegedly inferior human beings. They did not present inevitable extinction as speculation or theory to be further investigated for purposes of refuting or confirming it, which is what Erasmus Darwin would have insisted on. Instead, it had become a fact for them. They were so sure of it. It became a false fact. This enabled them to evade the problem of presenting evidence for their theory because inevitable extinction was not a theory to them, it was a fact.

As Darwin well knew, false facts do great harm to the study of science: "False facts are highly injurious to the progress of science, for they often endure long; but false views, if supported by some evidence, do little harm, for every one takes a salutary pleasure in proving their falseness; and when this is done, one path towards error is closed and the road to truth is often at the same time opened" (*Descent*, 676). This is precisely what Darwin and company were *not* doing with the idea of inevitable extinction of human beings. They were not opening any roads. They were closing them. The impending extinction of Natives was not a fact, it wasn't even a good theory. They turned it into a false fact. That was very different from what Erasmus Darwin was doing with all his speculations.

Erasmus was throwing out a hypothesis (of evolution) and pointing out several bits that it accounts for. You could say he was making a *prima facie* case, leaving a fuller proof to a future generation. One response is to shove his idea to the side and discourage any more thought about it. That is what the mainstream science of his day did. Another is to say: This is interesting, I wonder how much more evidence can be mustered in support. That was essentially his grandson's response, except that Charles never gave him full credit (in the *Autobiography*, 43, he makes a very weak statement that his grandfather and Lamarck may have had an influence on him).

Here are some of Erasmus's insights from that section in *Zoonomia*: he reviews many varieties of the breeds of domesticated animals (which he calls 'artificial or accidental cultivation'); he concludes that many horses, dogs, cattle, camels, sheep have "… undergone so total a transformation, that we are now ignorant from what species of wild animals they had their origin" (1.501; his grandson also pointed this out; see *Origin*, 40); how malleable is the human body which undergoes changes from exertions and disease; he believed in the inheritability of acquired characteristics (like Lamarck and his grandson who also accepted this to a limited extent); from the great similarities in warm-blooded animals, including mankind, he reasons that "they have alike been produced from a similar living filament" (1.502). He builds to this magnificent flight:

> would it be too bold to imagine, that in the great length of time, since the earth began to exist, perhaps millions of ages before the commencement of the history of mankind, would it be too bold to imagine, that all warm-blooded animals have arisen from one living filament, which THE GREAT FIRST CAUSE endued with animality, with the power of acquiring new parts, attended with new propensities … and thus possessing the faculty of continuing to improve by its own inherent activity and of delivering down those improvements by generation to its posterity, world without end? [1.505]

If it is not too bold, then it is a reasonable hypothesis to pursue.

Insofar as Erasmus Darwin offered a definition of 'generation' (i.e., evolution), it comes in the Additional Notes (p. 6) to *Temple*: generation is "the production of new organization." This covers both individual reproduction and the evolution of species (following his grandfather, Charles would write, "… *generation* of *species* like generation of *individuals*" in Notebook B 63; his emphases). In *Zoonomia*, Erasmus points out, "Owing to the imperfection of language the offspring is termed a *new* animal, but is in truth a branch or elongation of the parent … it may retain some of the habits of the parent system" (1.480; his emphasis). It is a combination of a continuation of most parental features with slight mutations giving something new. The process, as he says, "is still involved in impenetrable obscurity" (1.484).

There are more suggestions in section XXXIX.4.8 of *Zoonomia*. After considering cold-blooded animals and even insects, worms, and vegetables, he comes to the conclusion that all organic life may have arisen from "the same kind of living filament" (1.507); he refers to it as "this idea of the gradual formation and improvement of the animal world" and notes that geological observations support this (1.508); he brings up the importance of sexual selection, so that the strongest animals propagate the species (1.503); "all animals undergo perpetual transformations" (1.502). Geology also comes up in his poems. For example, he specifically mentions geology in *Temple* (note on I, 268) and alludes to it a couple of times (notes on I, 224 and 295). From the fact that some parts of the land are older than other parts, he concludes, "The juvenility of the earth shows, that it has had a beginning or birth" (note, I, 224). Reasoning back to a time when the earth was covered with water, he finds that "animal life began beneath the sea" (note, I, 295; he also deduces this from the resemblance of animal embryos to aquatic animals; same note and cf. note, IV, 359).

We should remember that the public had been made aware of the prominent role played by geology in evolutionary theory before Charles Darwin came along. We have Erasmus Darwin, Chambers, and Lamarck to thank for that. Benjamin Disraeli in his novel *Tancred* had some fun with the idea that we can see our past and perhaps our future written in the rocks. He probably had in mind *Vestiges* when he wrote this, and perhaps Erasmus Darwin's work as well. I quoted a much longer portion in *DR* (383-84). Here is a brief selection of what an aristocratic woman, enthusiastic about a book on this new science, tells the young hero of the novel:

> First, there was nothing, then there was something ... I think there were shells, then fishes; then we came ... Ah! that's it: we were fishes, and I believe we shall be crows. But you must read it ... it is all proved ... It is impossible to contradict anything in it. You understand, it is all science ... Everything is proved—by geology, you know. You see exactly how everything is made; how many worlds there have been; how long they lasted; what went before, what comes next. We are a link in the chain, as inferior animals were that preceded us: we in turn shall be inferior ... This is development. We had fins—we may have wings. [*Tancred*, 1.225-26]

The entire passage reads like a satire of *The Origin of Species*, except that it was published 12 years before in 1847. Almost everything in Charles Darwin's work was familiar to the public well before *Origin* appeared on the scene. Note well that Disraeli was sensitive to the belief of both Erasmus Darwin and Chambers that our most ancient origin was in the waters (while most critics were obsessed with accusing these naturalists of giving us monkey origins). As Chambers had written, "Life has, as it were, crept out of the sea upon the land" (*Explanations*, 165; cf. 70).

Erasmus Darwin's reference above to "perpetual transformations" (*Zoonomia*, 1.502) is a statement about the changes in individuals from conception to death, but as he proceeds, it is clear that he believes this to be also true of the organic life of species from generation to generation. In the recapitulation of this chapter, he reviews conception and birth and how "the outline or miniature of the new animal is produced gradually, but in no great length of time" (1.526) and what is true of individual life may also be true of how the inheritable characteristics of an animal were acquired, "which may have been gradually acquired during a million of generations, even from the infancy of the habitable earth" (ibid.). He calls this "the gradual generation of all things" (1.529). Gradual transformations, or evolution in other words. Animals "have constantly improved, and are still in a state of progressive improvement" (ibid.). As he says in *The Temple of Nature* (in a note on III, 411), "... the great globe itself, and all that it inhabit, appear to be in a perpetual state of mutation and improvement." This is probably his clearest statement of perpetual transformations in organic forms or species. That means we are linked to previous forms of life on this planet. The first sensations, motions, or volitions (all these terms are used in the same poem, especially in Canto III) probably arose "in some primeval site" (III, 427): "They link the reasoning reptile to mankind!" (III, 432).

Erasmus Darwin finishes up his section on gradual development in *Zoonomia* by summing up the views of Scottish philosopher David Hume who, he says, "... concludes, that the world itself might have been generated, rather than created; that is, it might have been gradually produced from very small beginnings, increasing by the activity of its inherent principles, rather than by a sudden evolution of the whole by the Almighty fiat.—What a magnificent idea of the infinite power of THE GREAT ARCHITECT! THE CAUSE OF CAUSES! PARENT OF PARENTS! ENS ENTIUM!" (1.509).

Note what appears to us as the very odd use of 'evolution' in the exact opposite way we mean it today, while he uses 'generation' in our sense of 'evolution'. The word 'evolution' obviously had nuances in his day that it no longer has. He uses 'sudden evolution' on other occasions—as when he discusses electric shocks and sparks (*Temple*, Additional Notes, p. 59) and earthquakes and vapors (*Economy*, note on I, 105). (Maybe it should not surprise us that his work was one of the sources of inspiration for Mary Shelley's *Frankenstein*.) Evolution here seems to mean production. But Erasmus Darwin was also capable of recognizing evolution in a gradual sense in the 1791 *The Economy of Vegetation* (in a note on I, 101): "From having observed the gradual evolution of the young animal or plant from its egg or seed ... philosophers [i.e., scientists] of all ages seem to have imagined, that the great world itself had likewise its infancy and its gradual progress to maturity." In the same poem, he also gave us "And the great seed evolves, disclosing all" (IV, 418).

(Rafinesque gave us, "… living swarms/ Of active moving bodies, gradually/ Evolving from each other, thro' the love/ Of reproduction and of changes …" [*World*, 1284-87]. But 'evolve' did not become a fixed term this early. Just as Spencer used 'the theory of evolution' once in an 1852 essay, not to be picked up again until after Darwin's book; see Spencer in Bibliography.)

There is more than just an analogy (comparing individual birth and species development) going on here. Erasmus Darwin was using individual generation/change to make an argument for the *reasonableness* of generation/ change in species based on the available evidence. The major objection at this time to the idea that all organic life on this planet developed by gradual changes from a common ancestor, "the same kind of living filament" (in Erasmus Darwin's phrase), was to ask: Look at the diversity of life we have— mammals, insects, plants and more—how could all these very different forms of life have come from the same source? In *Descent* (185), Charles Darwin took note that many still entertain this objection and consider it "monstrous" to believe that animals so distinct could have the same parents, but that, says Darwin, is because they "have not attended to the recent progress of natural history." Nor, he could have added but failed to, do they attend to the arguments of his grandfather.

Erasmus Darwin's answer was to say: Yes, let's look at the diversity of life, let's really look at it, let's see how fantastic is the entire life of almost any individual organism. One and the same organism is now a tadpole and now a frog; now a caterpillar and now a butterfly; now an embryo living in a fluid, or even earlier a mere germ, now an adult human with so many organs; now a seed, now a full-grown plant. If anyone had *only* a frog or butterfly or adult animal or beautiful orchid to study, could you guess how it started? No, you could not. It is all just too wonderful, too amazing. (Cf. Charles Darwin, Notebook D 62: "The change from caterpillar to butterfly—is not more wonderful than the body of a man undergoing a constant round." That is pure Erasmus Darwin.) The development of widely different species from one ancestor is no more or less fantastic. As an argument against gradual development, diversity is no argument. It is rather a point in favor of the development of species as it parallels what happens in the life of so many individual organisms.

It is also worth mentioning that the chain of being, which most naturalists believed in, also supports the idea that very different species are related. If each link is related to the next, then no matter how far apart two pieces may be in the chain, they must ultimately be related too.

One concise statement of his argument in *Zoonomia* runs thus (1.507):

> Shall we then say that the vegetable living filament was originally different from that of each tribe of animals above described? … as the earth and ocean were probably peopled with vegetable productions long before the existence of animals; and many families of these animals long before other families of them, shall we conjecture, that one and the same kind of living filaments is and has been the cause of all organic life?

And why should we engage in such conjecture? What is the evidence that makes it reasonable?

His basic evidence was the commonality of features and structures. Even something as apparently distinct from each other as vegetation and animals have much in common: Both breathe, both imbibe nourishment, both reproduce, both engage in a struggle for life—to acquire food and secure themselves from enemies—both begin as seeds or germs or eggs, some animals and plants use the same technique of camouflage to fool enemies, and most importantly, both have a system of heredity to pass on their traits to future generations, with both experiencing mutations as well. (Cf. Charles Darwin, Notebook D 68: "What takes place in the formation of a bud—the very same must take place in copulation.") That is quite a lot of evidence to make it a reasonable hypothesis (though not proof beyond all doubt) that all life on this planet comes from a common source.

Both animals and plants seem to acquire beneficial adaptations for survival. As Erasmus Darwin puts it for vegetation: "Many other changes seem to have arisen in them by their perpetual contest for light and air above ground, and for food or moisture beneath the soil" (*Zoonomia* 1.507). The sound conclusion appears to be that there are general laws of nature applicable to all forms of life and that would include a law of generation or evolution. There is certainly more than enough evidence to establish a *prima facie* case.

For good measure, as Erasmus noted, there is also the fossil record showing that there were similar but slightly different organisms in the past, rudimentary organs like male nipples which suggest that male and female sprung from a common source, and the artificial breeding of animals and plants which shows that malleability is a feature of living things. The more we look, the more evidence there is that life flows and develops from previous life forms and, indeed, can probably be traced back to one original life form. This was an exciting discovery to Erasmus and other early evolutionists.

I would not argue that Erasmus Darwin made his case beyond all doubt. But he certainly, absolutely, for sure, made it an extremely reasonable hypothesis worthy of further investigation. And that is the real sticking point in the history of this science: Mainstream scientists refused to recognize this accomplishment—just as they refused to admit that Robert Chambers made the development hypothesis more probable than not. They still refuse to see what Chambers and the first Darwin did. And Charles Darwin did no better on this score. He never acknowledged that his grandfather demonstrated the reasonableness of the hypothesis and Chambers the probability of it. Nowhere does Charles Darwin ever list all the evidence that Chambers brought to bear in the argument for evolution or the fewer but significant pieces in Erasmus's argument. To do so would have been tantamount to accusing establishment science of failing to see a rational argument and carrying out good science. That is not a bag of worms that Charles Darwin wanted to open. He was always ambitious to join the ranks of establishment science (as he tells us several times in his *Autobiography*, 67, 68, 115). He would do nothing to rock that boat. However good a scientist he was, he was always an even better politician of science. He would play down any accomplishment that might be upsetting to professional scientists.

It is all the sadder when you realize that Charles Darwin was quite capable of reasoning just like his grandfather. He knew in his own work the value of demonstrating reasonableness by pointing out the general common features shared by organisms. Here he is in Notebook C 154 proving to himself (that is, rehearsing an argument he desired to bring to public attention one day) that man is descended from, or genetically related to, lower animals:

> Animals have voice, so has man ... [s]hare of sickness, — death, unequal life,—stimulated by same passions—brought into the world same way ... Man has expression.—animals signals. (rabbit stamping ground) Man signals.—animals understand the language, they know the cries of pain, as well as we.

So much of the Notebooks and later works is like this: Arguing that a proposition is reasonable because a not insignificant pattern of evidence supports it. That is precisely what his grandfather was doing, yet grandson, as far as I know, would never publicly acknowledge this. Interestingly, in the same Notebook (C 123), he worries about being too far ahead of one's time: "Mention persecution of early Astronomers.—then add chief good of individual scientific men is to push their science a few years in advance only of their age." Erasmus Darwin was like one of those early astronomers. Too far ahead, not just a few years. Charles Darwin, while immensely admiring him, would not defend him, not even in retrospect.

Charles cannot be fairly described as a lone genius who single-handedly invented everything himself. Yet he himself had a tendency to see himself this way. In a letter to Richard Owen, he admitted that this is how he presented himself in a previous conversation he had with him, "You smiled at me for sticking myself up as a martyr" (Dec. 13, 1859; CCD 7.430). He begins *The Origin of Species* with an unrealistic sense of self-importance: "When on board H.M.S. *Beagle*, as naturalist, I was much struck with certain facts in the distribution of the inhabitants of South America, and in the geological relations of the present to the past inhabitants of that continent." And he was still thinking of himself this way in a late letter: "When I was on board the *Beagle* I believed in the permanence of species, but, as far as I can remember, vague doubts occasionally flitted across my mind. On my return home in the autumn of 1836 I immediately began to prepare my journal for publication, and then saw how many facts indicated the common descent of species" (ML 1.367). There is the myth in all its glory: Darwin takes a trip, is tantalized by doubts, comes home and assembles the facts he had gathered and sees the theory of evolution—I did this, I did that, I was struck, I believed, my mind having doubts, all without the slightest hint that certain facts and an outlook, both given to him by other naturalists, were bending his mind in a certain direction.

A myth is all it is. Darwin did not take that journey on the *Beagle* all by himself with a blank slate of a mind. His grandfather's and Lamarck's ideas and observations accompanied him. If Darwin had doubts about the immutability of species on his voyage, it is because his grandfather and Lamarck put them there. If he was struck by certain facts (as he says in that first sentence of *Origin*), it was because his grandfather and Lamarck had in effect told him to be on the lookout for such facts. He was gathering a wider range of facts, but he was looking for them because both these natural scientists had alerted him to a basic pattern of evidence for the transmutation of species. Not only were these previous scientists with him on the voyage, but when he returned and started keeping Notebooks to think all this through, he did not do this all by his lonesome self—*he kept returning to Erasmus Darwin and Jean-Baptiste Lamarck*. Having made his own observations, he still could not put his predecessors down. They helped him before, during, and after the voyage. Yet he keeps silent about that in *Origin* and in subsequent writings.

And if exaggerating the singularity of Charles Darwin's work is historically unfair, it is equally unfair to hold Erasmus and company responsible for the way their work was undervalued in their own time. Only consider how a little positive reinforcement about how interesting his ideas were might have prompted an Erasmus Darwin to think more upon it and look for more evidence. If he did not accomplish more, it is because his society made it impossible. The work of Charles Darwin's predecessors does not deserve to be belittled as less influential and world-changing, which it often is by the know-it-alls of academia who never had to live with the kind of opposition that these people faced. If anything, their work deserves to be celebrated as ground-breaking against all odds.

Here is a specific example of what I mean by the ground-breaking work of Erasmus. This comes from the note to III, 66 in *The Economy of Vegetation*. Erasmus Darwin observes that there are examples of common fossils of shells which are not in existence today, while some shells which are plentiful today are rarely found as fossils. He asks: "do some genera of animals perish by the increasing power of their enemies? Or do they still reside at inaccessible depths in the sea? Or do some animals change their forms gradually and become new genera?"

He was asking the right questions. That is not as easy as it looks. It is false to say he did not get as far as his grandson. It is true to say Charles Darwin started from a more advanced position, in part due to his grandfather. Extinction and the age of the earth were still open questions in the late 18th century. Erasmus Darwin had to look at all the possibilities. There was not enough solid information in his day to narrow them down. So extinction was one hypothesis. New evolved forms was another. A majority of scientists found these hypotheses literally unthinkable. What is great about Erasmus Darwin is that he can come up with these hypotheses. The confirmed opinion that transmutation of species could not possibly be taking place does not inhibit him from asking the right questions. He poses all the right hypotheses (and publicly no less!) no matter that contemporary scientific opinion automatically precluded some of them. How many really understand what an incredible accomplishment that is? It is almost impossible to think that clearly when the social pressure of established science is telling you to drop it.

Remember what Gertrude Stein once said: "No one is ahead of his time." True enough and it is no less true for Erasmus than it is for Charles. But she added: "it is only that the particular variety of creating his time is the one that his contemporaries who also are creating their own time refuse to accept … and the things refused are only important if unexpectedly somebody happens to need them" (*Masterpieces*, 27). They didn't need it when Erasmus was writing, they needed it when Charles was there. *That* is the essential difference between them, and not any inherent value in their work.

The point to reviewing all the evidence that Erasmus Darwin assembled for evolution (from geology to commonality of features to embryonic resemblance to aquatic life to artificial selection) is that he *thought* about this a lot. Generation or evolution was not simply a mystical or poetic idea that occurred to him and which he championed because he thought it was beautiful. The evidence that proved this is a real biological process mattered to him. Evidence means a deep impression of *truth* was made on him. But what probably hurt Erasmus Darwin's reputation more than anything else is that, like the other early evolutionists, he thought a lot about the *meaning* of this truth, and what he saw was not suitable to the age of war and conquest he lived in. He saw brotherly and sisterly connections among all earth's creatures.

In *The Temple of Nature*, not only is he quick to tell the reader that organic forms "rose from elemental strife" (I, 3-4) and that "Organic Life began beneath the waves" (I, 234), but he is not shy about extending this to mankind: Even "Imperious man ... Arose from rudiments of form and sense" (I, 309-14). The lesson of humility should be clear and he will drive home the point in the third Canto: "Stoop, selfish Pride! Survey thy kindred forms,/ Thy brother Emmets, and thy sister Worms!" (III, 433-34). We are linked to all forms of life, including the reasoning reptile (III, 432). Erasmus does not stop there. Nature has given us emotions and an ability to imitate. He describes Sympathy coming down from Heaven (III, 367), who "Opes the clench'd hand of Avarice to the poor,/ Unbars the prison, liberates the slave ... And charms the world with universal love" (III, 474-78). He pleads that nations and kings must listen to this (490). Like Rafinesque and Chambers, he does not merely tack on moral positions to his science, he derives these moral principles from his science because they are embedded in his scientific views.

It was Erasmus Darwin's expounding on the meaning of evolution that scared the hell out of upper class scientists. It was a legacy that Charles Darwin had to overcome, which he did very early in *Origin*, by the end of the second chapter, with his statement that the dominant species become ever more dominant. That's what the upper classes wanted to hear, and Charles Darwin gave it to them.

In Canto IV of *Temple*, Erasmus will acknowledge how violent life can be, in "vegetable war" (IV, 42) and "one great Slaughter-house the warring world" (IV, 66; also see his note on this). In a very personal comment, he admits that "e'en I ... wipe the secret tear-drops from my eyes,/ Hear through the night one universal groan" (IV, 123-27). But he does not want to draw lessons for human behavior from this. His ultimate point is not just that sympathy and love must triumph, but that we must not live in fear which destroys the quality of life. He qualifies his own emphasis on sympathy by advising that while children should be taught to sympathize, this should not be overdone to the point that it has a destructive impact on their own happiness (note on IV, 130). More interesting still is his expression of disgust for religious preachers who "inculcate the fear of death and of Hell." He calls this promotion of fear "intellectual cowardice" (note on IV, 87). Reason should teach us not to live in fear. His overall tendency is clear: Conquering and domination, or anything that creates fear and harm in creatures of the earth, hold no appeal for him; rather "That man should ever be the friend of man;/ Should eye with tenderness all living forms" (IV, 426-47), and that includes our brother ants and sister worms, and this is because his sense of evolution is that all of life is "a transmigrating mass" (420).

For all that Erasmus Darwin and Lamarck influenced him—how much Charles Darwin relied on them when he was gathering evidence on his round-the-world voyage—Charles was resistant to their holistic interpretation with its emphasis on connections, sharing of a common lifeblood, merging into a single whole. He wanted distinctions and grades, not a sumptuous whole warmly embracing all within. Chambers would give us the tender image of a pregnant woman as an analogy for evolution: "the production of new forms, as shewn in the pages of the geological record, has never been anything more than a new stage of progress in gestation, an event as simply natural ... as the silent advance of an ordinary mother from one week to another of her pregnancy" (*Vestiges*, 222-23). It is not "wonderful [i.e., amazing] or startling," he said, but simply natural. The world was pregnant with new forms of life, making both the development of each species and all of nature comparable to a fertile belly—and not at all frightening.

Chambers would not only unite all organisms in a single maternal bond, he would stretch his holism to include all of time, so that past, present, and future were united and nothing was ever really lost: "the thrill of the lover, the mother's smile on cherub infancy, the brightness of loving firesides, the aspirations of generous poets and philosophers ... the tear of penitence, the meekness of the suffering humble, the ardour of the strong in good causes ... that *all these* should be thus resolved; fleeting away whole 'equinoxes' into the past ... gone, lost, hushed in the stillness of a mightier death than has hitherto been thought of! ... making of all the far-extending Past but one intense Present, glorious and everlasting!" (*Explanations*, 188; his emphasis). His hope is that there is a wholeness to the experience of life on this planet that achieves a kind of eternity (in God's eye?). If his writing here was a little sentimental, his point was that ultimately there are no winners and losers, no superior and inferior, no game of domination, in life or in evolution. The weak are as valued as the strong. There is only life, the process of pregnancy, in which existence is good for all and at every stage.

Perhaps not all the early evolutionists emphasized that change should teach us tolerance and love as much as Erasmus Darwin or Chambers or Rafinesque did, but it did make them all kinder and more hopeful in one way or another. For these first evolutionists, evolution did not favor the dominant, the powerful, and the strong, as Charles Darwin would see it. Chambers expressed the hope in his statement, "The system has the fairness of a lottery, in which every one has the like chance of drawing the prize" (*Vestiges*, 377). One day a species is down, the next it is up. Chambers truly believed in the gift of chance that comes out of evolution or the development hypothesis.

Darwin is often credited with advocating this view of nature and evolution as random, but that is false. Darwin never favored the random in his interpretation of nature. (In *DR*, 356-65, I gave quite an extended discussion of this. Darwin sometimes denigrated chance by calling it so-called chance. He believed in "fixed and immutable laws" [*Variation*, 2.301]; see *DR*, 359, for the full context of this.) His system was geared to ensconce the dominant species in power and keep them there. This was fixed and determined, and not left to chance. In *Origin*, before he gets to the struggle for existence (Ch. III) and natural selection (Ch. IV), Darwin at the end of Chapter II is telling the reader that "throughout nature the forms of life which are now dominant tend to become still more dominant by leaving many modified and dominant descendants" (59). This is way too early in the book to be telling the reader this, but it makes sense when you realize that Darwin wanted to distinguish and distance himself from the previous evolutionists.

Up until the end of Chapter II, readers had not read anything in *Origin* with which they were not already familiar from the anonymous *Vestiges* and *Explanations*. Chapter I was devoted to arguing that artificial selection or breeding demonstrated that organisms are malleable and Chapter II that terms like 'variety' and 'species' are arbitrary. Robert Chambers had already given plenty of emphasis to both these points and had drawn the two conclusions that we are all connected in the wonderful system of nature and that the system is indeed a lottery giving hope to the poorly endowed that they might be favored one day. Darwin needed to toss these conclusions way and alert his upper class readers to the point that his system would be different in that it gave more hope to the dominant species or classes. He needed to let the reader know that even though everything they had read so far in Chapters I and II was just like the previous development hypothesis, he was actually headed in a different direction.

There is one important qualification to be made to this. I think that the wisest sentence Darwin ever wrote was in *Descent* (167): "Natural selection acts only tentatively." He had said the same thing in *Origin* (126) this way: "But which groups will ultimately prevail, no man can predict; for we well know that many groups, formerly most extensively developed, have now become extinct." And again (ibid.): "... of the species living at any one period, extremely few will transmit descendants to a remote futurity."

In theory, Darwin understood that natural selection gives nothing permanent. A species may think (if it could think) that its descendants will be around forever, but most will find disappointment in the long road ahead.

One could say this made Darwin and many of his contemporaries nervous. Our fate is out of our hands. The realization, which blossomed in the late 18th century, that extinction had happened often in organic history was a shock to western thought. How the west would respond to this knowledge turned out to be a true test of the moral character of the west.

Darwin's reaction to this was two-fold. One, he would choose not to harp on natural selection's tentative nature, and two, he would rather give emphasis to how a species could maximize its chances of surviving forever or for a very long time. The primary means was to become dominant and still more dominant and widespread (I will review this in the next chapter); in other words, the goal was to become a colonial power even if that meant decimating other peoples; better that extinction happen to them than to us. He put all his energy into thinking about dominant species and what is good for the dominant, acknowledging the tentativeness of it all only in theory and only in passing. The life of the dominant is what comes through in *The Origin of Species*, and not mortality and humility. For the holistic evolutionists like Chambers, the life of the small held more important lessons.

Chambers saw in evolution hope for the downtrodden and poor. Even if life handed you a disadvantage, it might make up for it in another way—so he continued after his remark on "the fairness of a lottery." (Emma Martin, as we will see in a few more pages, argued that there was no such thing as a defect.) This was not survival of the fittest, but survival of the doggedly industrious, regardless of fitness or unfitness or defects, the survival of the never-quitters, the ones who roll with the punches, the ones who gamble that life might hand them a blessing one day. Life is full of surprises, like a fish evolving into a human being. Who would have thunk it? And the reason no one knows what will happen next is that none of us know what the whole is up to. The whole is too big, beyond our comprehension, and has surprises in store for us. A combination of new scientific knowledge and humbling ignorance gives us hope.

This hopefulness about life expressed by Chambers and the other evolutionists did not sit well with the powerful who thought their job was to keep people down. The Chambers message of optimism was not founded on a dream, but on gaining solid knowledge of how nature works. With thoughtfully acquired information, you could accomplish almost anything. Gaining knowledge that would benefit everyone was a big deal to the kinder evolutionists. Because evolution was intimately connected with science and facts, it was also about knowledge and education. Chambers believed that the proper pursuit of knowledge would benefit the lower classes most of all.

Chambers's basic faith is that knowledge pursued with honest conviction can bring us "Daily health and comfort" (*Explanations*, 183) and might alleviate such ills as the death of children who die from "ignorance of the rules of health" (183). Though this came much later, I cannot help but note that Alfred Wallace, another holistic evolutionist, expressed concern for poor children suffering from the effects of air pollution. He concluded Chapter XIII of *Man's Place in the Universe* (1903), "For very shame do not let us say 'We *cannot* arrange matters so that our people may all breathe unpolluted, unpoisoned air!'" (his emphasis). These evolutionists were on a very different path than Darwin.

Chambers believed we need better knowledge of "the pestilences ravaging the haunts of poverty ... the neglect by the rich of the haplessness of their penury and disease-stricken neighbours ... the canker of discontent and crime, which eats into the vitals of a nation in consequence of an unlimited indulgence of acquisitiveness ... [and] degradation and misery which follow wars entered upon in the wantonness of pride, greed, and vanity" (184). All this is from *Explanations* but it's in the same spirit as *Vestiges*. There is, he is arguing, a law of life which dictates that from evil, evil comes. Sow bad seeds and you will get bad crops. What goes round comes round. What else should we expect?

The law of development (evolution) teaches us that "every act, thought, and emotion of theirs [of men] helps to determine their own future ..." (184). Screw others and it will come back to haunt you—which is precisely his argument against slavery, war, and one class in society taking advantage of other classes in *Vestiges* (382-83) where he says, as I quoted previously, "an individual, a party, a people, can no more act unjustly with safety, than I could with safety place my leg in the track of a coming train ..." (383). Unlike Darwin, *Chambers does not treat slavery as an isolated evil but classifies it together with other human evils*—like war and a social class acting to "grasp at some advantages injurious to the other sections of the people ... " (382). It is the philosophy of what goes round comes round. This is the fruit of holistic thinking. One part cannot do bad without other parts suffering. Goodness will reverberate too. This law of nature was more important than the law of dominance favored by Darwin.

Gaining knowledge was also a big reason why Emma Martin, an early British feminist, was so enthralled by the development theory. As a teenager, she was an ardent Christian, taking it to the streets, challenging freethinkers and atheists. But soon, she switched allegiance, taking up atheism with a vengeance and challenging religious people to debates, which she was fiercely good at. A lecture by one prominent socialist of the day, Alexander Campbell, in 1839 and her own independent studies had turned her mind around. She took up the cause of socialism and the rights of women. She said her change did not come overnight but was "the result of calm investigation." (For more on all this and her own development, see Taylor, 131-35.) She was a passionate speaker, attracting huge crowds, physically attacked on several occasions and at other times chased by crowds. She died in 1851, just shy of forty. In the last years of her life, one of her favorite lecture topics was teaching women to learn about their own bodies and take control of their lives away from male doctors (see Taylor, 155). She became a more dedicated atheist than most socialists were and lost some support from them. She pushed things to the limit, especially her belief in education and reason.

In the summer of 1844, just a few months before Chambers anonymously published *Vestiges* in October, she was in the streets again, handing out 4,000 copies of her tract, *First Conversation on the Being of God*, in which she argued for development theory. It is in the form of a dialogue between a Theist and a Querist. In one section (incorrectly labeled Theist, when it should be Querist), she explains:

> But suppose, we discover that the progression of development in general is matched by the progression in the development of individual being; for instance, every human being has passed through a variety of stages, each more advanced and complex then [*sic*] the previous one ... We know this is the case with the individual, may it not have been the case with the species also. [*First Conservation*, 5]

The embryo, she also says here, starts out as an animalcule, then resembles a "fish, and eventually becomes man." The main purpose of this pamphlet is to argue for materialism—the material world has a certain vitality in it which suffices to explain all of creation "without the intervention of an intelligent designer" (3). She goes on to argue that indeed man has developed from "the meanest insect" (6). We don't see new creations happening, "but they may nevertheless take place" (ibid.). She has caught on to the evolutionary insight that there is a creative power in the world that never lets up and that its imperceptibility to the human eye does not mean it is not happening.

After *Vestiges* and *Explanations* gained public attention, she gave a series of lectures on them in 1846. An editorial in one newspaper suggested that her followers resembled escaped inmates from the monkey ward at the Zoological Gardens (Secord, 318-19). Her teaching was the kind of thing that the professionals of science were afraid of. Novices, in their view, were using science to achieve radical social change. Why not, if all is in transformation? In another of her pamphlets, *God's Gifts and Man's Duties* (1843), Martin wrote, "I do not think that it can be *truly* said that there are *defects* in any department of nature ... [these varied operations] are not abberations [*sic*] from the laws of nature, but *portions* of it," and hence, she argues it is not really a defect, if it is part of the constitution of a thing (*God's Gifts*, 9; her emphases). There is that same generous spirit that you will find in the writings of Chambers, Rafinesque, and Erasmus Darwin. As Rafinesque had it, "Whatever has existence, must be true" (*World*, 5239).

"Go into the wide fields of nature, and by the process of an inductive philosophy, collect data which will teach you how to banish crime and poverty, and cause you no longer to be the victims of kings and priests" (*God's Gifts*, 16). This was not what scientists wanted to hear. Charles Darwin would have agreed with that last quote up to "collect data" but the rest of it would have baffled him. Note well that Martin was not preaching revolution for the sake of revolution. Her revolution was one that would be based on *collecting data*, on the secure knowledge of the true causes of the ailments of the poor and other disadvantaged groups. She desired that knowledge lead the way. Her own change, please recall, had come as "the result of calm investigation."

For Martin, all science had a social usefulness. Her main interest in development theory was that it was in accord with her atheism. It demonstrated that you did not need God to explain life on earth. But the development hypothesis was also part of her larger interest in education and science which she believed could be very useful to the forsaken classes. With thoughtfully acquired information, you could accomplish almost anything. When Martin said, "I would rather give my daughters a set of physiological and obstetric books for their perusal than allow them to read the Levitical Law ..." (in Taylor, 155), she was not thumbing her nose at the Bible or religion so much as at those who controlled knowledge. Development theory meant liberation, both from religion and the backward politics of secularists. Emma Martin took big risks promoting these ideas. And what did she get for it? Occasionally attacked at her lectures, her followers ridiculed as monkeys escaped from a zoo, poverty, sickness and an early death, and finally, mostly forgotten by academics who celebrate Charles Darwin as a courageous hero of science.

Some might wonder why I am always so hard on Darwin. It is true that I am critical of the way he distorted natural science by infusing it with racism and his callous attitude towards the extermination of Indigenous peoples. Most of my other criticisms, however, are not aimed at the real, historical Darwin. I accept the real man for what he was. The real Darwin did not take any risks to promote evolutionary theory and had no obligation to do so. Neither his safety nor his family's nor his finances nor his reputation were diminished or threatened in any way by the publication of *Origin*. All the previous evolutionists, but especially Chambers, had made it safe for Darwin to write about this. I am criticizing the fictional courageous Darwin who never had a real existence, and by extension and more importantly, I am critical of all the writers who have created and maintained this unreal iconic Darwin. What they have done with this fiction is to erase the people who really did risk something, who actually placed their lives and fortunes on the line.

It will be asked: What's wrong with creating a hero, someone young people can admire and imitate, even if the story we tell about him is a little false? It's more than a little false. Some will claim that our exaggerations about Darwin are relatively harmless and serve a good purpose. But it is not harmless. To manufacture a hero we have to suppress the real heroes and hide what happened to them—how they were treated in their time, what they lost, and how they have been treated ever since by historians. It is never good to obliterate the past. To accomplish that takes a lot of power and that much power is not good for anyone. The ones who have been kicked out of history will come back to challenge us. By getting rid of them we have left ourselves unprepared for the real costs of being a hero. They could have told us what was coming.

One incident, or rather two, may help to illustrate how academic solidarity has distorted the historical record and has hidden from us how the genuine risk-takers created a world in which someone like Darwin could publicly come out for evolution and not suffer for it. In 1847, at a meeting of the Geological Section of BAAS in Oxford, Robert Chambers appeared in person to present a paper on marine terraces and land elevation. While he was mostly a synthesizer of evidence discovered by other people, geology was the one science he did some original investigation in. At this point, most of these scientists were pretty sure he was the author of *Vestiges*, but a gentlemen's agreement honored anonymity. The assembled let him have it. They fiercely attacked his "audacious theorizing" as one called it (Secord, 434). Another observer, Andrew Ramsay, said that Chambers "got roughly handled" and that Lyell told him afterwards "he did so purposely that C[hambers]. might see that reasonings in the style of the author of *Vestiges* would not be tolerated among scientific men" (quoted in Desmond and Moore, *Darwin*, 348). The only one who had anything good to say about his paper was Darwin "who agreed with most of Chambers's conclusions …" (Secord, 435). Darwin had something that is unusual in a scholar and almost unheard of in an academic—he had a conscience. He even wrote to Chambers's family after Chambers died to apologize for his previous deprecation of his work (see further on). No one else did that.

Chambers had to have known that many of the scientists at that meeting knew who he was and still he faced them, fully aware of their harsh reaction to *Vestiges* and their likely impending attack at this public event. In church on the Sunday following the meeting, Chambers was also indirectly censured as 'halflearned', in a sermon before the assembled scientists, by the new Bishop of Oxford, Samuel Wilberforce. His is a famous name mainly because he later had a controversial debate with Thomas Huxley about *Origin*, which resulted in Huxley being rated a hero ever since and Wilberforce an enemy of science. The title of Wilberforce's sermon in 1847 was "Pride a Hindrance to True Knowledge". He indirectly berated Chambers as a speculative theorist who "grows to deal boldly with nature, instead of reverently following her guidance ... He has a theory to maintain, a solution which must not be disproved" (quoted at greater length in Secord, 436).

"Chambers, fuming in his pew, denounced it as an attempt to stifle progressive opinion," comment Desmond and Moore (*Darwin*, 348; apparently, Ramsay is the source for this also; Ramsay was approving of Wilberforce's sermon; see 708 n22). Secord reports that Chambers responded in an anonymous article in *Chambers's Journal* (the journal established by him and his brother). He said that the sermon seemed aimed "against the spread of knowledge" and that "the impression left on the mind was, upon the whole, of a discouraging nature. Once more the drag" (in Secord, 436). As usual, Chambers was right. On the efforts to suppress evolutionary thinking, Chambers was more perceptive and forceful than anyone of his time, including Darwin. Does brave even begin to describe Chambers in his career? When Wilberforce more than a dozen years later assailed *Origin*, Darwin's friends fairly leapt to his defense; wild horses could not have stopped them. Who befriended Chambers? Not one scientist. It took an outside source to offer some small aid. Says James Secord. "[T]he High Church *Guardian* condemned the 'great sparring march' [at the geological meeting] as disgraceful, Chambers being overwhelmed by sheer numbers" (ibid.)

The later Huxley-Wilberforce debate is a famous one in scientific circles and even in popular science histories. Huxley and others who spoke that day, like Darwin's other friend the botanist Joseph Hooker, are celebrated for their defense of scientific research against religious dogmatism. But the real origins and nature of this debate have been obscured by scholars. What historians do not like to remember is that it was scientists who made Wilberforce possible. They created the atmosphere in which a Wilberforce could flourish. On that infamous day in 1847, almost all the assembled scientists enthusiastically supported Wilberforce. They silently cheered him on. They had only themselves to blame when he attacked Darwin just over a dozen years later. These professional scientists had set that later attack in motion in 1847. The Huxley-Wilberforce debate is falsely presented as a conflict between religion and science. In reality, it was one more repercussion of an earlier moment when bad science (encouraging Wilberforce) tried to suppress better science (Chambers); except superficially, religion had nothing to do with it. What academic ever tells this side of history?

Adam Sedgwick, an illustrious geologist of the time, was another one who furiously attacked the Chambers book and much later Darwin. Sedgwick had written a scathing review of *Vestiges*, eighty-five pages long, in the *Edinburgh Review*, July 1845. (The review was anonymous, not unusual for reviews at that time, but everyone knew it was Sedgwick.) What has to be remembered for the sake of sheer truth-telling is that the Sedgwick and Wilberforce who attacked Darwin after 1859 were not the same Sedgwick and Wilberforce who had attacked Chambers so many years before. Chambers had significantly weakened them. He had performed a rope-a-dope on them, wearing them out, and then Darwin came along and polished them off. Chambers had never stopped coming out with edition after edition of his book (ten by 1853). Nothing intimidated him. It is true he had to publish anonymously. When a son-in-law asked him why he continued to remain anonymous, he said he had eleven reasons and pointed to his house in which his eleven children lived (Secord, 371). The threat to his family's security was real. Chambers once had to withdraw from a campaign for political office in Scotland because of rumors that he was the author of *Vestiges*. Darwin owed everything to him.

After Chambers died in 1871, still not officially revealed as the author, Darwin sent a note of apology to Annie Dowie, a daughter of Chambers: "I have always felt a most sincere respect for your father … Several years ago I perceived that I had not done full justice to a scientific work which I believed and still believe he was intimately connected with, and few things have struck me with more admiration than the perfect temper and liberality with which he treated my conduct" (CCD 19.208; this letter first appeared in another daughter's memoir, see Priestley, 41-42; also quoted in Secord, 510 n128).

Chambers's entire story is a lesson that the most dangerous forces arrayed against science come not from outside science, but from within. It is the scientists, who are ideologues and who shanghai scientific method to serve a selfish purpose (for power or material gain or the progress of western civilization), who do science the most damage. They set themselves against any fresh look at the evidence and they do it in the name of science. They pretend that science demands this evidence be suppressed. I cannot even begin to express how unholy that is. If professional science kept a more honest house, it would not have to worry about the dark forces outside its profession.

What probably hurt Chambers and Martin most of all is that they were working class, treading on upper class territory (i.e., science) and standing up for the working class. Why was development theory so appealing to workers? It meant everybody could develop and become something new. If the life of the individual recapitulated the history of species, as most development theorists believed, then the development of advanced forms of life in species gave hope that the individual could follow that path of advancement. Nothing was fixed and final. With the fixity of species giving way to ideas of transmutation, individuals could transform themselves as well. If nothing is fixed, then life is a lottery, as Chambers had said, and nature might favor those who took a chance.

Ah, but I have gone astray. I had been talking about Rafinesque way back, when I was waylaid by the temptation to keep connecting things leading to more things. Where was I? Oh yes, Rafinesque saw the possibility of tolerance and love in nature's fundamental principle of constant change. Change is almost always good in Rafinesque's eyes: God "Ever gives new forms,/ To beautify the whole by pleasing change" (*World*, 1963-64). But he was not all that interested in the physical cause of these transformations. He was more absorbed in the consequences and implications of the process. What conclusions could we draw about life, what natural system of religion would it give us? Constant change or instability, a creative process that never ends, organized within a larger system—this all implied tolerance and love as the overriding principles of life as far as he was concerned.

Rafinesque hated cruelty and intolerance. "Yet never dream to make all men the same/ In anything. It is beyond the bounds/ Of possibility ..." (*World*, 3789-91). To become less cruel was more important to Rafinesque than to become wise—eating the right foods would help us become of "milder mind" and "Not wiser, but less cruel" (3671-72). In this, we would be following God: "cruel rites/ Alone he hates, disclaims, and he desires/ To see abolished in ev'ry clime" (2084-86). Implicit in this was a theory of human rights: Ambition (or, one might say, arrogance and aggression) "tramples under feet, the human rights/ And duties; bathing oft in bloody gore" (3867-68). To repeat a quote I offered before, "Until [equality before the law is] secured, they deem themselves deprived/ Of common human rights or happiness" (the last lines from the Addition for verse 3116).

If the whole is putting its parts through a continual process of change, then the least that this demands of us is to tolerate change and love the variety, the constantly changing variety, that nature gives us. This is evident throughout *The World, or Instability*, but it is more explicit in some places than others. The following bits are quite typical of the poem as a whole:

> Every thing has chang'd, is changing yet,
> Must change; it is the mighty will of GOD.
> [3493-94]

Only God sees the whole truth, Rafinesque tells us next, and then:

> If we can teach from this survey of change,
> A law of God, that nothing can conform
> But for awhile, we shall not toil in vain.
>
> [3514-16]

And perhaps this is Rafinesque's ultimate statement on this:

> 'Twas wise and kind for him [God] to give us change
> In mind and matter, creeds, opinions, rites;
> As a sweet law to modify, improve,
> Adorn and beautify the whole of life.
> From this good law, let men at last receive
> The hint of toleration. ample full,
> Equal to liberty, in ev'ry case.
>
> [2253-59]

There it is, all put together in a few lines. The whole is overlooking this system of diversity and respect for each part. A couple of lines after this, he says, "Diversity controls the whole in pleasure,/ Dispelling gloomy uniformity." Diversity, instability, change—these were the great virtues of nature for Rafinesque. This was evolution. The idea that everything stays the same was a drag. You can almost hear Rafinesque say, as the earth spins and evolves, It's all good, or as he puts it, "Whatever has existence, must be true" (5239). He probably would have called Darwin's principle of the dominant becoming ever more dominant dullest uniformity.

The great lesson of evolution for him was simply: If God or the universe gives us constant change, then we should seek constant tolerance of this endless variety which is never fixed and seeks no fixed end. "Liberty of opinion and speech ... is the complement of tolerance and charity, fulfilling the law of instability" (Note 36; instability, recall, was one of his words for evolution). Drawing this conclusion from evolution was more important to him than finding the cause of evolution, more important even than assembling the evidence to prove that evolution was happening. "When shall we learn that toleration is/ A justice due to all, in any matter?" (3591-92).

It is not only never-ending change that should teach us tolerance. The biological bonds of all creatures should teach us the same. The earliest evolutionists remained truer to the evolutionary idea that organic beings are separated from each other by insensibly small steps and blend into each other, so that their deep connections remain intact. Darwin believed this only in the abstract. In practice, he was more attracted to the traditional and conservative idea that there are distinct rankings from lower to higher—everything is subordinated and not connected in a kind of equality. Holism gives us equality because the differences are insensibly small from creature to creature. A hierarchy of rankings gives us disconnections, which is fundamental to racism, whereas holism gives us connections, which is fundamental to antiracism. Hierarchy and holism could not be further apart.

As Jean-Baptiste Lamarck once put the holistic view, the very gradual gradations between species and genera mean that we have great "difficulty in determining what should be regarded as a species, and ... finding the boundaries ..." and, consequently, that "everything is more or less merged into everything else" (Lamarck, 37). This is much like Erasmus Darwin's webs unite, living web, whirling world, and transmigrating mass. This was holistic evolution. The lack of hard boundaries between creatures was crucial to these evolutionists. One life force, one set of organic laws, one mass of organisms blending into each other. Rafinesque called the earth an "organized animal rolling in space" (in Sullivan, 188). John Sullivan does not give a reference, but Rafinesque says pretty much the same thing in a passage that begins "Has not the earth her limbs and organs like/ The smaller bodies living there?" (*World*, 1325-26). Thus, the earth "moves and lives' thus has a soul" (1333). "Motion is life; but many motions claim/ The right of life ... in all directions leading" (1346-48).

Some of my favorite lines from Rafinesque are not his own but they do represent his thinking. They come from the school of Pythagoras and appeared in the one and only issue of his magazine *Western Minerva* (1821). Some of Rafinesque's fellow citizens of Lexington, Kentucky objected to his characterization of them as ignorant and uncouth. They went to the printer and had the magazine suppressed. In the 1949 republication, E.D. Merrill called it an example of early Americana. It is quite a hodge-podge on a range of subjects in the arts and sciences. The first entry is a collection of one hundred pieces of political wisdom from "Pythagoras and his Disciples," translated by Benjamin Franklin. The first three are these:

1. This world is but an atom, a small rolling ball.
    Let the plurality of worlds teach us humility.
2. The most powerful nation is but an ant hill,
    a bee hive. There is room for many on earth.
3. It is madness to dispute and fight for a few acres
    of ground, or for an unjust superiority. Let justice prevail.

"There is room for many on earth." It perfectly captures much of what Rafinesque's poem *The World* and holistic thinking are about. The above points read like an anti-colonialist tract. You can see why they appealed to him. If all you knew of evolution was Charles Darwin's exposition of it, you would never guess that evolution and anti-colonialism could be intertwined like this.

No. 39 in these bits of Pythagorean wisdom is "Where there is inequality of wealth, it is almost useless to speak of equality of rights." No. 61: "Tell to conquerors how many worlds there are to conquer." No. 69: "Beware of conquests, they are social robberies." And here is some real dynamite in No. 78, "All nations are equal, the earth on which they live is round, in order to prevent any pretext of precedence" (I think Tavis Smiley would particularly love that one) and in No. 98, "Do not despise other nations, else you will be despised by them. They are your equals. Avoid national jealousies, they lead to war." No. 100 ain't bad either: "Nations! do you want to know your friends? they are those who tell you the truth in spite of national pride and prejudices."

I have been selective in these quotations and I should point out that Rafinesque nowhere expressly agrees with any of this, but it is clear that most of these thoughts fit with his sense of evolution. The Pythagorean "room for many on earth" is so close to Rafinesque's sensibility. It is the opposite of Darwin's vision of the "dominant tend to become still more dominant." Rafinesque included Pythagoras for a reason in *Western Minerva* and that reason would have a lot to do with his feeling for the meaning of evolution. He was not the only evolutionist who connected the spirit of Pythagoras to the spirit of an ever evolving nature. Erasmus Darwin did it too.

Grandfather Darwin identified Pythagoras's doctrine as "the perpetual transmigration of matter from one body to another" and drew the conclusion that "all creatures thus became related to each other" (*Temple*, note on IV, 417). In verse form, it came out this way (IV, 425-28):

> … the moral plan,
> That man should ever be the friend of man;
> Should eye with tenderness all the living forms,
> His brother-emmets, and his sister-worms.

Yes, something happened before Charles Darwin came along. They were striving to create a world (all things netted) where science and justice were united. They didn't get there (there was too much opposition), but they kept trying.

~ 8 ~

Small and Broken

If we took away all of Darwin's letters, his *Diary*, and Notebooks, how much would we know about his racism? We'd know less, but we would still know a lot from *The Descent of Man*. What if we took that away as well? What if we removed all of his writings and were left only with *On the Origin of Species*? If that were the only book that Darwin left behind, could we still say that he gave us a science infected with racism? I think we could. Some of the clues are subtle and some are not very subtle at all. Altogether he leaves us in *Origin* with a very distinct impression about where all this was going in his view—some races are favored, some are not, and there is no brotherhood to relieve this situation of lethal competition.

The Origin of Species is a schizophrenic book. On the one hand, it is an objective work compiling the evidence to prove a thesis, or rather two, the general theory of evolutionary descent and the theory of natural selection, the means by which new forms are created. On the other hand, it is littered with dozens of comments coming from a European sense of entitlement and the right to conquest. It is very much a subjective examination of nature, as if it were out to justify European imperialism. Many have regretted that he put this into the subtitle, *The Preservation of Favoured Races in the Struggle for Life*. Richard Dawkins dismisses it as "ill-chosen and unfortunate", implying that it did not express anything deep in Darwin (*Greatest Show*, 62n). Tim Flannery agrees. He calls it "an unfortunate subtitle," as if it were a mere slip, and adds, "… only upon reading the entire book would one discover that the 'favoured races' did not explicitly include the British ruling class" (*Here on Earth*, 12-13).

I would reverse that and argue that it is the entire book that strongly conveys this impression. Some sentences are more explicit than others. Darwin notes the way organisms in Australia (*Origin*, 116) and New Zealand (337) fall before those introduced from Europe, and particularly those from Britain, and doubts their ability to compete with British and European life forms. He concludes: "Under this point of view, the productions of Great Britain may be said to be higher than those of New Zealand" (337). There is no reason to exclude human beings from what Darwin means by organic productions.

British forms easily take over in New Zealand (they "exterminate many of the natives," ibid.), but the reverse is not true; it is doubtful, he says, that New Zealand forms "would be enabled to seize on places now occupied by our native plants and animals" (ibid.). We can do it to them, they can't do it to us. Britain produces hardier races of organisms. It is a very small step to apply this kind of thinking to human groups and decide who is superior and who inferior. Darwin's readers would have had no trouble concluding that the British, and maybe especially the ruling class, were a "favoured race."

He has a similar take on Australia: "A set of animals, with their organisation but little diversified, could hardly compete with a set more perfectly diversified in structure ... In the Australian mammals, we see the process of diversification in an early and incomplete stage of development" (116; Darwin gives the example of Australian marsupials being unable to compete with our carnivorous, rodent mammals). His British readers would have had no doubts whatsoever about the meaning of this: We are more perfectly built (or carnivorous) than the Australian Aborigine. It is not very subtle at all. And it is very much like the racist argument, popular in Darwin's day, that the darker races were stuck in an infantile, incomplete stage of development.

Darwin had been warned about thinking like this by no less a botanist than his friend Joseph Hooker. In the year that Darwin was still working on *Origin*, Hooker practically begged him to consider that he was jumping to too big a conclusion from the fact that one species may destroy other species, when introduced into a new environment. I am not suggesting that Hooker was concerned about the implications for Aboriginal human beings, but he was extremely worried that Darwin was not being objective enough in his examination of the facts of nature.

On December 24, 1858, Darwin had written to Hooker, "The plants of Europe with Asia as being largest territory I look at as the most 'improved', & therefore as being able to withstand the less perfected Australian plants ... See how all the productions of N. Zealand yield to those of Europe" (CCD 7.221). I think it is right to conclude from this that Darwin was endorsing a concept of higher, though he does not use this word. Hooker certainly got the message. On December 26, Hooker responded, "I am horrified to find that you think Australian forms lower than Old World ones; because under *every method of determining high & low in Botany the Australian vegetation is the highest in the world*" (CCD 7.224; his emphases). He then gives six examples to illustrate his point and adds, "We cannot argue any thing by contrasting the multiplication of European forms in Australia & New Zealand with the absence of the converse in England." Here was Hooker registering a very strong objection to this manner of comparing organisms made by Darwin, even pointing out, "How often do I say all our arguments are edged swords."

One form wiping out other forms by its introduction to another environment is a bad way to measure what is higher.

Yet listen to how tortured is Darwin's reply (Dec. 31). He objects that he does not believe in lower and higher, but clearly he cannot and will not give them up (his emphases throughout):

> I do not think I said that I thought the productions of Asia were *higher* than those of Australia. I intend carefully to avoid this expression, for I do not think that any one has a definite idea what is meant by higher, except in classes which can loosely be compared to man [Note how he makes man an exception to the rule that there is no definite idea of higher] … I believe a greater number of the productions of Asia, the largest territory in the world, would beat those of Australia, than conversely … But this sort of highness (I wish I could invent some expression, and must try to do so) is different from highness in the common acceptation of word … [After giving some examples of one organism beating out another] I do not see how this "competitive highness" can be tested in any way by us … Not that I doubt a long course of "competitive highness" will *ultimately make the organisation higher* in every sense of the word; but it seems most difficult to test it … I should be sorry to be forced to give up view that an old and very large continuous territory would generally produce organisms higher in the competitive sense than a smaller territory. I may of course be quite wrong about plants of Australia (and your facts are of course quite new to me on their highness) but when I read the accounts of immense spreading of European plants in Australia, and think of the wool and corn brought thence to Europe [Note the appeal to imperialism], and not one plant naturalised, I can hardly avoid suspicion that Europe beats Australia in its productions … I want to clear my mind, as perhaps I should put a sentence or two in my abstract [i.e., *Origin*] on this subject. [CCD 7. 228-29]

He so clearly affirms his belief in what he calls "competitive highness" (an expression he never used again, as far as I am aware) and then incredibly adds (a little past mid-point in the above) that this will lead to "*higher* in every sense of the word" (his emphasis). What to make of all this? Did the senses of *higher* for Darwin include intellectually, morally, and aesthetically? Likely they did. (The ape whom Darwin drags into an admission of inferiority [see near the end of Ch. 2] has to admit he is inferior on all these levels; see *Descent*, 150-51.) This is not a man who was committed to avoiding concepts of higher and lower, however much he protested that he was. I think it is also not unfair to conclude that it looks like Darwin was affected by European colonialism's success and that he was using this colonial venture to guide his scientific thinking.

Perhaps most fascinating of all is that Darwin never incorporated any of Hooker's points in *The Origin of Species* even though he was in the midst of writing that book when this correspondence occurred. He never tells his readers that there is another point of view in which some of the organisms of places like Australia and New Zealand are indeed very high. This is all the more remarkable when you consider that Darwin is famous for entertaining objections to his theory (natural selection) and the general theory of evolution. He considers those objections because he knows he has a strong case and can answer them. But that is not the case with Hooker's objections to the very subjective judgment of what is high. Darwin had no answer to this criticism, so he just ignored it.

I think the reason so many scholars have failed to see Darwin's subjective approach, with its commitment to notions of higher and lower, is that they play up the younger Darwin who seemed to eschew the use of 'high' and 'low'. They admire the idealism of the youthful Darwin and imagine that this Darwin remained true to his ideals in his more mature years. Famous to many scholars is that, in his copy of the sixth edition of Chambers's *Vestiges*, Darwin reminded himself in a marginal note not to use 'higher' and 'lower' but only 'more complicated'. Ten years earlier, not yet thirty years old, he had written: "It is absurd to talk of one animal being higher than another" (Notebook B 74). But even idealizing this younger Darwin is a stretch. Not only did the older Darwin not remain true to this, his younger self had trouble staying true.

The young Darwin (say, up to 40 years) was stating an ideal to be lived up to, but not one he actually operated by. He could not remain consistent. When comparing the songs of birds from different nations, Darwin writes, "Their soft-billed birds are inferior to ours, & our lark ranks very high" (Notebook C 256). He could have said the notes of some birdsongs are more complicated and some more simple, but he did not. When he gets to savages, he regards their music as hideous (*Descent*, 116; cf. 636).

In a set of notes which he labeled "Old and Useless Notes" (from 1838 to 1840), he used the expression "production of higher animals" (OUN 37), which also appears at the very end of *Origin of Species* and at the end of the *1842* and *1844* essays, and he put man "at head of series in which special instincts decrease" (OUN 49). In another Notebook, he refers to "highness in scale" (D 156) and "lowest tribes" (D 157).

He also referred to "superiority of Christian over Heathen race" (OUN 38). He seems to be doing the same when he contrasts "The difference between civilized man & savage" (OUN 30ᵛ), though he does not use the words 'superior' or 'higher' here. He describes civilized man as "endeavoring to change that part of the moral sense which experience … shows does not tend to greatest good … The change our moral sense, is strictly analogous to change of instinct amongst animals." He does not go on to explain savages, but by implication, he seems to be saying that savages are like animals in that they live by a morality which is more like an unchangeable instinct, whereas civilized people use reason and experience to make necessary adjustments. Without using words of judgment, he nonetheless manages to make savages appear inferior and more animal-like. In Notebook C 196, he reminds himself that "Mans mind, in different races, being unequally developed." He similarly ranked religious views, as did most people in his time. He noted "how faint [love of deity or thought of eternity] in a Fuegian or Australian! why not gradation" (C 244). He saw savages stuck in "wildest imagination & superstitions" (ibid.).

Most famously perhaps, the young Darwin could wonder in his journal, as so many scientists of his day did, which was the lowest human culture on earth. For him, it was a toss-up between Fuegians and Australian Aborigines (*Narrative*, 235n; *Voyage*, 194). In the original *Diary* (125), he seems to have tilted more towards the Fuegians of whom he says, "I believe if the world was searched, no lower grade of man could be found." Darwin never, not even in his youth, eschewed notions of higher and lower.

All this makes for interesting history, but I am getting away from my point that even if we did not have all these other documents, we could see Darwin's subjective approach in *The Origin of Species* alone. The fact is that the mature Darwin in *Origin* definitely committed himself to ideas of higher and lower among nature's organisms, and worse yet, relied on an intuitive understanding of these terms, abandoning all precision. Discounting any uses of the following words in reference to artificial selection, and any other uses not relevant to the present point, these are the number of occurrences of these terms in *Origin*'s first edition: inferior(ity), 8 times; superior(ity), 4; low(er, est, ly), 31; and high(er, est, ly), 40; for a grand total of 83. He obviously preferred low-high to inferior-superior. "Low in the scale of nature" comes up 6 times and "high in the scale of nature" 7 times (he does not always use the full expression; sometimes the context makes it clear he means in the scale of nature). Add to this 61 uses of improve (and its variations, usually as improved or improvement) in respect to natural selection, and we have a very strong sense of progressive development in Darwin's thinking.

Twice Darwin tells us that organisms which came later in evolution are generally higher than organisms that developed earlier because they can beat and exterminate them (336-37, 476); "the more recent forms must, on my theory, be higher than the more ancient" (337), but he admits that "I can see no way of testing this sort of progress." The important point is that he believes lethal competition does give us progress. This is also where he asserts that Britain's organic productions are higher than those of New Zealand.

Look at what he says about the butterfly and caterpillar. He admits that "it is hardly possible to define clearly what is meant by the organization [of the parts of an organic being] being higher or lower" and then adds, as an example, that "no one probably will dispute that the butterfly is higher than the caterpillar," even though we don't know how to define that (*Origin*, 441). He does consider some ways that the larva may be higher in scale than the mature animal, but, again, he does all this with ill-defined ideas of higher and lower. It was the common view that no one disagreed with.

So too with the category of race and notions of superior and inferior. This was how groups of human beings were classified. Darwin saw no reason to dispute it. He was trapped. As Agnes Arber put it, "the general intellectual atmosphere of any given moment has an effect ... which is compulsive to a humiliating degree" (Arber, 7). Darwin was not out to revolutionize the categories of humankind or nature. He made that very clear in *The Origin of Species*. His goal was to explain and justify, not overturn, the rankings that his society already believed in. He accepted the system of classification as devised by naturalists over the centuries. He could now reveal the hidden spring (the hidden bond everyone had unconsciously been seeking, as he frequently said in one way or another in *Origin*, e.g., 413, 420, 426, 433, 449), but he never disagreed with ordering and ranking.

There are many places in *Origin* where Darwin was telling us what he thought a superior, or favored, race was. It is not just there in the subtitle or in that comment on the higher nature of British organic productions beating the productions of New Zealand. Darwin repeatedly uses words like colonists, colonise, intrude, and invade to describe the activities of species. What would a British reader think when he or she saw these expressions appear over and over again in *Origin*? Darwin never qualifies the use of any of these terms by saying something like 'I am of course speaking metaphorically.'

Any British imperialist would have been happy to read in the next to last paragraph of *Origin* Darwin's "prophetic glance into futurity ... it will be the common and *widely-spread species, belonging to the larger and dominant groups, which will ultimately prevail and procreate new and dominant species*"

(489; emphases added; he made the same point earlier on 350, 428-29). This isn't even highly coded language. It is a near-perfect formula to justify British imperialism, yet framed as an objective, scientific statement. Or how about this statement from *Origin* (205): "Hence, the inhabitants of one country, generally the smaller one, will often yield, as we see they do yield, to the inhabitants of another and generally larger country." So if we take over other, smaller countries, it's only natural.

Just prior to stating the above formula (on 489), Darwin tells us that most species become extinct at some point and leave no descendants. He also makes this point earlier in the book: "… of the species living at any one period, extremely few will transmit descendants to a remote futurity" (126). Only the widely ranging species have a better chance to leave future descendants. So if you want to leave descendants and create a mark, a memory, on posterity, you had better make an effort to supplant smaller, weaker groups. If you were not already inspired to be an imperialist, that idea would do it. Races supplanting and prevailing over other races (supplanting smaller and feebler groups, as he says on 428 of *Origin*) was on Darwin's mind from the beginning. Imperialism would have galloped along with or without Darwin, but reading Darwin could make you feel more comfortable with it, just in case you were having any doubts. And, as we have seen, there were plenty of humanitarians who were trying to instill doubt.

He also explains something important about what he means by ranging widely: "… we should never forget that to range widely implies not only the power of crossing barriers, but the more important power of *being victorious in distant lands in the struggle for life with foreign associates*" (405; emphasis added). If you don't hear *Hail Britannia* in that, that is only because you don't hail from that era. Then there is this: "As natural selection acts by competition … we need feel no surprise at the inhabitants of any one country, although … specially created and adapted for that country, being beaten and supplanted by the naturalised productions from another land" (472). So no matter how well adapted and fitted a species is in its own land, it is in a sense only natural if a species from a distant land overcomes it. It would be extraordinary if Darwin were clueless about the human implications of all these remarks. As we saw, he had already said as much in Notebook E 65, "man is not an *intruder*" (his emphasis); he has a natural right to invade other territories.

And what happens when two dominant groups, who developed in regions isolated from each other, come into contact? "… whenever their inhabitants [from the two isolated regions] met, the battle would be prolonged and severe … But in the course of time, the forms dominant in the highest degree, wherever produced, would tend everywhere to prevail. As they prevailed, they would cause the extinction of other and inferior forms …" (*Origin*, 326-27). Again, the application of this to British imperialistic efforts would be recognizable to Darwin's readers. They knew who the inferior forms were. Flannery has no grounds whatsoever for making his remark that Darwin's "'favoured races' did not explicitly include the British ruling class" (*Here on Earth*, 12-13). It may be impossible to conclusively prove that all these comments in *Origin* were modeled on British colonial activity. What is obvious, and hence provable, is that these comments so closely parallel imperialism. Coincidence? I think not.

The lesson to be drawn from *Origin* is that if you want to survive as a species for many generations to come, then the goal is to become common and widely spread—a perfect justification for colonialism, as I have said. Indeed, Darwin does draw such a conclusion in Chapter IV. "I conclude, looking to the future, that for terrestrial productions a large continental area ... will be the most favourable for the production of many new forms of life, likely to endure long and to spread widely" (107). The message is to spread out and find large areas of land to do it in. Then a little further on: "... it is the common species which afford the greatest number of recorded varieties ...Hence, rare species ... will consequently be beaten in the race for life by the modified descendants of the commoner species ... [some] will become rarer and rarer, and finally extinct" (110). In Darwin's world, the dominant become more dominant and the feeble feebler still (e.g., *Origin*, 125-26). It is not a good thing to be a rare, small culture. It is almost a sin in Darwin's eyes. To survive you must become numerous, common, and spread out. To those who have more will be given, and to those who have not or have little, even what little they have will be taken away and they will be left to disappear.

Whether or not it can be proven that Darwin intended these comments about 'widely-spread species' and 'dominant forms' to have implications for British imperialism, this much can be said: If Darwin wrote any of these lines without realizing that they served nicely to reinforce imperialism, then he was either the densest man who ever lived or the most self-deceptive. If you are wondering how Darwin could think of European colonialism as natural in *The Descent of Man* (and I will always wonder about this, I don't think anything could ever adequately explain how he could make such a mistake), you have to consider that he had already naturalized it in *The Origin of Species* and described it there, as illustrated by the above quotes and the next two which are from Chapter IV on natural selection. The first follows hard upon the last quote I gave: "... each new variety or species, during the progress of its formation, will generally press hardest on its nearest kindred, and tend to exterminate them" (*Origin*, 110). It does not matter if we are all human beings; we will exterminate those closely related to us. Then further on (126), Darwin gives us this: "Small and broken groups and sub-groups will finally tend to disappear." Supposedly he is not talking about human beings, but what a melancholy summation of much of human history that is. Broken groups, a broken people, destined to be eliminated. Darwin had already presaged in *Origin* what he believed would be the fate of Native peoples throughout the world, and in fact, said it in much starker language than he would in *Descent*.

Keep in mind that variety and species are just other ways of talking about human races (in *Descent*, 204, 210, he would prefer to call human groups sub-species). It is natural, says Darwin, for one group to exterminate a closely related group. Did human colonization and his own experience of it in his round the world trip from 1831 to 1836 influence the way he described nature in *Origin*? I don't know if that is provable beyond all reasonable doubt, but it is highly plausible.

He does not even mind using words taken directly from colonialism. Thus: "an intruder from the waters of a foreign country, would have a better chance of seizing on a place, than in the case of terrestrial colonists" (*Origin*, 388) and further on in that chapter he argues that better than the idea of independent creation is "the view of colonisation from the nearest and readiest source, together with the subsequent modification and better adaptation of the colonists to their new homes" (406).

One might have expected that when Darwin turned his attention to human beings in *Descent*, the colonial influence should have become more obvious. But that is not what happened. Darwin hid the horrors of colonialism in *Descent* and resorted to euphemisms (such as 'come into contact' and 'changed conditions of life' for what could more honestly be called invasion and dispossession). In *Origin*, because he was ostensibly writing about non-human nature, he could express his colonial leanings more openly. He is more poignant about the disappearance of groups (such as savages) in *Origin* (where he is supposedly not talking about human beings) than he is in *Descent*, such as in the comment about small and broken groups.

There is more. There always is when it comes to Darwin's racism. So many writers think that it is a stretch to find racism and imperialism in *The Origin of Species* because human beings are not present in that book. One of the most popular scholarly myths about *Origin* is that human beings are absent from it, with the one exception of an enigmatic sentence near the end. As a result of his theory of common descent by gradual changes, Darwin proposes that in some distant time, "Light will be thrown on the origin of man and his history" (488; in later editions, he made it 'Much light'). One cryptic sentence with the rest left unsaid. The scholarly world is nearly unanimous that, apart from that one sentence, you cannot find human beings in *The Origin of Species*. In *Darwin's Racism* (258-59), I gave about ten examples of writers who make this claim. Here are two of them.

Richard Dawkins in *The Greatest Show on Earth* (183) tells us that in *Origin*, "Darwin's treatment of human evolution ... is limited to twelve portentous words [the ones quoted above]." Adrian Desmond and James Moore say that Darwin was "defusing the *Origin* by removing the humans" (*Sacred Cause*, 346). In the introduction to their edition of Darwin's *Descent*, one section is entitled "Why Darwin Left Mankind Out Of The *Origin of Species*" (xxx). Essentially, they argue that Darwin did not want to be controversial. Darwin certainly left out a full-blown treatment, but that is not the same as leaving mankind entirely out of the book.

I am afraid that Agnes Arber's point is once again apt. The effect of the general intellectual atmosphere is compulsive to a humiliating degree. Once upon a time, someone said that Darwin did not include human beings in *The Origin of Species*, and everyone liked it so much, they kept on repeating it, and no one dared go back on it. They seemed to like the image of a cautious, modest Darwin who avoided controversy. It became a well-worn truism. It fits this mythical Darwin academia has been so very busy creating since the beginning. It's true that Darwin did not embrace controversy. He rarely responded to reviews and criticisms. He let Thomas Huxley, Alfred Wallace, and others do most of his fighting for him. But Darwin was not as cautious as the myth would have it and he certainly was not reluctant to allow some of his personal prejudices to enter the work and even to be obvious about it.

Darwin mentions human beings at least 16 times in *The Origin of Species*. My original count was 16. I realized very late in the day that I was undercounting, as I had missed some of the most obvious references to humans in the first chapter of his book. The most obvious things are often the hardest to spot and that is because of Agnes Arber's point. For example, I had missed "English breeders" (31), "pigeon-fancier" (32), and gardeners (37; 2x). These are all references to British imperialism and ability to improve stock. They are quite significant, as I will explain further on. Yet it took me a long time to see them. They were the last things I noticed. It is easier to blind oneself to the evidence than it is to see accurately.

As to the 16 more obvious mentions of human beings, most of them are inconsequential, but a few are not at all trivial, even if they don't tell us as much as we would like. Perhaps the most spectacular miss by Darwin mythmakers is on page 232 where Darwin uses the same language of 'light will be thrown' that he uses at the end, only here he is a lot less cryptic and, therefore, by the rules of academia, it must be forgotten. In discussing our ignorance of the unknown laws of variation, Darwin says he could also have illustrated this with "the differences between the races of man, which are so strongly marked; I may add that some little light can apparently be thrown on the origin of these differences, chiefly through sexual selection of a particular kind ..." (*Origin*, 199).

He is certainly not shy about mentioning racial differences. True, he is not saying anything here about which are superior and inferior, but most of his contemporaries would have had little doubt about the implications of racial differences. We must always keep in mind that natural selection is about two things: 1) common origin, and 2) the branching differences from the origin. The differences are as real to Darwin as the shared ancestry. The consequence of differentiation also applies to sexual selection. This comment on 232 is too brief to draw any conclusion about his belief in the equality or inequality of human races, but it's not nothing either and it is certainly more specific than the cryptic remark at the end of the book. Darwin is acknowledging that some racial differences are not slight (they are "so strongly marked") and that evolution by descent or by sexual selection produces great diversity and divergence of characteristics. He is affirming the European propensity to take note of human differences. (That divergence meant inequality was simply assumed by Darwin and others.)

Then there is Darwin's comment about Hottentots and Negroes. In making his point that the system of natural classification is really based on descent, Darwin offers the following hypothetical: "If it could be proved that the Hottentot had descended from the Negro, I think he would be classed under the Negro group, however much he might differ in colour and other important characters from negroes" (*Origin*, 424). There is so much that lies buried in this one statement. For one thing, Darwin is telling us that he does not count skin color as such a vital difference between humans, but it is important, he reminds his readers. One is left to wonder what he would say about white and black. At the time, everyone knew that Darwin probably believed we all have one common ancestor. There is an explicit statement about white and negro in his unpublished *1842* essay (53)—"Difficulty when asked *how* did white and negro become altered from common intermediate stock: no facts"—which was of course unknown to his contemporaries, but previous development theory, as for example in Robert Chambers's work, which emphasized common descent, made it a pretty safe conclusion in Darwin's case too.

In 1844, Chambers had written in *Vestiges*: "We are ignorant of the laws of variety production [a point Darwin would make over and over; e.g., *Origin*, 13, "The laws governing inheritance are quite unknown"]; but we see it going on as a principle in nature, and it is obviously favourable to the supposition that all the great families of men are of one stock" (*Vestiges*, 283; cf. 294, 305). Darwin's statement about Hottentot and Negro is a strong hint that humans have a common origin, and because of Chambers and others, the public knew what was coming. This remark also reveals the European arrogance of classifying everything on the planet, including other human beings. Darwin believed that we Europeans own the planet and that we can order it as we please. It hardly occurred to him that these other human beings might have something to say about that.

There is a brief reference to "mankind, so incomparably better known than any other animal" (*Origin*, 67). This comment might seem too slight to merit any attention, but then, if human beings are supposed to be so entirely absent from *Origin*, what is this comment doing here at all? He said almost the same thing in the *1844* essay (89). In *Descent* (203), we will get "Man has been studied more carefully than any other animal." It is a point he liked to keep returning to. He also asserted in *Descent* the possibility of "viewing him [man] in the same spirit as a naturalist would any other animal" (195), but given Darwin's own disgust with savages, that was a rather bold overstatement. Darwin appears only to be saying we have a lot of knowledge about humans, without indicating what that knowledge includes. The context of this remark reveals that there is more to it.

The reference to mankind being "better known than any other animal" comes near the beginning of Chapter III, "Struggle for Existence". He has already introduced the reader to natural selection a few pages earlier (61) and to "the doctrine of Malthus" which he sums up as "more individuals are produced than can possibly survive" (63). Then in one long paragraph (67-68), he discusses how difficult it is to identify all the checks that operate on population. "We know not exactly what the checks are in even one single instance" (67). But something must be checking the population (as Malthus, and now Darwin, argues), otherwise it would be spinning out of control. Even in mankind's case, "so incomparably better known," we don't know all the checks. By the end of the paragraph, he is reminding us of the great destruction in life, and particularly, the way the more vigorous kill the less vigorous (he uses plants as an example).

The average reader of *Origin* might have missed this, but some scientists would have realized that Darwin is clearly saying that human beings are subject to the Malthusian population principle (of course they are, that being the original point of the principle). We may not know all the checks in the case of man, but there must be some checks because man is subject to the same law of population. Since that law is one of the pillars of evolution by natural selection, there is a clear implication that mankind is subject to evolution by natural selection, and in particular, to the law of the more vigorous exterminating the less vigorous. No colonialist would have disagreed with Darwin's way of putting things.

Also, not a small point, his allusion to our knowledge of human beings is a kind of preemptive strike. He means European knowledge, upper class knowledge—and a European, upper class way of looking at things will displace any other way of looking at the world, including the view of human beings from below. The more vigorous are going to remove them anyway, so their knowledge does not count. Just as Walter Bagehot, who followed up on Darwin's ideas in a series of articles about ten years after *Origin's* publication, said of an aged savage who found western civilization "not worth the trouble," that "we need not take account of the mistaken ideas of unfit men and beaten races" (Bagehot, 209; Darwin called his work 'a remarkable series of articles;" *Descent*, 155 n5). The knowledge of disappeared and disappearing people does not count for much in the worldview of Darwin and so many others of his time. This also became the legal principle of dealing with Aborigines: Their laws and customs do not count; they are mistaken ideas; Aborigines are subject to European laws wherever Europeans arrive; hence, Europeans are not really intruding. It is extremely ironic that Darwin's statement about mankind being better known leads, in Bagehot's case, to a statement about erasing the points of view of other human beings. It is more likely than not that Darwin completely agreed. Is it knowledge they were seeking or conquest?

So those are three examples of Darwin's bringing human beings directly into his book. But the really extraordinary thing is that Darwin broke his "silence" on man in the very first chapter of *Origin*. No one has paid attention. It is so obvious that I could not see it until the umpteenth time I perused this chapter. Finally, I saw how often Darwin refers to human beings breeding animals and plants.

The overt purpose of this chapter is to demonstrate that the variability of domestic organisms tells us something about the malleability of all of nature's creations, and therefore, based on this one fact alone, we have good reason to suspect that species are not fixed but can be created over time. Darwin was not the first to see the significance of domestic breeding, or artificial selection, for the possibility of evolution in the wilds of nature. Almost all the previous evolutionists had made this point. His grandfather, Lamarck, and Chambers saw it. Charles Darwin was not even the first to draw a connection between artificial selection and natural selection. But he goes way beyond the idea of using breeding merely to establish that species evolve over time. He is after something more which his predecessors had no interest in.

Darwin's covert purpose here, which is not really all that hidden, is to set his conception of evolution on the path of *improving* as the goal of both human breeders and nature's breeding, and using this concept of *improving*, he is implying rather strongly that human beings who are better at *improving* nature's organisms, and hence better at imperialism, are superior to human beings, like savages, who do not do it nearly so well. The subtle point he is making is that there is a connection between man as a breeder of organisms and man as bred by evolution or natural selection.

Improving stock, a major professed goal of imperialism, is one theme of *Origin*'s opening chapter. Variations of 'improve' (usually as improvement or improved) appear 16 times in the 37 pages of this first chapter (7-43). That is about 0.43 occurrences per page, or almost one every other page. It is not nearly as frequent in the rest of the book, but the occurrences of derivatives of 'improve' in the next thirteen chapters is not negligible either. There are 61 in reference to natural selection in 447 pages, almost 0.14 per page, which is about a third of what it was in the first chapter. In a more objective science, there would have been closer to zero occurrences. I am not even counting other expressions used in the first chapter and the entire book, which also include the idea of improvement, such as "the best individual animals" (34; 36), "a slightly better variety" (37), "inferior birds" (42), and "usefulness to man" (38); except for this last one which I believe occurs only in the first chapter, similar expressions appear in the rest of the book.

Natural selection will improve organisms in the fight for survival. Darwin alludes to natural selection twice in the first chapter, but he already brought up the link between natural selection and improvement near the end of the Introduction, observing that "Natural Selection almost inevitably causes much Extinction of the less improved forms of life." Natural selection fosters improvement by eliminating the less improved. This is just like the roguing of unwanted plants which he brings up in Chapter I (32).

The constant use of variations of 'improve' in the first chapter has already set up a theme that both man and nature will breed superior organisms by eliminating the inferior. Improving implies there is a movement from inferior to superior, from worse to better, or lower to higher. Darwin was letting us know right off the bat that these categories of hierarchy will be important in understanding how natural selection works. Nor does he hesitate to tell us that the British are better at breeding than anyone else. But to fully appreciate what he is doing in the first chapter, it is important to understand the historical context of British imperialism and its claims to improve the world.

British imperialism considered itself very good at improving every part of the world it invaded. Savage ability to improve was quite inferior. We, the civilized, are the ultimate improvers and export our improvements—savages are far behind us as improvers, and hence, by implication, as survivors, since better plants and animals play a role in the survival of human beings. One might point out that this only demonstrates the superiority of Europeans in one very limited way, but superior as breeders carried a lot of weight in Darwin's world, and in a sense, would serve as a justification for imperialism.

For Darwin and his contemporaries, breeding was as much a symbol of general superiority as other symbols of imperialism.

"Through the most advanced knowledge and techniques, 'improvers' would organize the best possible future, both for those they expropriated and subordinated, as for themselves" (Drayton, 87). "British 'improvers' moved, at home and abroad, in the faith that they ultimately knew better than those on the ground. Their confidence depended, in part, on the assumption that they possessed a more profound understanding of how Nature worked" (90). There is more like this in Chapter 4 of Richard Drayton's *Nature's Government* and throughout the book. The British had better knowledge of nature and were out to improve the world, or so they said. At the end of the first paragraph of his first chapter, Darwin is noting, perhaps with some pride, "Our oldest cultivated plants, such as wheat, still often yield new varieties: our oldest domesticated animals are still capable of rapid improvement or modification." The book has just got under way, he has not finished the first paragraph yet, and already he is bragging about the superiority of British breeding practices.

In 1861, a flagpole flying the Union Jack was made from a Douglas fir from British Columbia. It was set up in Britain, towering over the surrounding trees, nearly twice their height. "Sir William Hooker [father of Joseph] pronounced it admirably calculated to impress on the public the 'size and bulk of the timber trees of one of our own colonies, British Columbia'" (Drayton, 207). Quinine was another such symbol. It was not only useful in defeating malaria but also served as "a symbol of the power of science to put nature on the side of imperialism" (208). Darwin himself wrote a letter in 1862 to the Superintendent of the Ceylon Botanic Garden to suggest a method for improving the tree from which quinine was obtained (209). It was, he said, "so important for mankind" (CCD 10.254). Breeding better plants and animals of all kinds was a major symbol of the purpose of imperialism, and would be used by Darwin as a model for how natural selection works. It is not an accident that explicit references to British imperialism appear in the opening chapter of *The Origin of Species*.

I said above that Darwin was not the first to draw a connection between natural and artificial selection. In 1649, Walter Blith published *The English Improover*, which he improved into *The English Improver Improved* in 1652. (I owe my awareness of Blith to Drayton, 52.) A declamation on the cover promises "the Improveableness of all Lands: Some to be under a double and Treble others under a Five or Six Fould. And many under a Tennfould, yea some under a Twenty-fould Improvement." There was a long tradition before Darwin celebrating English ability to breed and improve. Blith even drew a connection between God's (or nature's) selection and artificial selection. "So God was the Originall, and first Husbandman, the paterne [pattern] of all

Husbandry … And having given man such a Paterne both for precept and president [precedent?] for his incouragement … *Adam* [after expulsion from the Garden] is sent forth to till the Earth, and improve it" (Blith, pdf 74-75; pp. 3-4 in Ch. I). God breeds species and man can copy that. Blith presented God or Nature as providing a model, a pattern, for the human activity of selecting, breeding, and improving—humans in effect copying Nature— though in truth Blith (likewise Darwin) was using human breeders as a model to explain nature.

Take a long moment to think about that. Two hundred and ten years before Darwin's *Origin*, there was an author arguing that natural selection and artificial selection are essentially the same thing. Blith was implying that species in nature are not fixed, but are constantly being modified and improved by God. The more subtle implication is that nature will be a model and justification for imperialism—for improving the whole earth. Blith is actually not all that subtle about it. He laments that the English are not experienced enough in colonization: "… for though a new world [America] has been of late discovered, yet there is not an occupation or trade of finding them, nor are our English people very active in searching after them" (pdf 35). My point here is that as an early advocate for more imperialism, it is interesting that Blith felt a need to make nature complicit in the imperialist scheme.

Now we can turn back to what Darwin says in Chapter I of *Origin*. He directly states that civilized man is superior to savages in his ability to breed a better stock of animals and plants: "… neither Australia, the Cape of Good Hope, nor any other region inhabited by quite uncivilised man, has afforded us a single plant worth culture. It is not that these countries, so rich in species, do not by a strange chance possess the aboriginal stocks of any useful plants, but that the native plants have not been improved by continued selection up to a standard of perfection comparable with that given to plants in countries anciently civilized [i.e., Europe]" (*Origin*, 38). Darwin even told, or rather reminded, his British readers that English breeders are so good that they export their productions everywhere: "What English breeders have actually effected is proved by the enormous prices given for animals with a good pedigree; and these have now been exported to almost every quarter of the world" (31). Savages have for the most part done their selecting unconsciously (36), which gives limited results. Also, their nomadism limits them: "Wandering savages or the inhabitants of open plains rarely possess more than one breed of the same species" (42).

Statements like these would have been taken in Darwin's time as practically an explicit endorsement of western imperialism. That the British were a superior race of improvers is one unmistakable message of *Origin's* first chapter (the point is already there by the end of the first paragraph; see above), and it is strongly hinted that evolution has accomplished this. Deeply enmeshed in *Origin*'s Chapter I is a story of European man breeding his way to success and domination, while the savages' feebler efforts would lead them to languish—that is, if they survived at all. The savages' unconscious selecting is a less improved form of breeding, and those who engage in it are, according to the dictates of natural selection, destined for extinction. Even when "the lowest savages" today (34) engage in conscious selection, it is not nearly as good as what civilized people do (the first chapter as a whole makes this point). This implicit message in *Origin*—natural selection has bred the British to be better breeders than savages—would have been obvious and acceptable to most of Darwin's fellow Britons.

Just a little further below, I am going to explain three errors that Darwin made as he applied his system of thought to human beings. But underlying it all was Darwin's basic error—his insistence on looking at nature through the lens of improvement and that was improvement as Europeans understood it. When Darwin says natural selection *improves*, he means it (recall that there are 61 places in *Origin* where he links natural selection and improvement plus the 83 references to high, low, inferior, and superior). At the very start of *Origin*, in his first chapter, Darwin is reassuring his readers how committed he and his system are to improvement of the European kind. His notion of natural selection, or survival of the fittest, introduces teleology into nature. No matter how fiercely some people will deny this, a system geared to celebrate brutal survival is a system with a goal and values organized around survival.

On rare occasions, Darwin will give lip service to having no teleology, but he cannot stay true to it for very long. When he says "it is difficult to avoid personifying the word Nature," he explains, "I mean by Nature, only the aggregate action and product of many natural laws, and by laws the sequence of events as ascertained by us" (*Origin*, 6th, 109; he said the same thing a few years earlier in *Variation*, 17). He could easily have taken the opportunity here to advance a more objective statement of natural selection as the result of tendencies or forces in nature. Instead, in the paragraphs that follow in *Origin*, he goes right back to his personifications: "natural selection can do nothing [without increased variability]", "As man can produce ... so could natural selection", "... natural selection to fill up by improving some of the varying inhabitants", "She can act on every internal organ" and more (110-11 in 6th).

We quickly lose any sense of impersonal forces and are immersed again in a world of a powerful agent out to get things done. Darwin has gone well beyond using natural selection to sum up an aggregate of events, when he could have just stuck to the events and said: variations occur, some are inherited, there are many individuals being born, not enough food, some die, while others with certain mutations live. Why add a judgment of progress toward the higher? It is not at all difficult to avoid personifying nature, as Darwin claimed. He just did not want to do it.

Darwin goes beyond the basic description necessary to convey what natural selection is or is supposed to be. He envisions a nature which makes Europe's aggression towards other peoples appear very natural and acceptable— palatable as I said in the last chapter. "It has truly been said that all nature is at war; the strongest ultimately prevail, the weakest fail; and we well know that myriads of forms have disappeared from the face of the earth" (*Variation*, 16; cf. *Origin*, the last words of Ch. VII, "… let the strongest live and the weakest die," of which law, Darwin gives the Ichneumon wasp and slave-making ants as examples). Out of this sense of brutality in nature comes Darwin's admiration for queen bees killing the young queens (see previous chapter, a few pages in) and his sense of the necessity of Native peoples succumbing to foreign forces. He singled out his grandfather's description of nature as one great slaughter house as representing progress in modern thought (also previous chapter).

In the first chapter of the first edition of *Origin*, he only had to make one scientific point, which had been made by previous evolutionists. All Darwin had to do was point out that artificial selection is a sign of the plastic nature of organisms (he uses 'plastic' twice in Chapter I). That is a legitimate scientific step—one that the earlier evolutionists had taken. He was following them. But that was not enough for Darwin. He took a second step. This was the basic error I have been discussing. Darwin had to push it further and use artificial selection to draw a correlation between nature improving organisms and imperialism's improvements, and by doing this, he compromised the objectivity of his science. The fascinating thing is that while Darwin could get so much out of connecting natural and artificial selection, he separated them again when it came to understanding western imperialism's intrusion into Native countries. He should have seen imperialism as a form of artificial selection instead of as a sign of natural selection invading Indigenous territories. This gave rise to three major errors which slanted his science in a terribly biased direction.

The first error he made was not seeing the significance of the rapid decline of Native populations, which should have made him realize this was artificial selection at work. Darwin had always insisted that natural selection operates extremely slowly. He rejected the idea of catastrophes as playing a role in evolution. In Darwin's view, the extinction and birth of species had to be equally gradual. He insisted on perfect symmetry. Species must come in and go out with equal pacing. Somebody else might want to modify the theory to include occasional catastrophes or cataclysms as playing a role, but Darwin would have none of it. Even in his earliest approach to this, while he comments that sudden extermination may be possible (*1842*, 23, 26), he also says, "I shall doubt very sudden exterminations" (28). By the time he wrote the next essay, he no longer needed doubt. He was sure. Extermination is always gradual (*1844*, 145, 147, 180, 210, 245).

In *The Origin of Species*, he is forthright that catastrophes would never be incorporated in his thinking. "Natural selection … will … if it be a true principle, banish the belief … of any great and sudden modification in their [organic beings'] structure" (*Origin*, 95-96). He extends this to extinction. In explaining how natural selection can help us figure out the length of time in the history of fossils, he comments, "… species are produced and exterminated by slowly acting and still existing causes, and not by miraculous acts of creation and by catastrophes …" (487). In fact, Darwin believed that extinction is generally a slower process than the production of new species: "… species and groups of species gradually disappear … There is reason to believe that the complete extinction of the species of a group is generally a slower process than their production …" (317-18; cf. 321).

He knew this gradual extinction was not happening in the colonies, yet he continued to present imperial extermination of Native groups as if it were a matter of natural selection. He should have realized that *anything man actively undertakes to do* is artificial or a form of breeding. What was happening in the colonies was a cataclysm. All the signs were there, but Darwin ignored them.

Here is an interesting admission in *Descent* (217), in that section on the extinction of the races of man in Chapter 7: "One of my informants, Mr Coan, who was born on the [Hawaiian] islands, remarks that the natives have undergone a greater change in their habits of life in the course of fifty years than Englishman [*sic*] during a thousand years." Yet no bells went off for him that this was at odds with natural selection and, therefore, that this was a cultural phenomenon. It was artificial selection. All he can do is conclude that changed habits lead to lessened fertility, which is one of the points he harps on in this section. And a diminishing population leads inevitably to extinction, as Darwin dispassionately tells us: "even a slight degree of infertility … would sooner or later lead to extinction," as he says on the next page. Astoundingly, he can even note that "… infertility has coincided too closely with the arrival of the Europeans …" (219), and still no bells go off for him that we have a cultural problem here, which was tantamount to a catastrophe.

Years earlier, in his published journal, Darwin expressed his awareness of the rapidity of change in the colonies, far exceeding the extreme slowness of natural selection which he would come to insist on. Before *Origin* and before even the first two essays, he had a more honest sense of things. In the 1839 *Narrative*, he added this to his *Diary* comments about Tasmania: "Thirty years is a short period, in which to have banished the last aboriginal from his native island … I do not know a more striking instance of the comparative rate of increase of a civilized over a savage people" (*Narrative*, 533; the first sentence but not the second was retained in *Journal*, 447; and none of this made it into *Voyage*). 'Striking instance' is a kind of euphemism for unnatural. Since this was added after he had discovered natural selection, with its emphasis on the extremely slow appearance and disappearance of groups in the theater of life, I would have to guess that he realized how *unnatural* was the extermination of the Tasmanians, but it remained an unconscious realization. I don't know how significant it is that these thoughts gradually disappeared by the final *Voyage*. (I tend to think it is; it is as if he gradually eliminated from his consciousness the fact of rapid conquest because it did not comport with natural selection.) Judging from *Descent*, he gave up thinking about the European onslaught as unduly remarkable. It is another sign that natural selection had come to serve an imperialist agenda.

Ignoring the significance of the rapid changes in the colonies, which was not what natural selection would give us, was one error Darwin made, and building on this, he committed the second one of making out the extermination of Native peoples to be part of the process of natural selection. Extermination was much more like a horticulturalist weeding out unwanted plant varieties, which Darwin brought up in Chapter I of *Origin*. If there is a third error here, it is this: Darwin failed to see that Native resistance to colonialism was a case of natural selection resisting artificial selection. Darwin was very aware of this as a general phenomenon. He had discussed it in *The Variation of Animals and Plants under Domestication* (1868). As he sums it up in *Variation*, "Natural selection often checks man's comparatively feeble and capricious attempts at improvement" (2.297). It is quite possible to view rebellion by Natives as an example of natural selection reasserting itself against Europe's efforts at capricious, imperial selection. Darwin always assumed that natural selection primarily favors the dominant races. But when a smaller race tries to check the aggression of the stronger, that may be an even truer example of natural selection in action.

The Committee on Aborigines in Van Diemen's Land stated in its report, which Darwin read, that the Natives "sustained the most unjustifiable treatment in defending themselves against outrages which it was *not to be expected that any race of men should submit to without resistance*, or endure without imbibing a spirit of hatred and revenge" (Bischoff, 205; emphasis added). This Committee reminded Darwin that Native resistance was legitimate and natural, as it is something "any race of men" would do. But Darwin did not take it in. Even his own use of an expression in a letter to Lyell should have alerted Darwin to what was happening in imperialism. He had written, "White man is 'improving off the face of the earth' even races nearly his equals" and approved of Lyell's insight that "man now keeping down any new man which might be developed" (CCD 8.379; Sept. 23, 1860). White people "improving" and "keeping down" were signs that this was artificial selection. But Darwin ran right past all the warning signs and that was because he had made improvement a fundamental part of natural selection.

He took what was an obvious case of artificial selection (western barbarism) and renamed it natural selection, so that he could give it his full support and fool himself into thinking it was entirely natural. Darwin manipulated his concept of natural selection to make it apply wherever he wanted it to apply; politics intruded into his science, a fairly obvious fact that most scholars still stubbornly deny.

~ 9 ~

A Strange Coming and Going

A long time ago, I heard a magician say that adults are easier to fool than children. As I recall, he explained that adult human beings have their very fixed preconceptions about the way the world works. It is relatively easy to manipulate those preconceptions and make them look in one direction, while you the magician are engaged in some funny business in another place, even if it is right in front of their eyes. Children are different. They don't have as many preconceptions. They are restless and their eyes go wandering. They look in places they shouldn't be looking at (from the magician's point of view). You have to be extra skillful to fool them.

That is exactly right and gives us an important lesson about adults. Among adults, intellectuals are the easiest of all to fool. They have the most preconceptions. But in the case of academia, I would put it a little differently. They fool themselves—individually and collectively. They perform magic tricks on each other. Their specialty is making evidence disappear. They have strapped so much baggage onto themselves, in the form of ideologies and worldviews, and onto their colleagues, that being stuck has become their natural condition. They are sure that the less they see, the more they know. Knowledge for them is to be used to prevent themselves from seeing the evidence. Whereas to do history right, you have to be as light on your feet as Muhammad Ali was. Get rid of the baggage. Travel light. When academics convince themselves that they can see even when their heads are weighed down by all that baggage, that is the biggest magic trick of all.

The job of a good scientist and scholar is to become like children—to look in places where you should not be looking. Everyone will scream at you. But never mind them, though not minding can admittedly be very hard to do. Keep peering into unexpected places. There is gold in them hills, which is an awful imperialist thing to say, but as long as we take it metaphorically, it has some truth in it. 'Keep your eyes on the prize' is a better way to say it. The prize is always the evidence—not theories, not opinions, not ideas, but the evidence. And you can only see it when you have unburdened yourself of ideologies and preconceptions.

The scientific community and writers on science are fixated on understanding evolution and natural selection only as Darwin expounded it. They are sure they can dismiss anyone who came before; such predecessors could only have had an inferior idea of evolution. The true history of this science is worthless to our keepers of knowledge unless it elevates Darwin to premier status. I am afraid that even Stephen Gould contributed to this, but the more interesting side of Gould was his sensitive understanding of why we should study this history at all. He just did not apply it to Darwin.

Gould once wrote, "… in our arrogant approach to history, we choose to flay the past [as we do to Erasmus Darwin, Chambers, Rafinesque, and the rest, I would note], all the better to bask in our current wisdom …" (*Hen's Teeth*, 81). The only modification I would make to this is that I'm not sure that our current wisdom is worth basking in. At the end of the same essay, he said, "If we use the past only to create heroes for present purposes, we will never understand the richness of human thought or the plurality of ways of knowing" (93). Amen, a hundred times. He could also have mentioned a plurality of worldviews. We also might miss that some alleged goat might have grasped some points better than we do, as in Chambers's case with his keen sense of the unconscious forces that prevent progress in science and the need to confront those unconscious emotions.

Chambers had pointed out that professional scientists were just as liable to be emotional and in error as the average person: "there is such a thing in human nature as coming to venerate the prejudices … it is not surprising that scientific men view it [a new theory] with not less hostility than the common herd" (*Explanations*, 176). Scientists back then did not like hearing that anymore than scientists today want to hear it. Chambers understood that scientists could not escape their humanity and that this included the faults of being human—unexamined emotions, prejudices, narrow worldview, irrationality. His invaluable critique of practicing scientists—based on what science ideally should be, which is not to assume it is free of bias, but to constantly examine its preconceptions—made him, and still makes him, *persona non grata* in the halls of science. Chambers achieved the greatest thing one can in science: He made the unconscious conscious and, without that, all the evidence in the world will avail you nothing.

Chambers was there, making these essential points, at the beginning of evolutionary theory. Gould is rather a latecomer in this respect. Still, his is a welcome voice. In his book, *Time's Arrow, Time's Cycle*, Gould went on at greater length and struck a deeper note than in his brief remarks I quoted above:

> What harm is a bit of heroic folderol about an illusory past
> [and the idea that Darwin invented and proved evolutionary
> theory all by himself is as an illusory bit of history as one can
> get], especially if it makes us feel good about the progress of
> science? I would argue that we misrepresent history at our
> peril as *practicing* scientific researchers … we enshrine one
> narrow version of geological process as true *a priori*, and we
> lose the possibility of weighing reasonable alternatives …
> we will never understand how fact and theory interact with
> social context, and we will never grasp the biases in our own
> thinking (for we will simply designate our cherished beliefs
> as true by nature's dictates). [114-15]

It is so sad that no one lives up to this magnificent teaching from Gould. It is even sadder that no one paid attention to Chambers. Gould unwittingly presented all these perfect reasons for studying Chambers and Lamarck and Rafinesque and Erasmus Darwin in more detail. Gould's last point is particularly important. Historical accuracy is an important tool, maybe a necessary one, in teaching us humility and overturning the social biases in our thinking. Without it, we will replace discovery with merely designating our beliefs as true. I am sure Gould would have loved the way Saxe Bannister put it: "Nor is the past a mere worn-out tale" (*Humane* [1830], 42). It is alive and constantly whispering to us.

Olive Schreiner was not a scientist or historian and presumably has nothing to teach us about these subjects. But she had a very strong whisper. "All that is buried is not dead," she told us in her novel *The Story of an African Farm* (146). In my mind, I always link this with Bannister's equally succinct statement, "rights are never forgotten" (*Humane* [1830], 104). Like John Locke before them, and one can go even further back to the Torah, they took their stand in a humanitarian tradition that proclaimed that human rights take precedence over state power and state sovereignty. I hope to devote part of a future book to this.

Schreiner was a feminist and activist for social causes in South Africa in the late 19th century. She became famous in Britain for her novel, which is mostly free of plot and instead concentrates on the thoughts and feelings of several characters, especially Lyndall, a strong young woman who probably represents Schreiner's views. Lacking power to control one's own life is one theme. As Lyndall says to a young child who has just been whipped, "we will not be children always; we shall have the power too, some day" (142). The book is in a sense a song to the powerless to tell them that some of us know what you are going through. You are not alone. You are part of the wholeness of life.

While she may not have been a scientist, she grasped the holistic way of looking at the world. Perhaps she was influenced by Chambers (at one point, Lyndall uses the term 'vestige' when she talks about fossils and extinction). Schreiner captures very well the holistic approach to evolution in this novel (published 1883, a year after Darwin died). She notes how a number of diverse things resemble each other in form (the blood vessels in a dissected gander, a thorn-tree seen against the midwinter sky, metallic veins in a rock, the flow of water through some furrows, and the antlers on a horned beetle), and then ponders:

> How are these things related that such deep union should exist between them all? Is it chance? Or, are they not all the fine branches of one trunk, whose sap flows through us all? That would explain it … the earth ceases for us to be a weltering chaos … Nothing is despicable—all is meaningful; nothing is small—all is part of a whole, whose beginning and end we know not. [*African Farm*, 176-77]

This is deeply reminiscent of Chambers's point that everything has a place in the whole and Emma Martin's point that there are no defects. Implicit in all of them is that human rights are not small, but even if they are relegated to the small, they matter very much. I would add to Schreiner's last words above that nothing is fated to become extinct and lose its place in the whole, not as long as human beings inhabit the planet. We have choices. It is arrogant to think we don't. There is no manifest destiny.

Are these outward similarities of form, which Schreiner pointed to, a 'deep union,' as she claimed? Most scientists would say no (which I would not be so quick to agree with; there may well be a mathematical theory that explains why the diverse natural facts she mentions are so peculiarly similar). But the proper scientific response to this is not to dismiss it as mere poetry, rather it is to recognize that this is an interesting theory and to ask whether more precise evidence can be found to justify it. Schreiner was feeling her way to a vision that could be given more scientific support, if one knows where to look. While she may not have presented the best assortment of facts, sometimes the vision must come first, before we can see the evidence. Those who aren't busy being born every day, looking at things with fresh eyes, are busy dying.

Even Darwin might have agreed with that. As Darwin said in a letter to Lyell, "without the making of theories, I am convinced there would be no observation" (CCD 8.233; June 1, 1860) and later in the same year, to H.W. Bates, "I have an old belief that a good observer really means a good theorist" (CCD 8.484-85). Darwin was saying that we cannot see well unless we are guided by a good theory. The thinkers and writers who tried out holism were trying to see the world through another theory. They deserve great credit for that instead of ridicule. Darwin himself would have done no seeing if he had not been given the theory of evolution by those who came before him.

In the preface to the second edition of *African Farm*, Schreiner makes some remarks about storytelling which apply just as well to the study of history. Continual progress is how we want history to go in the stage version of human life, as she called it, with everything happening with "an immutable certainty" and everyone taking their bows. There is another kind of storytelling, she said, one in which:

> There is a strange coming and going of feet. Men appear, act and re-act upon each other, and pass away. When the crisis comes the man who would fit it does not return. When the curtain falls no one is ready. When the footlights are brightest they are blown out; and what the name of the play is no one knows. If there sits a spectator who knows, he sits so high that the players in the gaslight cannot hear his breathing. [8]

Real history is rarely neat or tidy. None of us know what's coming next and we won't be prepared for it, whatever it is. You can force history to be tidy only by sweeping a lot of things off the stage. Heroes don't always appear to save the day. Just the opposite. Great accomplishments turn out to have been not so great, if you take a closer look. Other genuine accomplishments are stomped into the ground until they are forgotten by all.

For those who think that Olive Schreiner was not as profound as I make her out to be, I will just say that if her thoughts are given the attention they deserve, there is a payoff. Instead of looking for eternal truths and manifest destiny—instead of pigeonholing historical figures as villains or heroes, which categories are so hard to undo, once fixed in an academic stone garden—we should be listening for that strange coming and going of feet. Have you ever noticed how strange history is when you really pay attention?

Thomas Robert Malthus was long ago selected to be a villain, a harsh man, an enemy of the poor. That is how he is remembered. We don't remember that he was very critical of Adam Smith for paying too much attention to the wealthy and not enough to the poor, whom Malthus often called the most important and numerous class in society. He was unhappy that Smith had not paid more attention to the phenomenon of an increase of the wealthy while the poor and the working poor were left behind. The true measure of the health of a society lies in how well the lower orders are doing, not in how the wealthiest are doing. (On all this, see Chapters XVI and XVII of the first edition of the *Essay*.) As examples: "The increasing wealth of the nation has had little or no tendency to better the condition of the labouring poor" (186); "it must be acknowledged, that the increase of wealth of late years has had no tendency to increase the happiness of the labouring poor" (189); and he considered luxuries, expensive items, and fortunes made in trade to provide "revenue only of the rich, and not of the society in general" (195). Personally, I think these thoughts were among his most brilliant insights.

Malthus favored a government that would decrease extreme wealth and extreme poverty: "… though we cannot possibly expect to exclude riches and poverty from society, yet if we could find out a mode of government by which the numbers in the extreme regions would be lessened and the numbers in the middle regions increased, it would be undoubtedly our duty to adopt it" (207). He did not believe that the interests of the wealthy and the middle class coincided. Perhaps it would not be a stretch to say that Malthus hated favoring any one class over another, unless it was the middle class. In the face of these obvious facts about Malthus, it is so strange that he gets to be remembered as an "apologist for greed" (see further below).

In the sixth edition, he continued to argue that most histories are of the upper classes and that we lack good knowledge of the lower classes (6th, 1.19), and continued as well to express his concern that while farmers and capitalists were getting richer, the condition of the lower classes was getting worse (6th, 1.22; it is possible that he was just describing here an economic state of affairs, but I sense a criticism of this situation). Ultimately, he seemed to believe that only small improvements could be made for the poor (1st, 176, 179, 198). Utopian schemes of grand progress bothered him as being against nature. The poor, he believed, had no natural right to be supported (6th, 2.337). It should also be said in defense of Malthus that he understood that great harm would result if poor laws were changed too drastically and too quickly; he was in favor of their gradual removal: "no man of humanity could venture to propose their immediate abolition" (6th, 2.336). Malthus, especially in his earliest stage, cannot easily be characterized as a political conservative or liberal.

We remember none of this and we especially erase his concern that increases in wealth do nothing for the poor. We carry over this misrepresentation of history to Malthus's influence on Darwin. Darwin is often remembered as "the gentler Darwin" (e.g., Desmond and Moore, *Sacred Cause*, 338), while Malthus is still vilified, *despite the obvious fact that Darwin put the population principle to harsher use than Malthus who warned against it*. Darwin was most likely inspired by the very first pages of the sixth edition of the *Essay* where Malthus had noted how prolific animals and plants are, while the means of subsistence was limited. But this principle of limited nourishment putting pressure on populations, which operates in its purest form in the wilds of nature, cannot be applied in the same way to human beings. To repeat a quote from Malthus which I offered in Chapter 4:

> plants and irrational animals … are all impelled by a powerful instinct to the increase of their species … interrupted by no doubts about providing for their offspring … [But in the case of man] Impelled to the increase of his species by an equally powerful instinct, *reason interrupts his career*, and asks him whether he may not bring beings into the world, for whom he cannot provide the means of support. [6th, 1.3; emphasis added]

As I said earlier, he might as well have said reason interrupts natural selection. Darwin paid this no mind and proceeded to apply Malthus's principle as ruthlessly to human beings as to the rest of nature. Yet Malthus is remembered as a villain and Darwin as a gentle hero. How is this possible?

Given his use of the population principle, it should come as no big surprise that Darwin would approve of the European extermination of Native peoples as a natural act, which no one as yet has reconciled with "the gentler Darwin." Not so Malthus. He was horrified by genocide. When it came to Europeans exterminating savages, Malthus stepped back: "the right of exterminating, or driving into a corner where they must starve … will be questioned in a moral view" (1.7), and as I also pointed out previously, he was appalled by the possibility that the Indians would be "ultimately exterminated" (1.8).

As far as Malthus was concerned, his population principle should never be used to justify the genocide of other peoples. Some will argue that Darwin was more consistent with the fundamental principle of Malthus than Malthus himself was. I cannot agree with that. For one thing, Malthus had convincingly pointed out that population pressure is not as perfectly severe for humans as it is for other animals, so he had good reason to drop the false consistency that would be maintained by Darwin. Some examples from Alfred Wallace immediately below will help clarify this. In the meantime, the only consistency I see is that writers consistently portray Darwin as a hero and Malthus as something of a bastard (not long ago, a well-known authority, Steven Stoll, unfairly characterized Malthus as "this apologist for greed" [*New York Times Book Review*, "Letters", Aug. 9, 2015]).

In July 1881, about nine months before Darwin died, Wallace, inspired by something he had read in a book by American socialist Henry George, wrote to tell Darwin that perhaps they had taken the Malthusian principle too far. He reminded Darwin that "both you and I have acknowledged ourselves indebted" to the principle of Malthus and then observed that "Mr. George, while admitting the main principle as self-evident and as actually operating in the case of animals and plants, denies that it ever has operated or can operate in the case of man, still less that it has any bearing whatever on the vast social and political questions which have been supported by a reference to it" (ARW 1.317). That was in fact Malthus's point, but both Wallace and Darwin seemed to have missed it. In Darwin's response (it was the last letter he wrote to Wallace), he was silent on this matter. The insight had come very late for Wallace, but at least he finally saw it.

Yet even on his own Wallace was capable of putting natural selection to more humanitarian use than Darwin would. Since he had discovered natural selection independently of Darwin, he maintained an independent relationship to it. In an 1893 interview (S736), Wallace thought of a way to bring together natural selection and his concern for social justice, in this case for women as well as for society as a whole. In one and the same interview, he pointed out the negative role of natural selection—"The method by which the animal and vegetable worlds have been improved and developed has been through weeding out. The survival of the fittest is really the extinction of the unfit"—and yet managed to argue that by letting women become the selecting force in choosing marriage partners, human society will advance.

Wallace looked forward to a future reformed society in which "no woman will be compelled, either by hunger, isolation, or social compulsion, to sell herself either in prostitution or uncongenial wedlock." He continued:

> As things are, women are constantly forced into marriage for a bare living or a comfortable home. They have practically no choice in the selection of their partners and the fathers of their children, and so long as this economic necessity for marriage presses upon the great bulk of women, men who are vicious, degraded, of feeble intellect and unsound bodies, will secure wives, and thus often perpetuate their infirmities and evil habits. But in a reformed society the vicious man, the man of degraded taste or of feeble intellect, will have little chance of finding a wife, and his bad qualities will die out with himself ... I hope I make it clear that women must be free to marry or not marry before there can be true natural selection in the most important relationship of life.

There were not too many people who were capable of combining science and social justice like this. He also stressed that in this future society, women "will have remunerative occupation," thus removing the economic necessity which usually forced them to marry unwisely. Wallace was willing to pay attention to certain facts that others ignored.

Darwin would never have used natural selection to reach such a conclusion about women. He had too many prejudices. Malthus was the inspiration for both Wallace and Darwin to come up with natural selection. Wallace praised Malthus just as much as Darwin did. Yet Wallace was not stuck with his population principle in the same way that Darwin was. In some ways, Wallace was a more original and creative thinker than Darwin. Darwin stuck to the premises of his system and his culture. To a great degree, he steadfastly followed these premises to their conclusion, or actually *one* conclusion. Was it the only conclusion one could draw? Wallace never stopped experimenting in his thoughts, combining and recombining ideas and stretching their logic. More importantly, he never stopped paying attention to the evidence. He was not as trapped as Darwin. He had the capacity to connect things you would think could not be connected, and this was because he always put the evidence first.

In his 1864 paper, "The Origin of Human Races and the Antiquity of Man Deduced From the Theory of 'Natural Selection'" (S093), where he defended Darwin's theory to the hilt (it was his own theory as well, but he always generously referred to it as Mr. Darwin's theory), he too took the extinction of savages for granted. He tried to follow Darwin as much as he could, even quoting the subtitle of Darwin's book. "It is the same great law of '*the preservation of favoured races in the struggle for life*,' which leads to the inevitable extinction of all those low and mentally undeveloped populations with which Europeans come in contact" ("Origin of Human Races", clxiv-clxv).

But in that same paper, Wallace also sees some of the positive signs in Native cultures. He recognizes that savages ("the rudest tribes") are "social and sympathetic" and take care of their sick and feeble, so that "The action of natural selection is therefore checked" (clxii). (Compare Wallace's 'checked' to Malthus's 'reason interrupts' the strict application of the population principle and take note: Two out of three great thinkers concluded that natural selection or the population principle does not work on humans as it does in nature at large.) These last points of Wallace on the sociability of Natives were something Darwin was unwilling to see. Darwin would never agree that natural selection was to any great degree checked and he objected to this positive assessment of savages as social. In his copy of Wallace's paper, next to the point about the social nature of savages, Darwin scribbled in the margin, "Does not act ... only civilized man!" (Quoted in Desmond and Moore, *Sacred Cause*, 344.) Already, despite all they had in common, Wallace was thinking a little differently about human beings. He was not prepared to be as ruthless towards savages as Darwin was, regardless of what both got from Malthus. *If* there was a bleakness in Malthus, Wallace struggled against it, Darwin did not.

Several years before Darwin wrote *The Descent of Man*, he told Wallace that he thought natural selection played a role in the constant battles among Australian savages (ARW 1.154). Wallace wrote back to tell him that he was oversimplifying. Wallace took Darwin to mean that the constant battles are "leading to selection of physical superiority" (ARW 1.156). He warned Darwin of simplifying too much and jumping to conclusions. "For instance, the strongest and bravest men would lead [in battle], and expose themselves most, and would therefore be most subject to wounds and death." (And therefore they would be less likely to leave progeny behind to give their characteristics to.) Darwin would incorporate this point in *Descent* (155), but did not give Wallace credit.

Wallace also pointed out that if one tribe was too bellicose, it might inspire all the other tribes to unite against it, leading to its own annihilation. Darwin ignored this point. According to Wallace, there were "so many exceptions and irregularities that it [constant battles] could produce no *definite* result" (Wallace's emphasis). He doubted very much that natural selection would in this case lead to any specific physical modifications "and can we imagine it to have had any part in producing the distinct races that now exist?" (ARW 1.157).

What Wallace was pointing to is that human life is more complex than that of any other animal. Humans in particular have an ability to cooperate, negotiate, and form alliances which makes survival far more complicated for them than it is for many animals for whom strength and speed may be the paramount qualities necessary in the struggle for existence. In the case of human beings, we are tempted to reduce it all to intelligence, but intelligence has many off-shoots; there is no one simple line in which it develops. Darwin never incorporated the human ability to negotiate and compromise as part of what is so important in our existence. These features contradicted his belief about the all-or-nothing quality of competition. He never even considered that human wars do not always end in complete annihilation of one side, but rather in peace settlements. For Darwin, in fact, wars never end and never even have to be declared, they are merely continued (as the poet Ingeborg Bachmann once wrote of our era of wars; I owe this to Ilya Kaminsky). Just remember that Darwin took his grandfather's remark about the world being one great slaughter house, full of rapacity and injustice, as "forecasting the progress of modern thought" ("Preliminary", 113; quoted previously, several pages into Chapter 7). Darwin so often let us know what was modern and important to him.

Competitiveness was a fixed value in Darwin's thinking. He never modified it. Variations of 'compete' appear about 70 times in *Origin*. He carried this over to human beings. Competition benefited society and anything that opposed or reduced it was bad. Early in Chapter 3, I quoted from a letter (CCD 20.323-24) in which he expressed his opposition to trade unions and cooperative societies because he believed they were harmful to the principle of competition in society. Wallace had the more nuanced view. Sometimes competition was good and sometimes it was bad. Darwin simplified everything.

In 1865, Alfred Wallace published an article, "On the Progress of Civilisation in Northern Celebes" (S104), in which he commented that "Competition and free trade are excellent things of themselves ..." He goes on to say that they cannot be imposed on a people not prepared for them:

> It appears to me, however, that we do an equally unwise and unjust thing when, having obtained power over a country inhabited by a savage people, we expose them at once to the full tide of competition with our highly elaborated civilisation, and expect them to thrive under it ... we have brought them into direct contact with English wealth and energy, vigorously developing itself for its own ends, and the result must inevitably be, sooner or later, the extermination of the native race ... we should hesitate in applying the principles of free competition to the relations between ourselves and savage races, if we ever expect them to advance in civilisation or even to maintain their existence upon the earth. [S104, 69]

Wallace recognized that it was not only overt violence that could be used to kill a people. One could compete them to death. Isn't that what the Walrus and the Carpenter do to the Oysters in Lewis Carroll's poem? The two colonizers wear the Oysters out on a long walk for which they are not suited—"They hadn't any feet" and besides which they are fat and easily out of breath. The Walrus and the Carpenter compete, improve, and civilize the Oysters off the face of the earth. But not before entertaining them with tales of civilization, and then they eat them all. The exercise and entertainment improved them right out of existence.

Wallace's response to this kind of injustice is: Do not drown the Natives with our overwhelming advantages; it is not a fair fight; let us scale down our competitive drive; let us not wear them down. He makes essentially the same points in *Malay* (1.256-57), which Darwin read, but there his focus is on free trade—the merchants get rich, but the people "relapse into poverty and barbarism." Much like Malthus's point that an increase in wealth leaves the working poor behind. In 1898, exactly one hundred years after the first edition of Malthus's *Essay*, Wallace more firmly came around to this Malthusian idea that no one (not even Wallace) calls Malthusian. At least three times in *The Wonderful Century*, he pointed out that capitalism benefits the wealthiest without diminishing poverty, lamenting that we have an economic system "resulting in great accumulations of private wealth, but not sensibly ameliorating the condition of the people at large" (368; cf. 344, 357) and expressing his disappointment in "our modern civilization—more correctly barbarism" (368-69)—Darwin's remote future making an appearance once again before the 19ᵗʰ century was over.

Wallace was a thoughtful man, always putting justice ahead of "pure scientific" thought. In the Celebes essay (S104, 67), he comments (my emphasis): "We know, or *think we know*, that the education and industry, and the common usages of civilised man, are superior to those of savage life ..." (also in *Malay*, 1.254-55). I love that he added that qualification of we "think we know." He was always willing to entertain doubts about so much, including who is superior and inferior. It was his concern for justice that brought on such doubts.

As he once said in a letter to the journal *Nature* ("Government Aid", Jan. 13, 1870; S157), "... though I love nature much I love justice more." He was objecting to government funding of science (which would potentially have been of much use to him) because he perceived that it would benefit the upper classes most of all. "... if we once admit the right of the Government to support institutions for the benefit of any class of students or amateurs however large and respectable, we adopt a principle which will enable us to offer but a feeble resistance to the claims of less and less extensive interests whenever they happen to become the fashion." Wallace often takes my breath away.

As should now be obvious, Darwin could have cared less about what happens to Aboriginal peoples. If they are eliminated, so much the better. Darwin's vision of competition was monolithic. It was always good, everywhere, for all organisms, at all times. It was not to be applied with thoughtfulness, but imposed as the only lifestyle choice possible. But he must have lacked some confidence in his own position, no? Darwin never offers a compelling rejoinder to Wallace's thinking. He never considers that competition might sometimes be bad. This seems to have been his practice with ideas he could not defeat. Not only does he not respond to Wallace and others, he does not even acknowledge their different point of view. The existence of another way of thinking about all this could not be tolerated by Darwin. He preferred to look the other way and not look back.

Despite Wallace's brilliant ability to stay faithful to the evidence and to always try to reason from the evidence to conclusions rather than from conclusions to the evidence, most scholars consider him a second-rate scientist compared to Darwin. They grudgingly acknowledge that he independently discovered natural selection, but that is all they will give him. They refuse to see that he was less hampered by prejudice than Darwin was.

I suppose the point to all this is that an idea like natural selection, or any idea, does not have to have just one logical path. Logic does not deploy itself. It has to be manipulated by people who have emotions and cultural biases, and therefore, it can have multiple paths, depending on what your other premises, inclinations, and prejudices are. Logic cannot tell you what your ultimate hopes and dreams are or what your first premise should be. And it cannot tell you which pieces of evidence to focus on. It cannot even tell you what it means to be a human being. Those decisions come from somewhere else.

We have three thinkers who thought hard about the same principle, the population principle, which in one form is natural selection. Each used it in different ways. Is this not a strange coming and going of feet? Darwin's theory was more than just a theory with a built-in logic. It could be, and was, handled in a variety of ways by each person who was inspired by it. How does anyone begin to explain the different paths that this one theory gave us? How does anyone understand how scholars have taken the strangeness of human thought with its multiple byways and reduced it to simple theories marching to one logical drumbeat?

Until the world and the people who make it up become strange to us again, *through a detailed look at the evidence*, we will never see let alone understand what is happening all around us and what brought us to where we are. How did we normalize Darwin's racism and make his science seem objective? How did we estrange the humanitarians and make them seem like loose fanatics who deserve no attention? How did a beautiful family man like Darwin become a racist in the first place, indifferent to the suffering of Aboriginal families? How did a hero do this, and equally strange, how did we pick this man to be a hero? How did beautiful thinkers like Gerland, Wallace, Rafinesque, Ward, and all the rest get cast into obscurity, shut up in the asylum of outcast protesters?

I don't have answers to most of the questions I have asked in this last chapter. Maybe they are unanswerable, maybe not. I only know, or think I know, that it is more important to see the strangeness of the world than to insist on answers. Too many academics have gotten us to stop wondering about these things. They have put an end to looking in places we shouldn't be looking into and given us presumed knowledge instead—a knowledge about destiny and the way things were meant to be. Yet somehow we're always surprised by the next turn of events. How does that happen? Anything that does not fit into destiny is declared defective, forgettable, and scheduled for disappearance. Darwin was great, the first discoverers of evolution were not. Western civilization is great, other civilizations are not. But what if Emma Martin was right? What if there are no defects? What if everything that was born, God wanted to be born?

Bibliography

A bold, capital **H** designates editions which can be found at hathitrust.org. For any old book not so designated, I used a modern paperback reprint, but some of these can be found at Hathitrust as well. The works of Charles Darwin are listed, under his name below, alphabetically by the abbreviations and abbreviated titles used in the text of this book. The essays of A.R. Wallace can be found at the Charles Smith website: http://people.wku.edu/charles.smith/wallace.Sxxx.htm. For xxx, just substitute the three digit number given in parentheses after the title of each essay found below under his name. All his books can be found at **H**.

Arber, Agnes, *The Mind and the Eye: A Study of the Biologist's Standpoint*. Cambridge: Cambridge University Press, 1954.

[H] Bagehot, Walter, *Physics and Politics: Thoughts on the Application of the Principles of "Natural Selection" and "Inheritance" to Political Society*. New York: D. Appleton and Company, 1873. (Originally a series of articles in *Fortnightly Review*, 1867-1869.)

[H] Bannister, Saxe, *British Colonization and Coloured Tribes*. London: William Ball, 1838.

[H] _____, *Humane Policy; or Justice to the Aborigines of New Settlements*. London: Thomas and George Underwood, 1830.

[H] _____, *Humane Policy; or The Protection of Aborigines Secured by a Just System of Colonization*. Second edition. London: Fisher, Son, & Co., [1840?].

[H] _____, *Remarks on the Indians of North America in a Letter to an Edinburgh Reviewer*. London: Thomas and George Underwood, 1822. (I believe this is the same book which at a later time was referred to as *Defence of the Indians of North America*.)

[H] Bischoff, James, *Sketch of the History of Van Diemen's Land*. London: John Richardson, Royal Exchange, 1832.

[H] Blith, Walter, *The English Improver Improved, or, the Survey of Husbandry Surveyed, Discovering the Improvableness of All Lands.* London: John Wright, 1652. Third edition? (Originally *The English Improover, or, A New Survey of Husbandry*, 1649.) About the first sixty pages, a series of prefatory epistles to various personages, are unnumbered. As a result, this is the only book I reference by pdf page number. The book proper begins on pdf 72 and Chapter I on pdf 74.

[H] Bonwick, James, *The Last of the Tasmanians: Or the Black War of Van Diemen's Land.* London: Sampson Low, Son, & Marston, 1870. (Reprinted by Forgotten Books, 2012.)

[H] _____, *The Lost Tasmanian Race.* London: Sampson Low, Marston, Searle, and Rivington, 1884.

Boulukos, George, *The Grateful Slave: The emergence of race in eighteenth-century British and American culture.* Cambridge: Cambridge University Press, 2008.

Boyce, James, *Van Diemen's Land.* Melbourne, Australia: Black, Inc., 2010. (Originally 2008.)

Butler, Hubert, *Independent Spirit: Essays.* New York: Farrar, Straus and Giroux, 1996.

Chambers, Robert, *Explanations: A Sequel to Vestiges of the Natural History of Creation.* Second Edition. London: John Churchill, 1846. (Reprinted by Cambridge University Press, 2009; see *Vestiges*, Fifth, below.) All his books were originally anonymous.

_____, *Vestiges of the Natural History of Creation.* London: John Churchill, 1844. (Reprinted by British Library Historical Print Collections.) This is the first edition. The Sixth was in 1847, the Tenth in 1853, and the Eleventh in 1860. (Darwin read the first and sixth, and likely the tenth.) A pdf version for the 1844 first edition can be found at Google Books. Pdf files for the sixth and eleventh editions can be found at **H** and BHL. I could not find a digital version of the tenth edition anywhere.

_____, *Vestiges*, Fifth edition (London: John Churchill, 1846), and *Explanations: A Sequel* (see above), reprinted together with separate pagination for each book by Cambridge University Press, 2009.

[H] _____, *Vestiges*, Sixth edition. London: John Churchill, 1847.

[H] _____, *Vestiges*, Eleventh edition. London: John Churchill, 1860.

[H] Coates, Dandeson, *et al*, *Christianity the Means of Civilization: Shown in the Evidence. Given before a Committee of the House of Commons, on Aborigines.* London: R.B. Seeley and W. Burnside, 1837.

Damasio, Antonio R., *Descartes' Error: Emotion, Reason, and the Human Brain.* New York: Avon Books, 1994.

Darwin, Charles, *1842* and *1844* essays. See Darwin, Francis, *Foundation.*

_____, *Autobiography* – *The Autobiography of Charles Darwin, 1809-1882*, edited by his grand-daughter Nora Barlow with her Notes and Appendix and original omissions restored. New York and London: W.W. Norton & Company, 2005. (Originally London: Collins, 1958.)

_____, CCD – *The Correspondence of Charles Darwin*, edited by Frederick Burkhardt *et al.* Cambridge: Cambridge University Press. Multi-volumes. Vol. 1 (1821-1836), 1985. As of this writing, they are up to the mid-1870s, over 20 volumes. Vol. 16 (1868) is the only one that takes up two books, but the pagination is continuous from one book to the next.

_____, *Descent* – *The Descent of Man, and Selection in Relation to Sex.* Second Edition (1874). With an Introduction and other editorial material by James Moore and Adrian Desmond. London and New York: Penguin Books, 2004. This edition contains all three parts in one volume. (Originally published in two volumes; Volume 1 on the descent of man, first edition in 1871, second in 1874; Vol. 1, 1871, available at BHL. The New York publication of second edition of entire book in one volume available at **H**; no date given.)

_____, *Diary* (or *Beagle Diary*) – *Charles Darwin's Beagle Diary*, edited by Richard Darwin Keynes. Cambridge: Cambridge University Press, 2001. (Originally 1988.)

[H]_____, *Journal* – *Journal of Researches into the Natural History and Geology of the Countries Visited during the Voyage of H.M.S. Beagle Round the World*, Charles Darwin. Second edition. London: John Murray, 1845. (The first edition under this title was just a reprint of *Narrative*, Vol. 3, in late 1839.)

_____, "Letter on Vivisection" – in London *Times*, April 18, 1881. Available at D-O.

[H]_____, LL – *The Life and Letters of Charles Darwin*, edited by Francis Darwin. London: John Murray, 1888. Three volumes.

[H]_____, ML – *More Letters of Charles Darwin*, edited by Francis Darwin. London: John Murray, 1903. Two volumes.

[H]_____, *Narrative* – Volume 3 of *Narrative of the Surveying Voyages of His Majesty's Ships Adventure and Beagle, between the Years 1826 and 1836.* Three volumes. London: Henry Colburn, 1839. Vol. 3, *Journal and Remarks, 1832-1836,* was Darwin's contribution. Citations to *Narrative* are always to Vol. 3 unless otherwise noted. Vol. 2, *Proceedings of the Second Expedition, 1831-1836,* was by Captain Robert FitzRoy. Vol. 1, *Proceedings of the First Expedition, 1826-1830,* was by Captain P. Parker King.

_____, Notebooks – *Charles Darwin's Notebooks, 1836-1844: Geology, Transmutation of Species, Metaphysical Enquiries.* Transcribed and edited by Paul H. Barrett *et al.* Cambridge: Cambridge University Press, 2008. (Originally 1987.)

_____, *Origin – On the Origin of Species by Means of Natural Selection, or the Preservation of Favoured Races in the Struggle for Life,* by Charles Darwin. Originally London: John Murray, 1859. This edition has been reprinted many times over with varying pagination. My page references are from the original edition. All page references to *Origin* are from this first edition, unless otherwise noted. The "Historical Sketch" was not added until the third edition, but is usually included in current reprints of *Origin's* first edition. A searchable pdf version of the first British edition of *Origin* can be found at BHL. The following is information on later editions of *Origin* referred to in the text of this book: The original British fourth (1866) and fifth (1869) editions (both London: John Murray) are available at **H**; the fifth was the one that first used 'survival of the fittest'. The sixth edition (originally 1872) is still in print in America; New York: The Modern Library, 1993. All the editions can also be found at D-O, but as of this writing, this site does not have searchable digital formats.

[H]_____, "Preliminary Notice" – See Krause.

_____, "Supplementary Notes on Gerland's book" – Darwin's Notes [1868?]. A link to this can be found on the same web page for Gerland's book at BHL. There are 6 sheets (12 numbered pages) altogether. The first four pages are in one handwriting (Darwin's, I believe) and were scanned into the web site out of order: 2, 1, 3, 4. The last eight are in another's handwriting, possibly that of his daughter Henrietta Darwin. I don't know whether she made these notes for him based on her own reading or he dictated them to her.

_____, *Testimony on Vivisection* – Darwin's testimony before a Royal Commission in *Report of the Royal Commission on the Practice of Subjecting Live Animals to Experiments for Scientific Purposes,* London, 1876, 233-234; testimony taken on Nov. 3, 1875. Available at D-O.

[H] _____, *Variation – The Variation of Animals and Plants under Domestication.* With a preface by Asa Gray. New York: Orange Judd & Company, 1868. Two volumes. (Originally London: John Murray, 1868.)

_____, *Voyage – The Voyage of the Beagle*. Introduction by Catherine A. Henze. New York: Barnes & Noble, 2004. (Originally 1909.)

[H] Darwin, Erasmus, *The Botanic Garden, A Poem in Two Parts: The Economy of Vegetation and the Loves of the Plants, with Philosophical Notes*. London: Jones & Company, 1825. (*Economy* originally published 1791 and *Loves* 1789.)

[H] _____, *The Poetical Works of Erasmus Darwin*. In three volumes with Philosophical Notes and Plates. Vol. 2: *The Loves of the Plants*. Vol. 3: *The Temple of Nature*. London: J. Johnson, 1806.

[H] _____, *The Temple of Nature, or, The Origin of Society, A Poem with Philosophical Notes*. London: J. Johnson, 1803. This is the first edition. Also available at BHL along with notes on passages marked by Charles Darwin.

[H] _____, *Zoonomia; or, The Laws of Organic Life*. London: J. Johnson, 1794. Two volumes.

Darwin, Francis, editor, *The Foundation of the Origin of Species: Two Essays Written in 1842 and 1844 by Charles Darwin*. Cambridge and London: Cambridge University Press, 2009. Pagination is continuous from one essay to the next. (Originally 1909.)

Dawkins, Richard, *The Greatest Show on Earth: The Evidence for Evolution*. New York: Free Press, 2009.

Desmond, Adrian, and Moore, James, *Darwin: The Life of a Tormented Evolutionist*. New York and London: W.W. Norton & Company, 1994. (Originally London: Penguin Books, 1991.)

_____, *Darwin's Sacred Cause: How a Hatred of Slavery Shaped Darwin's Views on Human Evolution*. Boston and New York: Houghton Mifflin Harcourt, 2009. (Subtitle changed to *Race, Slavery, and the Quest for Human Origins* for paperback edition.)

[H] Disraeli, Benjamin, M.P., *Tancred: or, The New Crusade*. London: Henry Colburn, 1847. Three volumes. (Also, Leipzig: Berhard Tauchnitz, 1847, two vols., also available at **H**. The satirical fin and wings passage is at 1.124 in the German edition.)

Drayton, Richard, *Nature's Government: Science, Imperial Britain, and the 'Improvement' of the World*. New Haven and London: Yale University Press, 2000.

[H] Fitzpatrick, T.J., *Rafinesque: A Sketch of His Life with Bibliography*. Des Moines: The Historical Department of Iowa, 1911.

Flannery, Tim, *Here on Earth: A Natural History of the Planet*. New York: Atlantic Monthly Press, 2010. (Originally published by The Text Publishing Company, Melbourne, 2010.)

Ford, Lisa, *Settler Sovereignty: Jurisdiction and Indigenous People in America and Australia, 1788-1836*. Cambridge and London: Harvard University Press, 2010.

Gerland, Georg, *De l'extinction des peoples naturels*. Marc Géraud's French translation of Gerland's book originally in German (below). Paris: L'Harmattan, 2011.

_____, *Über das Aussterben der Naturvölker*. Leipzig: Friedrich Fleischer, 1868. (Darwin's copy of this book, with marginal annotations, available at BHL.)

Glick, Thomas F., *What about Darwin?: All Species of Opinion from Scientists, Sages, Friends, and Enemies who Met, Read, and Discussed the Naturalist who Changed the World*. Baltimore: The John Hopkins University Press, 2010.

Gopnik, Adam, *Angels and Ages: A Short Book about Darwin, Lincoln, and Modern Life*. New York: Alfred A. Knopf, 2009.

Gould, Stephen Jay, *Hen's Teeth and Horse's Toes*. New York and London: W.W. Norton & Company, 1983.

_____, *The Mismeasure of Man*. Revised and expanded. New York: W.W. Norton & Company, 1996. (Originally 1981.)

_____, *Time's Arrow, Time's Cycle: Myth and Metaphor in the Discovery of Geological Time*. Cambridge, MA, and London: Harvard University Press, 1987.

Heuman, Gad J., *Between Black and White: Race, Politics, and the Free Coloreds in Jamaica, 1792-1865*. Westport, CT: Greenwood Press, 1981.

Himes, Chester, *My Life of Absurdity: The Later Years: The Autobiography of Chester Himes*. New York: Paragon House, 1990. (Originally, 1976.)

[H] Hoare, Prince, *Memoirs of Granville Sharp, Esq., Composed from his own Manuscripts, and Other Authentic Documents in the Possession of his Family and of the African Institution*. London: Henry Colburn and Co., 1820.

Holt, Thomas C., *The Problem of Freedom: Race, Labor, and Politics in Jamaica and Britain, 1832-1938*. Baltimore and London: The John Hopkins University Press, 1992.

[H] Humboldt, Alexander de, *Personal Narrative of Travels to the Equinoctial Regions of the New Continent, 1799-1804*. Translated by Helen Maria Williams. Vol. V. London: Longman, Hurst, Rees, 1821.

[H] Huxley, Thomas, *Lectures & Lay Sermons*. London: J.M. Dent & Sons, Ltd., and New York: E.P. Dutton & Co., [1910?].

[H] Irving, Washington, *The Sketch Book*. Philadelphia: Henry Altemus Company, [1848?]. (Originally around 1819?)

Kaminsky, Ilya, "Red Ripening", review of *The Girl from the Metropol Hotel* by Ludmilla Petrushevskaya, in *The New York Times Book Review*, February 12, 2017, p. 20.

Knox, Henry, Enclosure, 15 June 1789, to George Washington. This can be obtained online at Founders (see Abbreviations).

[H] Krause, Ernst, *Erasmus Darwin*. Translated from the German by W.S. Dallas. With a Preliminary Notice (biography of Erasmus Darwin) by Charles Darwin. London: John Murray, 1879.

[H] Lamarck, Jean-Baptiste, *Philosophie Zoologique*. Nouvelle Édition. Two volumes. Vol. 1: Paris: Germer Baillière, 1830. Vol.2: Paris: J.B. Baillière, 1830. (Originally 1809.)

[H] _____, *Zoological Philosophy: An Exposition with Regard to the Natural History of Animals*. Translated with an Introduction by Hugh Elliot. London: MacMillan and Co., 1914.

Lindqvist, Sven, *"Exterminate All the Brutes"*. New York: The New Press, 1996. (Originally Stockholm, Sweden, 1992[?].) Translated from the Swedish by Joan Tate.

_____, *The Skull Measurer's Mistake: And Other Portraits of Men and Women Who Spoke Out Against Racism*. New York: The New Press, 1997. (Originally Stockholm, Sweden, 1995.) Translated from the Swedish by Joan Tate.

[H] Lyell, Charles, *Travels in North America*. London: John Murray, 1845. Two volumes.

MacMillan, Margaret, "Neither War Nor Peace", a review of Robert Gerwarth's *The Vanquished: Why the First World War Failed to End*, in *The New York Times Book Review*, December 11, 2016, p. 16.

Malthus, Thomas Robert, *An Essay on the Principle of Population* and *A Summary View of the Principle of Population*. With an introduction by Antony Flew. London and New York: Penguin Books, 1970. (Originally published in 1798 [*Essay*] and 1830 [*Summary*]. See "Explanations" at beginning of this book for further information.)

[H] _____, *An Essay on the Principle of Population; or, A View of Its Past and Present Effects on Human Happiness.* Sixth edition. London: John Murray, 1826. Two volumes.

Manne, Robert, editor, *Whitewash: On Keith Windschuttle's Fabrication of Aboriginal History.* Melbourne, Australia: Black Inc. Agenda, 2003. Collection of essays by various writers, including Robert Manne, James Boyce, Henry Reynolds, Shaye Breen, Lyndall Ryan, and more.

[H] Marchant, James, editor, *Alfred Russel Wallace: Letters and Reminiscences.* London and New York: Cassell and Company, Ltd., 1916. Two volumes.

Martin, Emma, *First Conversation on the Being of God.* London: Self-published pamphlet, [1844?]. Available at Google books.

_____, *God's Gifts and Man's Duties, Being the Substance of a Lecture.* October 9, 1843. Third edition. London: Etherington, [1844?]. Includes "An Address to the Minister" and "A Letter" to the Minister. Available online (I found it in the Columbia University Library website, which had a link to another site, but I have lost track of that information.)

Melish, Joanne Pope, *Disowning Slavery: Gradual Emancipation and "Race" in New England, 1780-1860.* Ithaca and London: Cornell University Press, 1998.

[H] Merivale, Herman, *Lectures on Colonization and Colonies, Delivered before the University of Oxford in 1839, 1840, and 1841.* London: Longman, Orme, Brown, Green, and Longmans, 1841. Two volumes (Vol. 2 is 1842).

Minardi, Margot, *Making Slavery History: Abolitionism and the Politics of Memory in Massachusetts.* New York: Oxford University Press, 2010.

Napier, Charles James, *Colonization: Particularly in Southern Australia, with Some Remarks on Small Farms and Overpopulation.* London: T. & W. Boone, 1835. (Reprinted New York: Augustus M. Kelley, 1969.) Also available in a pdf version at Google Books.

Newsome, Daniel, letter to editor, under heading "Darwin in Full", *New York Times Book Review*, February 15, 2009, p.6.

North, Christopher, (pseud. for John Wilson), *The Comedy of the Noctes Ambrosianæ.* Selected and arranged by John Skelton. Edinburgh and London: William Blackwood and Sons, 1876. (Originally appearing in installments in *Blackwood's Magazine*, 1825-1835.)

[H] Peron, M.F., *A Voyage of Discovery to the Southern Hemisphere, 1801-1804*. Translated from the French. London: Richard Phillips, 1809.

Plomley, N.J.B., editor, *Weep in Silence: A History of the Flinders Island Aboriginal Settlement*. A collection of primary sources, including George Robinson's Flinders Island Journal, 1835-1839. Hobart: Blubber Head Press, 1987.

[H] Priestley, Lady (Eliza Chambers), *The Story of a Lifetime*. London: Kegan Paul, Trench, Trübner & Co., Ltd, 1908.

Pye, Michael, *The Edge of the World: A Cultural History of the North Sea and the Transformation of Europe*. New York: Pegasus Books, 2015.

Quinn, Peter, letter to editor under heading "Darwin in Full", *New York Times Book Review*, February 15, 2009, p. 6.

[H] Rafinesque, Constantine Samuel, *Hebarium Rafinesquianum*. Philadelphia: Atlantic Journal, Extra of No. 6, First Part, 1833.

[H] _____, *Ichthyologia Ohiensis, or, Natural History of the Fishes Inhabiting the River Ohio and Its Tributary Streams*. A reprint of the original by Richard Ellsworth Call. Cleveland: The Burrows Brothers Co., 1899.

[H] _____, *The Pleasures and Duties of Wealth*. Philadelphia: The Eleutherium of Knowledge, 1840.

[H] _____, *Western Minerva, or American Annals of Knowledge and Literature*. First volume. Lexington, KY: Thomas Smith, 1821. Reprinted in 1949 by Peter Smith.

[H] _____, *The World, or, Instability: A Poem in Twenty Parts*. Philadelphia: J. Dobson, 1836. And London: O. Rich, 1836.

[H] *Report from the Select Committee on Aborigines (British Settlements), with the Minutes of Evidence*. House of Commons, June 26, 1837. The *Report* is on pp. 3-92. The "Minutes of Evidence" are appended and separately paginated, 1-108.

Reynolds, Henry, *An Indelible Stain? The Question of Genocide in Australia's History*. Ringwood, Australia and New York: Viking Penguin Books, 2001.

_____, *This Whispering in Our Hearts*. St. Leonards, Australia: Allen & Unwin, 1998.

[H] Rusden, G.W., *History of Australia*. London: Chapman and Hall, Ltd., 1883. Three volumes.

Rush, Benjamin, *An Address to the Inhabitants of the British Settlements, on the Slavery of the Negroes in America*. Philadelphia: John Dunlap, 1773. Second edition. Appended and paginated separately is *A Vindication of the Address*, in response to a pro-slavery pamphlet. Available at NYPL website.

[H] Schreiner, Olive (under the pseudonym Ralph Iron), *The Story of an African Farm*. Second edition. Chicago: M.A. Donahue & Co., [1883?]. Also available in paperback.

Secord, James A., *Victorian Sensation: The Extraordinary Publication, Reception, and Secret Authorship of* Vestiges of the Natural History of Creation. Chicago and London: The University of Chicago Press, 2000.

Semmel, Bernard, *Democracy Versus Empire: The Jamaica Riots of 1865 and the Governor Eyre Controversy*. New York: Doubleday Anchor, 1969. (Two previous editions: In 1962, under the title *The Governor Eyre Controversy*, MacGibbon & Kee Ltd; and in 1963, under the title *Jamaican Blood and Victorian Conscience: The Governor Eyre Controversy*, Houghton Mifflin Company.)

Sharp, Granville, *A Representation of the Injustice and Dangerous Tendency of Tolerating Slavery*. London: Benjamin White, 1769. Available in a pdf file through the NYPL website. Also available in paperback.

Smiley, Jane, *A Thousand Acres*. New York: Anchor Books, 2003. (Originally 1991.)

[H] Spencer, Herbert, *Essays: Scientific, Political, and Speculative*. London: Longman, Brown, Green, Longmans, and Roberts, 1858. The essay "The Development Hypothesis" is identified as one of the Haythorne Papers, originally published between January 1852 and May 1854 in the *Leader*. Revisions to this essay, if any, would have been made in 1857. Thus, the expression "theory of evolution", which Spencer uses in this essay, predates Darwin's *Origin*.

[H] _____, *The Principles of Biology*. London: Williams and Norgate, 1864. Two volumes.

Stein, Gertrude, *What Are Masterpieces?* New York: Pitman Publishing Corporation, 1940.

[H] Stokes, John Lort, *Discoveries in Australia: With an Account of the Coasts and Rivers Explored and Surveyed During the Voyage of H.M.S. Beagle in the years 1837-1843*. London: T. and W. Boone, 1846. Two volumes.

[H] Stuart, Charles, *A Memoir of Granville Sharp, to which Is Added Sharp's "Law of Passive Obedience," and an Extract from his "Law of Retribution."* New York: The American Anti-Slavery Society, 1836.

Sullivan, John Jeremiah, *Pulphead*. New York: Farrar, Straus, and Giroux, 2011.

Taylor, Barbara, *Eve and the New Jerusalem: Socialism and Feminism in the Nineteenth Century*. Cambridge, MA: Harvard University Press, 1993. (Originally 1983.)

Uys, Cornelis J., *In the Era of Shepstone: Being a Study of British Experience in Southern Africa, 1842-1877*. South Africa: Lovedale Press, 1934.

[H] Waitz, Theodor, *Introduction to Anthropology*. Volume the First. Edited by J. Frederick Collingwood. London: Longman, Green, Longman, and Roberts, 1863. Originally *Anthropologie der Naturvölker*, Vol. 1.

Wallace, Alfred Russel, *Alfred Russel Wallace: Letters and Reminiscences*. See Marchant.

_____, "Government Aid to Science" (S157), letter to Editor, *Nature*, January 13, 1870, 288-289.

_____, "How to Civilize Savages" (S113orig for the original 1865 version; S113 for the expanded 1900 version), *Reader*, June 17, 1865, 671-672.

_____, Interview 1893 (S736)—"Woman and Natural Selection. Interview with Dr. Alfred Russel Wallace", *The Daily Chronicle*, December 4, 1893, 3, by unknown interviewer.

[H] _____, *The Malay Archipelago: The Land of the Orang-Utan, and the Bird of Paradise, A Narrative of Travel*. London: MacMillan and Co., 1869. Two volumes. (The 1890 Tenth Edition is reprinted in one paperback volume by Kessinger Legacy Reprints.)

[H] _____, *Man's Place in the Universe: A Study of the Results of Scientific Research in Relation to the Unity or Plurality of Worlds*. Originally New York: McClure, Phillips & Co., 1903. (Also, facsimile reprint by Kessinger Legacy Reprints.)

_____, "On the Progress of Civilisation in Northern Celebes" (S104), read at a meeting of the Ethnological Society of London on January 24, 1865. Published same year in the Society's *Transactions*.

_____, "The Origin of Human Races and the Antiquity of Man Deduced from the Theory of 'Natural Selection'" (S093), originally delivered March 1, 1864 at the Anthropological Society of London. Published in the *Journal of the Anthropological Society of London*, Volume 2, 1864, clviii-clxx. Includes the discussion that followed, clxx-clxxxvii.

_____, *The Wonderful Century: Its Successes and its Failures*. Cambridge and New York: Cambridge University Press, 2011. (Originally 1898; also at **H**.)

Ward, Alan, *A Show of Justice: Racial "Amalgamation" in Nineteenth Century New Zealand*. Auckland: Auckland University Press, 1995. (Originally Australian National University Press, 1974.)

Ward, J. Langfield, *Colonization in its Bearing on the Extinction of the Aboriginal Races*. Leek: William Clemesha, 1874.

[H] West, John, *The History of Tasmania*. Tasmania: Henry Dowling, 1852. Two volumes.

Wood, Michael, review of *The Story of Alice* by Robert Douglas-Fairhurst, *New York Times Book Review*, June 14, 2015, p. 15.

Zitzer, Leon, *Darwin's Racism: The Definitive Case, Along With a Close Look at Some of the Forgotten, Genuine Humanitarians of That Time*. Bloomington, IN: iUniverse, 2016.

Index